T0325987

TWISTED TURBAN

A THOUGHT-PROVOKING JOURNEY
ALONG CULTURAL BORDERLANDS

Naginder Sehmi

TWISTED TURBAN

A THOUGHT-PROVOKING JOURNEY
ALONG CULTURAL BORDERLANDS

MEREO
Cirencester

Published by Mereo

Mereo is an imprint of Memoirs Publishing

1A The Wool Market, Cirencester, Gloucestershire, GL7 2PR
info@memoirsbooks.co.uk   www.memoirspublishing.com

Copyright ©Naginder Sehmi, 2013

The moral right of Naginder Sehmi to be identified as the author of this work has been asserted by him in accordance with the Copyright, Designs and Patents Act, 1988

First published in England, 2013

Book jacket design Ray Lipscombe

ISBN 978-1-86151-024-2

All rights reserved.

No part of this publication may be reproduced, stored in a retrieval system, or transmitted in any form or by any means, electronic, mechanical, photocopying, recording or otherwise without the prior permission of Memoirs.

Although the author and publisher have made every effort to ensure that the information in this book was correct when going to press, we do not assume and hereby disclaim any liability to any party for any loss, damage, or disruption caused by errors or omissions, whether such errors or omissions result from negligence, accident, or any other cause. The views expressed in this book are purely the author's.

Printed in England

In memory of my wife Jiti, who tragically departed
this life on Christmas Day 1991, leaving a permanent
void in our lives.

ACKNOWLEDGEMENTS

The generous offer by Roopinder Singh, Deputy Editor of The Tribune, Chandigarh, India, to review the first draft of Twisted Turban provided me with the stimulus I longed for. He found the story of Inder interesting and encouraged me to work on it with the help of an editor familiar with the background. I could not have found a better person than Rupi Mangat, travel/environment writer and journalist with The Nation, Nairobi, Kenya. With her I was able to focus and almost rewrite every chapter.

I received precious comments and suggestions from my daughter Upi, President of Alliance Française, Santa Rosa, California and editor of its monthly bulletin until she moved to San Jose recently, and my nephew Harminder Sehmi, Springhill, Oxford, England.

My heartfelt gratitude goes to my editor, Chris Newton and Tony Tingle of Memoirs Publishing. Without their help and guidance the book would not have seen the light of day.

I am indebted to my colleague and friend Valerie Mitchell, Geneva, Switzerland, for carefully correcting the printed proof.

CONTENTS

CHAPTER 1

INDER

In 1946, I was nine. I did not know my real name. My father appeared for the first time in four years in my aunt's village, and took me to my village on his new Raleigh bicycle. I do not remember him hugging me. All I remember is that I sat on the back carrier.

At a bridge over a small irrigation canal, there were deep ruts made by carts across the bank. My father did not see them. When the bicycle bumped over the first one, I was airborne long enough for the bicycle to continue without me and I landed on my bum in the middle of the dusty cart-tracks.

My father jolted his way over the second track and happily continued pedalling. Suddenly he sensed something amiss and realized I was not on the bike. That is when for the first time he called me by my real name, Inder, for he did not know me by another name.

Later I learned that my mother had insisted on naming me Inder after Indra, the king of all Indian gods – the almighty rain-god. Europeans named him Jupiter and Zeus. Why? It's anybody's guess. Punjabis find it difficult to twist their tongues to pronounce the double consonant 'dr'. For them it is easier to say Inder, a monosyllable short and simple. The name of the super-god Indra appears in a bulk of male and female Indian names like Inderjeet,

Parminder, Surendra, Rabindranath. Indira, a diminutive of mighty Indra, does not match Indira Gandhi, the Indian prime minister well known to the world and killed by her own turbanned bodyguards – it was a dangerous folly to equate herself with the indestructible, all-powerful Lord Indra.

Another diminutive of Indra is Indri, a word that arouses the image of the linga and yoni, or phallus and vagina. A linga, usually standing in a yoni, is the symbol of life-giving force and the focal point in daily worship of devotees of Shiva. It gives form to many a famous temple, some several storeys tall like the one in Bhubaneswar.

I was not born in Punjab, the land of five rivers, the land of my ancestors, but in Kenya, East Africa. I'm writing an introspective because if I don't, nobody else will. My story is no more engaging than yours or anyone else's. It is like everybody else's story. But I am different from everyone else. We all are.

Like all normal children, my earliest childhood memories are of my mother – a mother I lost before I was five years old. When I lost her, I lost my childhood. My father is a distant memory, for he was absent for long stretches of time earning a living in Africa to support us. Remembering now what I have achieved and not achieved gives meaning to time, for without memory, time has no meaning. So I time-travel and zoom back to people and places I have not seen in years.

Eldore – the name fills me with nostalgia, for it is the place of my birth. In the 1930s, it was a white settlers' town in the White Highlands – a vestige of the British colonial rule, for the land was exclusively owned by the whites. Today it is no longer the White Highlands but the home of the famous long-distance Kenyan runners who dominate the world's racetracks. From here, chance, events and circumstances took me to unexpected places on different continents. Finally I found myself living in a heavenly country, the land of snow-capped mountains, forests and lakes, Rolex watches and banks – Switzerland, a paradise. The truth, however, is that I did not choose to go there; it happened. Is it destiny? Yet I rebuff the idea that destiny manipulates us like puppets.

I have navigated the storms of life. Family, friends and acquaintances, living here or in the unending cosmic flow, are active in my mind. I chat with them all the time. I encounter fellow passengers and share their actions and thoughts. I develop real and imaginary relationships with them and mistake them for real. Am I also a shadow? I join my voice with fellow travellers to expose truths that seem to be twisted like the turban I once wore – real truths which only the fool would disagree with.

I have to write this story because it is so different from your life in Europe where you were born and raised, as I tell my children. I have to tell you how rigid the society was in which boys and girls were not allowed to talk to each other, for girls had to be chaste and be married to boys chosen by their parents. Don't get me wrong, it was not a harsh life, but it was a simple life unless you wanted to be different – like Malika, my first and greatest love, and me.

I grew up shy. Imagining what others thought of me tortured me. I found that the way out was to stop thinking about other people, a good way of staying happy but not for mental peace and improvement.

My turbanned head made me look different - more authoritative. When I took it off to play football or run a race, or at home, I did not feel the same person. I lost my assertiveness and became a normal person. The turban has its status. Its size and quality can indicate a person's opulence and point to his taste and elegance. A splendid turban is not a sign of goodness, which is the driving force of spirituality. The track I followed was as twisted as my turban, and I often took wrong turnings. My too-direct speech offended people. But hate does not have a place in my mind. This is my way of communicating.

CHAPTER 2

PENTHOUSE

⮌

Often things just happen. A nebulous, invisible, yet palpable flow carries people and everything else with it. Some manage to navigate through it - others are buffeted along. Nothing that I planned for worked out.

On a hot Indian summer day in our village in Punjab, in a small mud penthouse on the rooftop, my mother asked me "Where is bai?" It is the word for father. Raising my chubby arm with a finger pointing towards the door I prattled like a parrot, "Doooor… Freeca" - far in Africa. This is my earliest childhood memory. It does not include my older sister or younger brother. On such hot days my mother would take me to the airy penthouse, which appeared enormous then, but all it held was a single bed.

Three years later the same rooftop became a scene of disaster when my mother slipped off it accidentally. She died a few months later. My siblings and I were left motherless.

Nineteen years later, I found myself in another penthouse, this time in Eldore. Eldore is a Maasai word that means 'stony river'. Millions of tourists have seen and photographed tall, slim, proud Maasais wearing ochre-coloured togas, hair matted with ochre, holding a spear and often seen standing on one leg. A pastoral people speaking a Nilotic language, they once grazed their cattle herds in some of the best grazing savannahs of Kenya and Tanzania, much of which now forms the world-famous wildlife reserves. Their lives and livelihoods revolved around their herds. They roamed the Eldore high plateau.

At some point the name of the small settlement was changed to Eldoret, probably by the Nandi tribe that displaced the Maasai. The names of many towns and people in this area end with 'et' or 'at': Kapsabet, Kabarnet, Kaptagat, Kaplagat, Chemnoet. I stick to the original name - Eldore. Thirty kilometres north of the Equator one would expect this little town to be hot and humid, raining perpetually. However, it sits in the middle of a serene and undulating plateau perched two thousand metres above sea level on the western flank of the Great African Rift Valley. It remains cool throughout the year and the air is dry even during the rainy season. The signboard at the town boundary boasts of the best climate in the world. Until the beginning of the twentieth century, the Maasai cattle shared this virgin land with the African wildlife. In no time, it became the gun-carrying sportsman's paradise and hell for the lion, buffalo, and elephant. The latter once roamed from the thick forests of Mount Elgon, now forming the border with Uganda, to Cherangani Hills on the edge of the Great Rift Valley and supplied the finest ivory.

The Stony River cascades over a very stony bed. The tall, trim people of the Nandi tribe replaced the Maasai, but not for long. The whites found Eldore very attractive, as it reminded them of the Downs of southern England. By 1930, it had become the largest white settlement in Kenya. The majority were Dutch people from South Africa. Eldore was also offered to the Zionist movement.

When a Zionist party of experts and scientists camped for the night on the escarpment, the Dutch, with the help of the Nandis, beat drums to chase the wild animals towards the camp. Frightened, the party abandoned the investigation and reported adversely on the scheme. To attract white settlers, land was offered at between £1 and £2 an acre - land suitable for growing wheat, maize, coffee and raising herds of dairy cattle.

The luxurious house on the hillside was in the transition zone between the Whites and the Asians. Eldore's 7000 inhabitants lived in racial zones divided according to the colour of the skin. The house belonged to Roshan's father, one of the few well-to-do Indian businessmen, who had scaled one rung higher on the racial ladder. Blacks were yet to follow. Roshan, my fellow teacher, arranged my rendezvous in this hide.

"Do you know it is exactly fifty years ago that we made our vows?" Malika reminded me when we finally spoke over the phone in yet another continent. Malika had never spoken to anyone about those secret vows, a memory of half a century ago.

It was four in the afternoon. I approached the house by the back street to avoid suspicious eyes. Parking my bicycle on the side of the driveway, I entered the house nervously. Roshan's smile assured me a little. In a hushed voice, she guided me upstairs, "She's waiting for you up there", she whispered. "Mother is in the kitchen at the back, she will not know you are here."

Roshan led me to the little penthouse. Malika stood in the middle, her jet-black hair combed into two pigtails, exaggerating her wide forehead and beautiful black eyes. Her pastel-coloured printed kamiz (long Indian shirt) over white salwar (pantaloons) revealed a slim bodyline which traumatized me. I was speechless for a moment. We had grown up together, but this meeting was different. Malika had arranged this rendezvous. We taught at the same school and sought each other out at school and social gatherings. On occasions when we could not talk, our eyes met and said a lot. A year of teaching together had passed in a flash.

I sat down next to her and she felt warm and soft so close to me.

I had never touched a woman before and I dared not touch her, so unsure and afraid was I. I was afraid to tell her that I loved her. Nervously, I held her hand. Her hand was sure.

A state of timelessness followed. Suddenly Malika enquired, "Why did you break your engagement with Santi?"

I reeled back, surprised by the sudden question. Then, almost angrily, I told her, "I was blackmailed into it. How can I marry a girl whose family is against all Sikhs being members of one Sikh temple?"

Was I looking for excuses? Absolutely not. I was in love with Malika, not Santi.

I was firm in my stand against constructing another Sikh temple in our small town which would divide us according to the caste system that was against the Sikh way.

"I've nothing against Santi," I defended myself. "She is a nice girl, but I'm not attracted to her and I do not fancy her family."

It seemed Malika was deaf to what I said. "Did you break it because of me?" she persisted.

I was stupefied. Did she not hear me?

Roshan called from below "You have little time left."

We had not even started to talk. I put my hand on her knee, imploring her to believe me. My hand slid a little higher. We embraced. My hand stopped just below her breast. The sensation was electric.

Malika broke the silence. "We should go, Roshan's brother will arrive any time", she said. We hurried down the stairs to the first floor bedroom. An incredibly powerful magnet seemed to be drawing us together. Our lips met and we were lost in eternity.

Roshan called again– this time afraid. But our lips pressed harder together. It was an unforgettable first kiss. I walked out in my seventh heaven.

The following morning at school, Malika's lips were swollen. She pouted at me playfully.

"I'm sorry, I didn't know they were so delicate," I whispered. "No one noticed at home?"

"Mother did in the morning. I told her I got scalded drinking hot milk from the metal glass last night," she smiled coquettishly.

I resisted the temptation to touch her again. The teachers were watching us. Our fate was sealed – we were going to get married, even though all the odds were stacked against us because we were from different castes.

CHAPTER 3

TWISTS OF FATE

Before the outbreak of World War Two, my mother and I sailed to India in a dhow. What was the voyage like? I cannot tell; I was only an infant. It was 1939, the year Vakil, my mother's younger brother, was getting married in Punjab. The women in Eldore were not overjoyed at this, for my mother was one of the few literate members of the group. With her away, there would be no one to read or write their letters. Vakil Uncle (as we Easterners say instead of Uncle Vakil) was in the British Indian Army Corps of Engineers. His duty would take him to faraway lands to fight the European world war.

Whenever I mention that I was born in Eldore, the European ear equates it with Eldorado of South America. The first time Eldore achieved world fame was at the Mexico City Olympics in 1968, when the unknown Kipchoge Kieno and his team-mates won a handful of gold medals. Long-distance European runners were quick to discover the secret of their fantastic prowess – high-altitude training in the mountains surrounding Eldore. Eldore is now a famous training ground where European athletes crowd the training camps before major athletic events. Westerners are of course envious and now claim that the predominant runners, in particular of the Kalengin tribe, are genetically predisposed to running. Some researchers say this is not the case. It is sheer hard work, intense training six days a week, discipline and determination. Coming from an impoverished background, the only option they have to earn money is to run. I drew my first breath here. My seventy-five-year-old lungs can still pump enough oxygen to run half marathons.

Hardly thirty-five kilometres to the east, as the crow flies, I have often stood on the edge of the plateau to look down into the Great Rift Valley, a thousand metres below my feet. Showing off to first timers, I would pull out my handkerchief and let it drift away. They expected it to land on the floor of the valley, but the strong eddy rising from below would blow the handkerchief over our heads and land it behind us. No one has ever succeeded in sending a handkerchief down to the valley floor.

Growing up in Eldore, I often ventured into the savannah woods to watch herds of elephants and giraffes snipping delicate leaves from the tops of the acacia trees. Herds of zebra grazed in the soft sun, watched by prides of lions browsing under green thickets where motherly lionesses let their playful cubs tug their tails. Antelopes frolicked in the tawny grass. Baboons and monkeys chattered in the trees. Tick birds accompanied the wild animals, pecking the bloodthirsty parasites off their hosts. Hundreds of other species lodged in the numerous marshes: sunbirds, kingfishers, cuckoos, wild ducks, ibis and hawks. Under this heavenly bowl, the noble Maasai grazed their herds of cattle unruffled by the wild animals.

White settlers replaced the natural grasslands with wheat and maize fields, eliminating most of the wild animals and pushing the few left into remote unprotected areas. Often on Sundays, I would go to the one surviving part of the savannah, near a village called Soi, twenty-five kilometres to the west, to watch the animals. But even Soi with its mud-and-thatch roof huts has changed.

I could not foretell that many years later Soi would become a fateful turning pointing of my life. One day I might meet the spirit of my first wife here. She died in a head-on collision on Soi River

Bridge on Christmas Eve 1991. We were returning from a safari to Lake Turkana in the northern deserts of Kenya. Sitting on the passenger seat, she unbuckled her belt to turn around and hand a bottle of Coca Cola to our teenage daughter, Atima, in the back seat. Atima had not even finished her sentence, "Mummy put on your belt…" when an oncoming van driven by a drunk driver swerved to the right, hitting our car head on.

Why did it happen? Where was Jesus? The Three Wise Men from the East were busy counting the rosary beads, waiting for Jesus to be born.

Nevertheless, if I had the choice, I would return to Eldore in my next life, even though the town has mushroomed into a city, and live there like Mohi, my younger brother, who never left this town.

Until the controversial elections in Kenya at the end of 2007, few had heard of Eldore. On New Year's Day, inter-tribal violence gripped this peaceful town. Power-hungry, corrupt and irresponsible politicians triggered gruesome ethnic killings in and around Eldore. Machete-wielding gangs set fire to a church, burning it to the ground with dozens of families sheltering in it. Hundreds died and thousands quit the district to become refugees in their own country. Another Rwanda? No, it will pass, I am convinced.

My father knew only how to sign his name in the Gurmukhi script; he preferred to use his thumb. Yet many an educated person in Eldore sought his advice. Back in his village, Jatpur, he was convinced that he was incapable of learning to read and write. He did not even try. He cultivated his land and provided a service to farmers by making and repairing their tools. His earnings were not sufficient to feed the family and at the same time repay the loan that his elder brother, Santa, had taken to finance his travel to Kenya in 1930.

Two years later Santa advised him to come to Kenya as well. There he worked as a technician in various sawmills owned by people from nearby villages in the Punjab. His simplicity and rustic wisdom endeared him to all. In later days, he worked in H. I. Flourmill. He could write numbers just well enough to count the sacks of grain that a truck delivered and the number of bags of flour he loaded. He ran the mill and installed and maintained the machines as well as take deliveries of wheat and maize.

In those days safety measures were almost unknown. One day in 1952, my father's shirt, dangling out of his loose trousers, was caught in the main shaft turning the grinders. It quickly started to wrap round, pulling him over it. He held himself on hands and feet curved over the shaft until all his clothes were torn away, making a thick spindle. He escaped with a badly-burnt belly.

When I returned from school, I was surprised to see my father lying in his bed, for I had never seen him ill. Next to him sat a neighbour, Achhara. Describing the incident, my father said, "I was not afraid of dying. I did what I could". He was a very strong man, the stalwart of the town's tug-of-war team.

Achhara turned to me and asked, "What would you have done if your father had been killed?" Without much thought I replied, "We would have managed as we did before". I showed little emotion because that is how I had grown up.

In 1969, my father suffered a massive heart attack during the night. Next morning Mohi drove him down a hundred kilometres of rough road to the newly-built hospital on the shores of Lake Victoria where I was stationed.

"What happened, Mzee?" the Czech doctor, who was a heart specialist and my friend, asked him in Kiswahili. Mzee is Kiswahili for a respected old man.

"Late at night, I had a severe pain in the chest. With my fist, I hit hard on it and called my son. He gave me some whisky. I lay down and waited. I was not afraid of death."

"Mzee, you're strong", the doctor complimented him, examining his cardiogram. "Another person wouldn't have survived."

As if it were predestined, every time my father returned to India he lost a member of his small family. The first time he returned, my mother died. The second time, in the mid 1940s, he came to take us with him to Kenya. This time my grandmother, Mahan, passed away.

Mahan was a special woman. Five days after her last child, a daughter, was born, her husband died. She refused to breast-feed the child. Little Premo had to be fed drop by drop, the milk squeezed from cotton wool. She named her Bahkto, bad luck. She refused to allow Santa Uncle to go to Africa. But he escaped and caught a train at Jagraon twenty-five kilometres away. Only my father knew of this. But after three continuous days of his mother's threats, he told her.

"He has gone to Africa," my father blurted out. Great Grandma then walked to Jagraon to bring Santa back, but found that the bird had flown. In Mumbai he had his passport made, earned some money and took an Arab dhow to Mombasa that cost ninety-five rupees, quite a sum for a poor man in those days. Without consulting anybody Mahan bought a buffalo that died three days later. She comforted the seller, "Do not worry about payment, I will pay you. My son will send money from Africa".

Mahan was a professional mourner. She had to be in every Jatpur village team going to mourn someone in another village. When asked why she wept every day, she replied, "Why do you sing, Asa di Var, the morning prayer, every day?"

My father quickly arranged the marriage of my sixteen-year-old sister to a boy from a nearby village. Marrying a daughter was a burden. Moreover, he wanted to return to Kenya, taking his two sons with him. Santa instead decided to leave Kenya and return to his motherland. He was an intellectual, a good musician, a skilful technician and a bit of a politician. "What I do in Eldore I can do better in Jatpur," he reasoned.

During my father's third trip, my sister died of typhoid, leaving behind two teenage children and a lazy husband. Finally, my father returned to India for good in 1970 and lived there for ten years. In 1979 he decided to visit Mohi in Kenya and then to see me in Europe. He had never travelled in an aeroplane before. Yet he organised his trip himself.

Back in the village, two months later, in February 1980, he died quietly of a heart attack while brewing his morning tea in the kitchen. I retain only a vague memory of my sister: she is making chapattis on the round hotplate sitting beside the hearth with flaming wood in it and my grandmother being angry with her. I cannot explain why I remember this particular image and automatically think of the expression I learnt in school: from the frying pan into the fire!

Looking back now, there are so many loved ones I lost early in life – mother, father, sister and then my wife, forever. But my first love, Malika, I lost to another man. I fell in love and tried to plan a happy fairytale ending. It was a disaster. I brood over this episode when my mind has nothing else to occupy it. It has left me emotionally charred. Looking back, I think that marrying Malika would have been more than getting a wife; she would have given me the mother's love I never had.

Happily, on other fronts things worked out well for me. I deal with the present and let the future sort itself out. I attribute much of my success to a reaction to my sore relationship with the society, my unfulfilled motherly love and my failure to obtain my first soulmate. My desire to meet Malika again – even after half a century - was unrelenting. In January 2008, I plucked up the courage to phone her. I had heard that she was ill.

Malika reminded me, "In 1958 our parents nearly succeeded in leading us to a Romeo and Juliet ending."

What seems easy to talk about now is the tragic ending of our love – we had been ready to die for each other. Having survived the incident, I became determined to succeed in life. Was I ever unhappy?

I just did not care. There were many who warned me that I would not be able to marry Malika, but no one to guide me how to get over this hurdle. Malika's father, Shera, led the struggle to unite the town's Sikhs as a model for other towns where farmer and artisan castes had built separate gurdwaras. I helped him. Under his guidance the small multi-caste group promoted equality and a casteless society.

"Let's talk to my father," Malika proposed. "He loves me. He will do anything for me." I was also convinced that Shera would give us permission to marry in order to justify what he had been preaching – unity amongst castes. We did not realise that the caste wall overrides all religious and moral values. Very few have succeeded in getting across it.

CHAPTER 4

MILKING A MALE BUFFALO

~

Crouched near the bus, my father held me in his arms. Did I see tears rolling into his black beard? His sombre face did not fully reveal his sadness. I was too young to notice it. His narrow and short flowing beard made his face look long. He was neither fair nor dark. A stocky, bearded bus driver growled at his assistant-cum ticket-collector: *Teri bhen di chut*, (Your sister's cunt) – put some more coal in it. No one can be more abusive than a Punjabi. Buses were rare in those days. This was the first one I had seen. It operated with gas produced with coal burnt in an old petrol drum crudely strapped to the back of the bus, ready to take off from Raikot.

In the spring of 1942, I turned five and my younger brother, Mohi, was three and a half. A small family group watched us, looking agonizingly sad. My mother had died after a prolonged sickness resulting from the accident. I was too young to know the exact details but I remember an outing with her not long before she died.

Raikot is a dusty country town forty kilometres south-east of Ludhiana, now a mushrooming industrial city. I treasure precious childhood memories of Raikot. Once I went to the annual fair. I saw people crowding to watch someone performing magic tricks. I was too short to see them. After that, I remember relishing hot jalebys – fried dough ringlets soaked in sugary syrup. On another occasion, I remember sitting on a tricycle at my uncle's cycle repair shop. Another time I recall holding my mother's hand and walking from Jatpur four dusty long kilometres to Raikot. She had dressed me in maroon velvet shorts which she must have brought from Kenya. In those days in the village, no one wore western shorts. The shorts had become too small for me. The shoulder straps pulled them up so high that my balls were squeezed, causing excruciating pain. Halfway there, someone noticed my discomfort and my mother slid the straps off my shoulders. It was a relief. We entered the haveli (manor) of the town chief, a Muslim descendant of the Rais (chiefs) of Raikot. He owned a large tract of land around Ludhiana, which once belonged to the Mogul emperors. The compound of the haveli was full of people, mainly Sikh, waiting to see the sacred flask, the Ganga Sagar. It once belonged to the tenth Guru of the Sikhs. Once a year it was brought out for people to see. I perched on my mother's shoulder to see the chief come out holding a long-necked brass flask.

"The belly of the flask has two hundred and eighty-eight micro holes," he announced. "You can see fine sand pouring out. Now I will replace the sand with water. Not a drop has come out." With hands folded, many bent their heads in awe and genuflected in front of it.

He then narrated the legend. "Guru Gobind Singhji was retreating after fighting the imperial army and the Hindu rajas. He took shelter in the Bumper Forest near Raikot in January 1705. It was a cold frosty morning. My great-grandfather, Rai Kalha's herdsman, Noor Mahi, was grazing his buffaloes there. He came across the Guru. The Guru asked Noor Mahi for some milk. Respectfully, the herdsman said that he had already milked the buffaloes at home. The Guru handed him the Ganga Sagar and pointed towards a buffalo, some claim it was a male buffalo, and asked him to milk it. Noor obeyed. He was wonderstruck when the buffalo produced milk and not even a drop poured out through the holes in the flask. Noor hurried home to inform his master. Rai Kalha immediately invited Guru Gobind to his manor and gave him shelter and assistance. In return, the Guru gave him the Ganga Sagar. It has protected our family from all upheavals since then."

My mother lifted me higher so that I could also have a darshan, a holy sighting so to speak, of the miraculous flask. The Rai family migrated to Pakistan in 1947 and took the sacred flask with it.

After a silent goodbye, my father returned to Africa. Freshly motherless, I felt abandoned, an orphan. Then I heard a child cry hysterically and someone said "chalo, chalo" (let's go).

Childhood memory flashes became frequent. How many months or years since the bus stop scene, I do not recall. When I turned fifty, I decided to computerise my family tree. I tried to work out how old my mother was when she died. In rural Punjab to find someone's date of birth, you first have to find the date of death. It proves the Indian dictum: death is life. Our culture does not require people to remember such dates. People come and go; the wheel of life keeps spinning, and everything merges into a sort of flowing miasma, Rub, God, only knows.

I was lucky to have Vakil Uncle. Sixteen years younger than my mother, he was one of the many villagers who in the British Indian Army became a civil engineer (and not an advocate as his name implies). He rose to be a colonel. The occasional letters from him during my youth were the only stimulus that turned me into an optimist. In reply to my inquiry, Vakil sent a note in 1987:

"I went to Hardwar on the holy Ganges River. At the Ghat I checked with the pundits and finally one of them dug into his old ledgers and found the following entry: 'Bibi Shyam Kaur (mother of Kartaro, Inder and Mohi): Baba Hazara Singh took last mortal remains of Bibi Shyam Kaur his granddaughter to Hardwar in Phagum 1998 Bikrami'. As Bikrami is fifty-six years more than the

Christian year this converts to 1998 - 56 = 1942, March." How my great-grandfather travelled to holy Hardwar, three hundred kilometres away, is anybody's guess. All that I know of my mother's death is from my Aunt Bibo, my mother's sister, who visited us for the first time in February 2001 to mourn Mohi's death.

"Sister fell from the roof. She made a clay baoli, crib, for placing Diwali lamps in it. She took a few steps back to look at her creation but fell in the neighbour's yard. She suffered a severe internal pelvic injury".

"Didn't they take her to the hospital?"

"Who bothered about injuries in villages in those times? I was only eleven then. I heard people talk that sister was pregnant."

I vaguely remember my mother's face. I imagined her smiling face when looking at the baoli.

"I recall that sister was brought to my village in a rath, to see Dr Gopal Singh."

I interrupted, "Why in a rath?"

"A rath is a light chariot, a little more comfortable than a common cart. A bullock can draw it faster."

"I think I have ridden in one at a cousin's wedding."

"Yes, people used a rath instead of a Rolls Royce in those days to take the newly-wed girl to her husband's home. Sister became sicker. People talked about infectious toxins that had spread inside her. She was rushed to Raikot for an abortion. Everything was done late. She succumbed and died a month after Diwali. She must have passed away in January 1942, aged only thirty-eight."

"So she was born in 1904" I calculated.

"She died of TB, having lost her left lung," Bibo shook her head sadly.

Back to the Raikot memory flash. The bus drove off with my father. A flux of intense heat left behind by the coal drum hit me in the face, leaving me baffled. Another aunt, my father's elder sister, took me to her village, Thikrival, not far from the desert of Rajasthan. Her husband was in Uganda. Alone she managed a full house - four daughters and a son, all older than I did. When I arrived, my cousins nicknamed me Chhota, Junior. For four years, I did not know my true name, until my father appeared in Thikrival and took me to Jatpur on his new Raleigh bicycle.

In the spring of 1948, my father took me to Eldore, where I finished school. After completing university in Ireland I returned to Kenya to earn a living until I was thirty-three. Then I migrated to another continent. I know north Indian languages, including Urdu, and am an amateur player-singer of Indian music steeped in Indian culture. I have aspired to help people. For that, my heart goes unflinchingly to Kenya and Africa in general. I also wanted to return to Jatpur and link up with my childhood images. Twenty years later, I returned with my wife and three-year old daughter. Nothing looked as before. What was far and big then appears so near and small now.

CHAPTER 5

JUNIOR TWO

I did not see who took my baby brother, Mohi, from the Raikot bus stop when my father left for Africa. In those days, travelling to Africa meant riding buses and trains to Mumbai and then boarding an Arab dhow to cross the Arabian Sea. A month later, my father landed at Mombasa's old port. My maternal grandmother took Mohi to her village, Bassian, on the road to Jagraon.

"Why should he go away when we are still alive?" bemoaned Bibo when she came to mourn Mohi's death. Her breath got stuck in her throat for a few moments before she continued. "When he was brought to my village, he cried day and night. He would not eat or drink. The entire family used to cry with him. It took a long time before he compensated the loss of mother with my sister-in-law who took care of him like her own son, if not more."

Bibo had mellowed with age. Nobody ever saw her cry and she demanded that others face life in her way. However, on that day she broke down as if a dam had burst, unleashing a flood of tears.

During my four years in Thikrival, I saw Mohi only twice.

Mohi did not even know that he had a brother. He was the youngest in the new family, so everyone called him "Chhota", Junior. I saw him wearing good clothes. He had plenty to eat: milk, butter, fresh saag made from freshly collected leaves of the mustard plant, with buttered missian rotian, mixed-flour chapattis. In Thikrival, I had to often miss meals and sleep hungry. Mohi was secure and well surrounded. Probably the most striking thing that I envied was Mohi's friendship with our great-grandfather, Hazara Singh, everyone's Baba. He was short and sturdy and always on the move like a soldier. Three generations after him ended up being soldiers. I remember staying with Baba in 1945. He was hunchbacked with age and died at the age of a hundred and four. He had never been sick in his life.

Once Mohi was out of his crying stage, he and Baba were inseparable. He slept in Baba's bed. Wherever he went, Mohi was sure to go with him. The biggest attraction for him was a stock of health-giving rustic buns Baba made from flour, nuts, dried fruit and many other ingredients, still a secret. The two connived to take the buns from a secret niche in the house. One bun in the morning and one in the evening after meals was their dessert. No one else had the right to relish them. I remember it was a little hard, not too sweet but yummy.

Baba always carried a lathi, a staff, as tall as he was, every time he went out, which was nearly always. There was always some work in the farms, like repairing the tools or training young oxen to draw the plough and the cart. Once, he took me along. Baba cut a big acacia branch and yoked a young white ox to it. Mohi was happy and sat on the branch, but I, frightened, sat as far possible from the ox's kicks. The ox dragged the branch and gradually started trotting, Baba carefully controlling it. All that I remember next is that I lost my hold of the branch and fell to the ground, and the thorny branch passed over me. When I got back on to my feet, I felt something pierce my right toe. Baba examined it, but could see nothing.

"Probably it's come out", he said. I felt no pain, but an unusual stiffness when I bent the toe. I forgot all about it when I went out to play. A month later when back with my aunt, I noticed a sharp cone at the top of the toe. I did not have shoes and was barefoot all the time. While sweeping the yard, broom thistles sliced the top of the cone. Noticing a black sharp point, I pulled it out. It was a half-inch long acacia thorn. It had worked its way upwards through the joint painlessly.

My next flashback is of grandfather lying very sick in bed. He died a few days later in 1946.

Such memory flashes, and what little I have heard, help me to understand Mohi's fibre. Physically strong and daring, he hid a tender side. To outsiders this shell looked stern. Speaking hesitantly, he always came out with genuine help, advice and lasting friendship. However, he was unable to exteriorise his childhood sentiments. He revealed this during the last hours of the fateful day of 13 January 2001. Six months earlier, he had been the strongest golfer in town, hitting the golf ball farthest and in the right direction, playing the role of the club captain. On that day, Mohi seemed troubled by a bed sheet on his knee. He wanted to take it off, but there was no sheet on his leg. Every one tried to help him get over this delusion.

"It's me, Mohi, do you see me?" I asked.

"Yes I see you, but what is this doing here? Why don't you put it aside? *aih ki karda aithey? Iss noon passey kardo na!*" he reacted in Punjabi.

It was a pleading voice, curiously different and tender. He hugged me for the last time. Where had I heard this voice before? It was that of the innocent motherless baby crying at the bus stop. Recalling the old scene, I broke down, but holding my feelings back I tried to divert Mohi's mind to see beautiful images.

"We are walking in Eldore Club golf course. You are holding Arti's hand. Tall green trees: do you see them? That's the one you love hitting the ball over." He shook his head. "Hear the birds sing. The sun is beautiful…"

It was more than Mohi's brain could accommodate. Toxic fluids from the sick liver had overpowered it. Arti, his wife joined in. "Let's sit in the garden. You take the white chair. Look at the lilies I planted. They are so beautiful." She mentioned the names of their three sons and five grandchildren playing on the lawn.

Just after midday, like the beautiful sunset he frequently watched in Eldore, Mohi passed away. It must be perfectly serene there. Has the mother he was longing for embraced him in her loving arms? The only mother he knew was the little photo in her passport.

"You have a wheel under your foot," Mohi used to tell me. "You are always travelling, whereas I rarely leave Eldore. It's all in our karma, nothing to do with God or Allah or Waheguru, or whatever name people give it."

Mohi lived his entire life in Eldore after leaving India. He started school there. His colleague and closest friend, Happy Klaus, read out an appreciation at the Stony River cremation ghat of which Mohi was the manager:

"Mohi, born in Eldore in 1938, was a truly outstanding and remarkable man. He was humble and unselfish, he was dedicated, kind, and loving, yet he was strong and very charismatic. In addition, he was a perfectionist in everything he undertook.

He was, firstly, a good son. His father, a skilled technician, came to Kenya to seek employment, working first at a sawmill near Timboroa, then for H. I. Flour Mill, and later for Elgeyo Sawmills. When Mohi was not yet four years old he lost his mother. His father had to care for their two sons on his own: not easy for him, and not easy for Inder and Mohi.

Secondly, he was a loving and caring husband. He married Arti in Eldore in 1958. They were married for forty years. From small beginnings, they became a happy couple living in a house they built themselves.

Mohi was, thirdly, a loving and caring father and grandfather. The entire family came from distant lands to be with Mohi and Arti when they learned how ill he was. They gave him a great deal of pleasure, and he was overjoyed to see them all again. Mohi had a very special relationship with his family and in the last few weeks of his life, their companionship and support were the most important thing they could have given him. They did this wholeheartedly, and I know he was very proud of them all.

As a brother, Mohi had a unique and very special relationship with Inder. They were from the time they were very young inseparable.

The same high standards were evident in whatever Mohi did, whether as a student, a sportsman, a businessperson, a colleague or a friend. He never compromised his principles, and his honesty and kindness meant that he cared for others more than for himself. I quote here an email received today from a tennis-playing friend: 'I remember him as having perfect manners, both off and on the court'.

As a student, he struggled, at his own expense, to qualify as an ACCA accountant, while still working full time. As an employee, Mohi's first job was as an accounts clerk with the Eldore Magistrates' Court. He later moved to the County Council. Then he joined East African Tanning Extract Company as an assistant accountant, rising through various posts to become Finance Director. After twenty-five years of service, he went into partnership and set a firm of accountants, well respected in Eldore. Soon with his youngest son, he started Africaland, the first Internet service provider in Eldore.

Mohi was chairman or committee member of many organizations such as Lions Club, Gurdwara Singh Sabha, this Shamshan Bhumi, Eldore Club, Eldore Academy and others, and his achievements and the respect he commanded were legendary. This is exemplified by the fact that he served for over twenty years as Chairman of the Eldore Sikh Union.

As a Mason, he was totally dedicated and was held in high esteem by all those who knew him, achieving a very high rank - that of a Grand Officer in one of the orders.

His organizing ability endeared him to all, and he was often asked to be spokesperson at functions. His sporting achievements were numerous, especially at hockey where he was picked to play against international teams. He was also an all-rounder, playing tennis, badminton and golf with equal flair, and was a member of the Kenya Golfing Society and the Senior Golfers' Society. He loved a good game of cards.

As a friend, he was unequalled. His sense of humour and concern for others, particularly in times of sorrow or hardship, were well known. Mohi will be greatly missed by many who relied on him for counsel and advice, which he gave unstintingly. His friends came from all walks of life and from all communities, as you can see today. Many of his closest friends are from his schooldays and from his childhood, and he valued them very much.

Finally, as a patient, he was truly remarkable. When the doctor told him of the diagnosis of cancer, he remained composed and mentally strong, as he did throughout the course of his illness, right to the end. He made known his appreciation of all that his family were doing for him. I am sure they are proud to have done it for this most outstanding man. May he rest in peace, Eldore, January 2001."

I felt an emotional emptiness. Courage seemed to have seeped away. No one wanted to go through what Mohi had left behind in his office. I was amazed to see the number of charity organizations, sports clubs, religious and social bodies that he helped with accounts. I felt deeply proud of my younger brother.

CHAPTER 6

MALIKA

1998. I am in California. I had tried to forget Malika, but her image refused to leave my mind. On the last day of the stay, after visiting Yosemite National Park and Silicon Valley, I had to call her. Malika lives in one of the burgeoning South Bay cities. She was curt, almost brutal.

"I would like you not to phone. It will upset my family," she said. "No one knows about our past and I want to keep it that way."

"I have no problem. My family knows our story."

"Inder, it's over," Malika interrupted. "We have our own lives to live, children and grandchildren to look after. Let's not disturb silent waters. I do not see any purpose in maintaining contact. I wish you happiness". She did not wait to hear my reply and cut me off. I take in such treatment badly. I waste my energy especially when handling such emotional contacts. Why did I call her? This question continued to perturb me for many days. Should I react the way she did and cut her off? I still love her. As I grow older, I feel a greater need to be loved in return. Then I realized that she must have the same need for love. No one can escape the course of life. Prayer cannot stop what is happening, it may give strength to resist or overcome emotions. Soon my emotions fell back to normal.

2008. I am in California again. A hidden hand pushes me to call her again. A voice responds, "Who am I talking to?" The accent is more British than American. A current passes through my body. Not sure of her voice and afraid that I might be talking to her daughter I ask, "Is it possible to talk to Mrs Malika?"

"Speaking."

"It's Inder. I do not want to disturb you. I just wanted to know how you are. Is it OK? Can you spare a minute?" I stammered. Nervous.

"No problem, I have time," she replied calmly.

Obviously, she had forgotten her previous stipulation. We chatted for an hour. Now I have to stretch my brain to remember what we talked about. I am either becoming senile or getting emotionally wild. I was just happy to know that she would communicate with me by email. What had made her change her mind?

"Roshan mentioned that you are not well. What is it?" I inquired.

Without hesitation she replied, "Breast cancer. I'm in the exit line. Diagnosis revealed that it's the nasty type. Funny. I was seventy last week. Until then I was not afraid of going away. Now I don't want to leave so quickly."

She talked so intimately as if we had been together all the time – all those years apart vanished. "I'm waiting for the report of the latest tests to know how far it has spread," she said in a matter-of-fact way. Not having the vaguest idea what she looked like now, talking to her or even thinking about her did not hurt or upset me any more.

Roshan was my only source of information. Even she has not met Malika for ten years. Talking to Malika brought an intense desire to meet her and talk to her in person. Her voice made my old heart throb. The brief encounter in London twenty-six years earlier had become hazy. The prospect of seeing her again aroused new expectations. I spent a fitful night speculating – having coffee with her somewhere romantic. The spiritual ointment of eternal union of souls in afterlife did not console me. A wound in the present life has to be treated here. God, if he exists, has no role to play in it. Yet I whispered, "Oh God! I want to complete the cycle, see what she is like".

To calm my nerves I called Roshan. "You know a miracle has happened. Malika talked to me for nearly an hour. I asked her if I could meet her. Her response was: Let's sleep over it. Can you believe that?"

"I'll suggest to her to come and stay with me for a few days so we can have a get-together," Roshan suggested. "I'll contact other school-time friends to come as well. She has confined herself to her clan and nothing else. Call me when you're back."

Still feeling restless, I emailed Malika. "I'm overwhelmed having talked to you. I had lost all hope of ever talking to you. I'm worried about you," I blurted like a love-torn teen. "Last week I spent four days just a ten-minute drive from where you live. This morning I forgot to tell you that I had attended a wedding in South Bay and you know the family. I thought you would be there. I met Sewa and his wife. What a reunion after forty years. Naturally, they asked about you, opening up old wounds. I told them I did not even know where you were and asked them for information. You are on my mind all the time. Sorry, I jumped from one subject to another. That meeting in the penthouse has always been with me. Yet I don't even know what you look like now. You can see me on my website. The way you describe things gives me the impression that you have a very caring and loving family. I know you are very brave. I wish I can do something for you. I have the time and means. Can I talk to you again before I fly back in two days?"

Had I reacted too quickly? Had I said too much? Would she respond?

At midnight, she emailed. I burst with joy. Twenty-six years had passed since we saw each other. Would I recognize her if we met in the street? I still see her sitting in the front row in the official photograph of schoolteachers, slim and beautiful, wearing an elegant Punjabi dress.

Malika wrote back, "Thanks for the sweet email. The phone call was a complete surprise, but, what a pleasant one! You worried that I would be curt to you - I am not that bad! I looked at your website - wow! Your accomplishments are very impressive. Congratulations! One of these days, I would love to read your writings. Call tomorrow morning and we will see how our timetable works. I imagine you want to spend time with your family. Enjoy your loved ones. They are precious. Life is very uncertain. Best wishes."

Her voice shook me. Would meeting her trigger an emotional earthquake? I sensed that she remembered every moment of our pristine love, a word she dare not utter. A love nipped in the bud because of the horrible caste system. Blinded by love we naïvely braved to change the society, its traditions and rituals but it was too much for us. We decided against eloping to another country; it would go against our vow to marry within the social setting with full parental consent, to set an example, a model for future generations. We wanted to put into practice what our parents had taught us - that we were one people. Malika was convinced that people would be pleased with our courageous action. We were too far ahead of our time – naïve idealists or idiots.

CHAPTER 7

LIFE IS A TRAIN

⌒

Sobha has an elder brother, Guma. He was born in Eldore. When he was four years old, his father opted for an early retirement from the East African Railways and returned to the Punjab to manage the family farm in his ancestral village, Kishangarh. After the first year in a country college in Sadhar, Guma quit. His father sent him to Utter Pradesh to manage a recently acquired big farm near Dudwa Wild Life Reserve not far from the Nepal border. The adjoining farm belonged to my father-in-law and his elder brother, who had sold their flourishing sawmill business near Eldore to retire in India, away from relatives in the Punjab. They were quite old when they left Kenya. Guma lived with them in relative luxury and drove around in their Mercedes; he did not have much else to do on the farm. He longed to leave India and join his grandparents, uncle and aunts in Eldore. I visited the farm in 1978 on my way back from the Far East.

"What are you doing here?" I asked Guma. "You should be in college." Guma was driving me to a bar in Palia, a small and dusty town.

"I want to go to Canada."

"What will you do there? You must learn a trade."

"I will learn there."

"At least improve your English."

"I know a little. Again I will learn there."

I found Guma so determined that I did not pursue the line. When I next heard of Guma three years later, he was married to a girl in Vancouver and had no difficulty in finding a job in a lumber mill. He lost two fingers to a saw there. On the side he studied real estate trade and joined a well-known estate company. A few years later he went into a successful house construction business. His good nature and humility have brought him success. I meet him and his family often, in India, in Kenya, in North America or Europe – a continuation of a symbiotic relationship of the two families for more than seventy-five years. Soon after Guma left the farm my father-in-law passed away. The farm was sold and the family dispersed.

Guma's half-sister's daughter was getting married. A marriage in the family was a good reason for relatives and friends in different continents to flock to South Bay. Entire families of uncles, aunts, cousins and friends flew in from as far as Australia and Africa. Celebrations started a week earlier.

"Uncle, we expect you on Monday," Guma phoned a fortnight earlier from Vancouver. I'm leaving today, everyone else is already there. Uncle Satti from Perth has come. They are all waiting for you."

I realised why Guma was so insistent; to give company to the oldies who were unable to pass time. I arrived on Friday evening.

"Uncleji," said Guma giving me a welcoming hug. "Father and others are waiting in the marquise at the back. I'm bringing tea. You relax today. Tomorrow is Jaago and we'll be up all night."

Jaago literally means 'wake up'. As elsewhere, Californian Sikhs have revived this dying folkloric ceremony. Women, young and old, perform the Jaago dance. I could not take my eyes off the elegant ladies showing off their colourful silk Punjabi costumes. One young woman placed a decorated earthen pot lit with candles on her head. Its mouth was covered with a red cloth tied with a ceremonial red-yellow-white string. She danced provocatively to the rhythmic clapping and Jaago folk songs. Other women joined her in turns; the pot was transferred to the head of another woman and the dance continued for hours. Jaago songs typically tease elders. In the conservative rural Punjab, Jaago is one of the few social occasions when women can dance publicly, giving men the opportunity to appreciate them.

I did not have a wife, but I was looking for the girl who would have been the one fifty years earlier. I heard someone mention her name. In the guise of a photographer, I scrutinized the face of every female who could have been her. Guma tapped my shoulder bringing me back to the present. "Uncle, Sewa is here". I had no difficulty recognising the unchangeable, eternal Sewa with the same scanty but greyed beard revealing his round young unwrinkled face and small intelligent eyes. He was sitting at the long dining table with his wife and talking to Satti and a few others. He was my fellow teacher, a few years older. I sat opposite them without interrupting their conversation. Then I put in a word. The two looked at me for being rude.

Suddenly Sewa stood up and said, "That is Inder's voice". The last time we had spoken was forty years ago in Narok, a remote Maasai town in Kenya. The only difference was that I wore a turban then. In a flash we were in each other's arms in an unrelenting hug, followed by an equally long hug with his wife, an act that would not have been tolerated in the good old days. I felt a spiritual reunion of long lost souls. Sewa is kind and ahead of his time. He took me aside and asked, "Are you in touch with Malika? How is she?"

Many in the gathering knew the episode, but no one talked about it. Sewa had tried to help us marry. Painful memories of a love lost flooded from half a century.

"You know Malika is being taken to India" Sewa had said. "Her train leaves tomorrow evening. I have invited her family for dinner today. Do you have a message for her?"

I had a gold ring made for Malika. The inside of the ring bore my crudely-carved initials. I was looking for an opportunity to put it on her finger.

"Yes, please give this to her," I pleaded.

Later Sewa told me, "She took the ring reluctantly but did not know how to hide it from her parents. When alone in the kitchen with my wife, she told Malika to tie it to her trouser string."

The following day, I went to the railway station to bid farewell to the family. Her father, Shera, told me that he would write when it was appropriate for me to join them in India. That was never to happen. I only saw the train steam away; Malika was not allowed to show herself in the window and bid farewell. By allowing me to come to the station, Shera left a public image that everything had been amicably sorted out. The train became a phantom rolling away never to return to its station.

The day before I left California, I received a second email from Malika, "This one in particular is very close to my heart and I refuse to take no for an answer in forwarding it, especially, to those who have either completed or are about to complete a stay of seven decades on God's earth... so here it is ... Tell me if it doesn't tug at your heart."

It was past midnight when I started to read it on a full screen with colourful images and words in large letters delicately emerging and fading accompanied by soft music.

'Life is like a train ride. We get on. We ride. We get off. We get back on and ride some more. There are accidents and then there are delays. Some people on the train will leave an everlasting impression when they get off... We will sometimes be upset that some passengers whom we love will choose to sit in another compartment and leave us to travel on our own. Once sought out and found, we may not even be able to sit next to them, because that seat will already be taken. Personally, I know I'll be sad to make my final stop - I'm sure of it! But then again, I'm certain that one day I'll get to the main station only to meet up with everyone else. I'll be glad to see them again.'

Was it a coincidence that she sent the train-poem to remind me that we had boarded a train of life together?

"Do you remember the note you handed me when I took the train at Nairobi station?" Malika asked when I called the next morning.

"Yes, you received your diploma a few days earlier so that the girls could return to their towns not accompanied by any of us lads. We knew when you were leaving and we came to see you off. I took the train two days later. But we had boarded the train of life earlier when we travelled from Eldore to Nairobi for the last term".

"You mean when my father could not be the guard on that train", she chuckled.

"Yes, that was our last train journey to Nairobi together. I came to your cabin."

Her father had asked a Muslim colleague to keep an eye on her.

"You were in my cabin," continued Malika, "The guard knocked at the door, I was petrified. We kept silent. After some time he went away. You know, he reported that to my father. Father looked very upset when we met a few days later. I explained to him that I was passing a letter from Santi to you. I didn't want the guard to see us. He accepted my explanation and told me to be careful in future. He trusted me".

"That day changed my life," I replied. "I was worried. It was going to be our last ride in the same train, never again with you. I would be married to Santi. No more train rides, no contacts. You sanctioned my marriage to her with that letter. I had no desire to read Santi's letter. Instead I expressed my feelings towards you. I was embarrassed by my clumsiness, worried that I might offend you by not appreciating the message from the girl I was engaged to. I don't know if you remember, I apologized, touched your foot and you let me. At that moment I boarded the train of life. Ever since I've been riding that train, the train of love, I went along wherever it took me."

CHAPTER 8

JATPUR

⌒

The train took us from Delhi to Ludhiana and then a bus dropped us near Raikot's old gate. Carrying a heavy suitcase, as wheeled cases were not yet in fashion, I struggled through the crowd of people into the narrow gate. I asked my wife, who was on her first visit to India, to follow me. She was carrying our three-year-old daughter.

Someone grabbed my arm and hugged me very tight. It was Bhag, my cousin, the son of my father's elder brother, Santa. Crying and laughing at the same time, he asked how I was. We were meeting after twenty years, in 1968. That time we were boys, now we were men.

We got into a three-wheeler, the big rustic type, locally called a tatoo, a mule, powered by a single-cylinder diesel engine placed precariously above the front wheel. The four-kilometre dirt road to Jatpur was muddy after the rain, much worse than I remembered. The three-wheeler had to skirt many deep puddles. Bhag, following us on his bicycle, had to get off and push us a few times. We stopped in front of a brick house which had been painted white. I looked around curiously and asked Bhag, "Where is our house?"

"A few years ago, the land consolidation exercise changed the village layout" he said. "Like many others, we gave up our old houses in the village centre and moved to the new one on the new ring road to Raikot."

"I recognize nothing," I confessed. "Take me to our old house, the workshops, and the village pond." I was nostalgic, wanting to see my childhood haunts.

"There isn't much to see of that now," said Bhag.

"Is the crumbling brick gate next to our house still there? And the narrow alley winding through the village to the watch tower on the main road?"

I remembered the smelly drain in the middle of this alley. It served as the children's toilet and we had to jump from side to side to avoid the shit. But so much had changed, and I felt lost.

"Bhag, where are our fields?"

"This house is in our field. In the land reshuffle you were allocated the one next to us." Bhag pointed. I looked lost.

"What about our old house?" I asked.

Not used to speaking the village Punjabi, I spoke in short sentences. It did not take long before I became a villager again. Twenty years suddenly collapsed after lunch.

In the afternoon Bhag guided me along the ring road and then into the old main road. "The watchtower used to be here," he said, pointing towards a two-metre high dirt ramp on the left.

"This slope looked so steep before" I remarked. From there I remembered all the houses and the occupants. "Everything is so near and small. That's Pooran's house and Karam lived in the one opposite. On the corner is Gurdit's workshop." I pointed, excited. "Sometimes I used to sleep in his house. His son, Hukam, made us do one hundred sit-ups. That red brick house opposite is Gurdial's. It looks so small now – even the glass-panelled windows."

Forgotten memories were flooding back of the houses and the people I had left. I recalled a Muslim woman, her hair dyed with henna, lying on a low charpoy in the hall on a hot day and asking us – the little children - to pour cold water on her head. It was not easy to draw water with our little hands from the well.

By now we were by the village temple, the gurdwara, and close to it still stood the ox-drawn flour mill. We reached another house. "Isn't this where the woman lived whose lover murdered her husband?" I asked. The scandalous affair had rocked our village. To add to the drama, the lover had been the husband's best friend.

"Yes and then he buried him in a sand dune near Nurpura. He was of course arrested."

It was light-hearted banter as we walked on. "The lover was brought to the numberdar's [chief's] house and tortured. We heard his screams" I recalled. "His palms were placed under the legs of the charpoy (bed). A policeman jumped on it. They say that made him admit his crime quickly."

"Do you remember Taru?" asked Bhag, pointing to the rustic mud house.

"I don't think anyone could forget him," I laughed. Taru, a nice quiet guy who decided to joined the Nihang order of Sikhs. Nihangs regard themselves as an elite corps with a mission to defend the Khalsa and promote traditional martial arts. Wearing blue garments they roam the country on horseback. Sticklers for Khalsa code, they are colourful and reckless but cannot give up cannabis and opium.

A few months later the Nihang group found out that Taru had lapsed and betrayed the order by trimming his beard and smoking. Nihangs returned and camped under a banyan in our school compound. A few of them started preparing a drink, grinding poppy seeds in a big metal bowl with a pestle made with a thick wooden pole tied to a branch. I still carry the nauseating odour of the opium they smoked. Others were busy making mincemeat out of this defector in a small side room. The entire school heard his screams. We saw him brought out soaked in blood, supported by two Nihangs holding thick bloodied cudgels. I cannot forget the image of Taru's bloodied half dead body.

"That's how Nihangs punish deserters. It is difficult to escape them," Bhag confirmed.

In the square we reached the spot where the old village gate was supposed to be. The old gate, which had been a landmark, had been pulled down many years before. We were standing by our old village houses, which looked really small. "I can't imagine how we lived in them, four families crammed in them," I remarked.

Each house was just one room, three of them with tiny penthouses on the their roofs. Other than the outer wall, the houses had been cleared away and the space was occupied by six buffaloes. "That is hardly enough for the beasts," I gasped. A few families who did not own farmland still lived in the old houses. Many others had crumbled, silenced by the passage of time. In my childhood there was always laughter, talk, quarrels and women in the courtyards stitching costumes, weaving rugs with simple patterns or feeding and milking the cows. We were at the dera, the monastery, across the street.

"We used to beat gongs standing in a circle in the evenings here," I recalled.

Next to it stood the goldsmith Dhanu's shop with the inscription still above the door: 1936 DHNI RAM.

"In the shop, uncle used to play an ancient game called Sooa that in English would be Nine Man Morris, or simply Mill, traced on the floor with charcoal with each player using nine pebbles. I can still hear him quarrelling over some disputed move. His voice could be heard above all others, proving that he was the village hymn singer. They came out with black hands." I have seen a similar game played by Africans in Eldore.

We entered the narrow lane I wanted to see. The lane is the same, but it is neatly paved with red bricks with a drain on each side. The watchtower from which the guard in times past warned the villagers of invaders is no more. We entered a yard lined with many small houses inhabited by the lower caste people. In the old days, this was quite filthy and I was surprised by the transformation.

"It is the same street. Now all houses are made of brick," said

Bhag. "They do not practise traditional menial trades. They have learnt our skills and trades. They are now carpenters, masons, mechanics, plumbers, electricians, tailors, shopkeepers, clerks, and bankers, you name it."

Forty years later, on a bright and warm spring morning, I was cooling down in the front courtyard after a jog, this time to Burmi village four kilometres away, when Bhag walked in.

"Sat Sri Akal, Bhag Singh", I greeted him. (Literarily: the True, Reverend, Timeless One.) "Have you woken up Guru Baba?"

Even after many weeks, this daily remark about the holy Sikh Book-guru Granth, which I call Book-guru, made him laugh aloud.

"The Guruji is always awake."

"This morning, I heard you singing the hymns in the gurdwara much louder than those from the other two loudspeakers. Have you bought a new amplifier?" I joked.

"No. After singing the hymns in the gurdwara I came to Dial's house. He had asked me to sing to mark the finishing of the ceremony of three days' uninterrupted reading of Book-guru."

Bhag is Jatpur's principal ragi, musician and hymn singer. Following in the footsteps of his grandfather and his father, he conducts prayers and religious ceremonies for any gurdwara or any person of any caste. He accepts no offerings. Devotees who do not know him place money on his harmonium. Invariably at the end of the ceremony, he places it in front of Book-guru with the other offerings. For other ragis, singing is their livelihood. They are unhappy with Bhag. Out of respect, at private functions, he is given time to sing one or two hymns, no more, because he must not shorten the performance time of paid singers.

Jatpur's history is mainly the story of Jats and Tarkhans. Bhag is one of the few who remember a good part.

"You have told me bits of the history of Jatpur. I want to hear it all," I said.

After dinner, we huddled together on his big charpoy to hear him.

"Once you told me that our forefathers migrated from Puneval, near the town of Dhuri. Why?" I asked.

"Well, before irrigation canals brought water to that area, sand dunes covered large tracts. That's where our aunt took you when your father returned to Africa".

"Yes, I remember the sand dunes near my school on the way to Barnala."

"At the time of Maharaja Ranjit Singh, about one hundred and seventy years ago, the rains failed and people had little to eat there. The region south of the Sutlej River was under the British protection. Ranjit Singh was scouting in the famine-struck region trying to negotiate with small Sikh rajas of Patiala and Nabha and others to bring them within his fold. The rajas could not make up their minds. Ranjit, a clever strategist taking up the cause of poor peasants, started to help them in order to win them over to his side. The majority of them were Jats, like him. The maharaja then negotiated with the local Muslim administrator at Punewal and obtained land from a big landowner named Tajedin. Our forefathers moved here and set up the village."

"That is how our village got its name?" I asked.

"That's correct. Tajedin was the chief and the village came to be known as Tajpur, and not Jatpur as you insist calling it. He lived and died here. His grave was in the dera [monastery], in front of our old house. I do not know what happened to it".

"Does the dera still exist?"

"Yes, the house is still there, somebody lives in it. One day I'll take you there. Villages around Jatpur came later, for example Navanpind (New Village) hardly a mile away. Originally it was called

Chhanna, the name of a deep round cast-metal dish. The thatched roofs of its shacks looked like an inverted Chhanna. Not long ago villagers got the name changed to Kishangarh."

"Are we the direct descendants of original settlers?"

"Our patti [wing or ward] of the village is named after the Khangura, a jat clan. Almost all jat and our tarkhan (artisan) families living on this road are descendants of original settlers. A few lower caste families also came with us. Khanguras and we have always collaborated in everything. Later on, other families, many of them relatives from nearby villages, moved in and formed the second wing, called Jhuja patti."

"I remember we used to pass through the chamar [leather workers'] street on the way to our fields", I recalled.

"It is the continuation of our patti, but you do not see stuffed smelly hides of cattle hanging on wooden bars stuffed with chopped acacia bark to produce tanned leather. Nobody makes shoes now. The animal mortuary does not exist, nor do you see vultures tugging at the corpses. After land consolidation, we built new houses in our fields. The chamar ward has become the village centre. We were allocated equivalent farmland in the east."

"I remember there was only one gurdwara on the edge of the pond, with three big banyan trees in front. To frighten us, the older boys told us that ghosts and spirits lived in them at night."

"Now you have mentioned it, I remember that."

"I remember something else. In 1943 the monsoon rains failed. The hot summer sun parched the land, crops withered and a famine loomed. Even in our food-rich area people were scared. To entreat Almighty Waheguru for rain we had a special uninterrupted reading of Book-guru. Even a Brahmin priest was invited to perform havan, the butter-burning sacred fire Hindu ceremony at the gurdwara. He chanted mantras and poured precious ghee mixture on a small sacrificial wood fire, invoking all three hundred and thirty million

Hindu gods and beseeching them to dispatch Meghraj, the rain god. But to no avail. Under the banyan trees, hefty men prepared the sacred sweet flour pudding and a maize porridge in two huge steel cauldrons posed on fire-pits dug in the ground. To please the gods, they distributed this food to the poor and the hungry. They also fed a cow, the holy mother. The village replicated yajna, the ceremony that Vedic people performed thousands of years ago but without sacrificing a bull or cow. I do not remember if it rained, do you?" I asked Bhag.

"How come you remember all that? It had all escaped my memory."

"You are getting old".

"None of the gods budged. I remember father was furious with these un-Sikh rituals. Human beings cannot change Waheguru's will."

"Is that why he joined the rival Jhuja jat clan, to construct a separate gurdwara in his patti?"

"Partly. The real reasons are different. First was the rivalry between the two pattis. Each one wanted to stay in power. Every jat wants to be a leader. Then it was the gurdwara's caretaker priest, a depraved person. He was using the donated funds for sexual services."

"So uncle changed sides?"

"Father's protesting did not change anything. The split was between the two dominating farmer families: Khangura and Jhuja. Father was the only musician and hymn singer of the village as well as one of its wise men. He wanted people to live according to the teachings of Book-guru. He performed most of the prayers and ceremonies. In the Jhuja patti, Jeta Singh was the strong man, a big landowner, active politically and a cultured person. He started the first school of the village in his haveli, manor, and you went there".

"You mean I was carried there?"

"Yes, you refused to go to school, and aunty insisted that you must go. It used to be a big drama. Two boys carried you like a sack of wheat to school." Bhag laughed. "You know, some of Jeta's children completed university. Later one of them became a Member of the Punjab Assembly. Father was like a member of that family. Without his advice they would not do anything."

"What happened to the priest?"

"The patti leaders supported him. Naturally, Jeta and father decided to build Jhuja patti's own gurdwara, near Jeta's house. There was a dung and waste dump, the smelliest part of the village. In this way Jeta got rid of the dump. His house was the biggest and the nicest in the village."

"So religious differences were not the cause of the split?"

"Not at all. As I said earlier, it was the question of leadership."

"When uncle died in 1995, you assumed his responsibilities. I'm glad that you sing in all gurdwaras. But you should take pity on me," I pleaded with hands joined.

"You have committed no crime" Bhag said uneasily.

"You wake me up every morning at five, mercilessly pouring out verses from powerful loudspeakers. You make me feel guilty. My half-hearted attempts to get up and join you fail miserably. I go to sleep again with a valid excuse: I do not know from which gurdwara you are singing. It's total confusion with all gurdwaras on air," I joked.

"You have seen that we have replaced the gurdwara with a bigger one."

"Yes, it looks beautiful. I also saw you have made provision for installing bigger loudspeakers in its dome. Is that to stop lazy people like me from falling back to sleep? I hope you will not feel bad if I said that all I hear is noise, not heavenly music. When I come the next time I will hold on to the earplugs I get in the aeroplane. I think that people use the latest audio systems in the gurdwaras to prove that God is not dead."

"Well, now the Ramdasis have built a third gurdwara," said Bhag.

"Do you mean dalit and harijan Sikhs, the untouchables?"

"Yes."

"Can't they pray in the other gurdwaras? Aren't they Sikh?"

"Now, no one objects. But it's too late, the harm was done a long time ago."

"In the old days, I recall, low caste devotees, sweepers and shoemakers, sat outside the worship hall even on cold winter mornings in case they contaminated Book-guru."

"That was when the wrong was done. Jats in particular wanted to keep them out. The excuse was that they were smelly. Steel plates and glasses used by dalits to eat from the communal kitchen were passed through fire to purify them."

"I know Saint Ravidas was a cobbler who tanned leather and made shoes. All his hymns are in Book-guru," I pointed out.

"Father tried hard to stop that practice and often sang his songs. Even Ravidas would not have been allowed in" Bhag laughed. "Protected by new laws, they have exerted their right and built their own gurdwara. They feel proud of it even though the building is not impressive. You even see an official signpost on the main road near our house, but none for the other two."

Inter-caste relations have improved. The change in attitudes does not originate from the Sikh institutions or guardians of Book-guru but from economic forcing. Dalits are doing well in various trades. Financially stronger and politically united, they exercise their power effectively in village politics. Without their support no party can win. They have used their right to build their own gurdwara. The three gurdwaras celebrate in turn the main religious festivals and all attend. But Dalits celebrate, in addition, the birthday of Ravidas.

The architecture of the new gurdwaras has evolved towards elegance, sleeker pillars and pointed arches. Conical long spouts of loudspeakers dangling from posts or fixed to walls are disappearing. They have been replaced with four mega-decibel speakers lodged in the graceful onion-shaped central dome. From a distance they look like holes pierced by cannonballs. Are they intended to represent the bullet-holes in Akal Takht made by Operation Blue Star on Amritsar? The dark holes blemish the beauty of the curve of the shining dome. Hopefully someone would install hole-covers, giving a seamless dome without restricting the flow of Book-guru's word. I was taught that if I saw a piece of paper on the ground with words from Book-guru on it I must pick it up and burn it to save the word from defilement. Now I feel that page after page is being torn from Book-guru and flung out through these loudspeakers.

It was time for the evening prayer. I invited Jas, Bhag's grandson, to walk with me in the village. Jas is a chemistry graduate from a rural college: a book degree. His level of education and knowledge is little better than that of other villagers.

Suddenly, the three gurdwaras switched on their audio systems, filling the air with the same prayer.

"I'm half deaf. Can you make out what you hear?" I asked.

"They are braying, not praying," replied Jas. I had to laugh.

"You're young and educated, why not propose that the gurdwaras use the loudspeakers in turn on a weekly basis?"

"It is very difficult to do anything here. Things will change when they will," Jas lamented. "Jats want to lead. You rightly call it Jatpur."

"Jatpur also means castepur. Tell me another thing. A jat boy can marry a tarkhan girl but a jat will not allow his daughter to marry a tarkhan boy or outside his clan?"

"Nothing has changed here. To save honour a father can still kill his daughter. In cities things have changed, especially in universities and colleges".

So the change is the result of education and not the teachings of Book-guru."

"You dare not promote such ideas openly in the village or in the gurdwara." Back home Jas's father, Bhola, greeted us sarcastically, "Anything new in the village?"

"Not really. But Jas told me that people in general tolerate inter-caste marriages."

To the surprise of my friends, I spent the summer of 2008 at home. Then an invitation to a wedding brought me to Jatpur. My brother and I had inherited our father's house that he had built some forty years earlier. The house I bought thirty years ago in Chandigarh had been taken by the government because the estate agent did not inform me of a small legal hitch. A petition to the Supreme Court needed to be arranged. Never before had I spent more than a day or two in Jatpur. The month passed like a whirlwind. The October sun had not yet lost its vigour. The cold was approaching.

Spring is short. The harvest season was in full swing when I left Jatpur. On the train to Delhi I thought of the simple rig that had been used to drill an eighty-metre deep borehole in my Jatpur plot in five days - a day was lost because the driller's mother died. To ensure success, the technicians recited two prayers to please the underworld gods and goddesses – first with sweet rice when the drill pierced through the layer of clay and when the lower aquifer was struck. The submersible pump installed at a depth of about forty metres gushed out fresh water, to everyone's delight. I recall clean water was abundant in the Punjab plains at the depth of less than ten metres. Now heavy-duty pumps have emptied this upper aquifer to meet the needs of the green revolution, and what remains has been seriously polluted by rural latrine pits and unchecked industrial effluents in the cities. Now the aquifer, more than eighty metres deep, is being tapped and its level is lowering fast, a major concern for the government. It was no wonder that everyone was happy to take the first sip of clean drinkable water, a blessing.

In the rural Punjab three Ms indicate absolute certainty - miti, mukhi and muchhar - dust, flies and mosquitoes. It reminds me of three Ws that people associate with unpredictability in England:

weather, wine and women. I survived the first three until the day my plane brought me home at nine in the morning. At one o'clock I was warming up to run the annual seven and a quarter kilometre race in the old town of Calvin's city. I was able to get into a portable toilet moments before the start.

It was 1963, the year of Kenya's Uhuru, independence. I felt claustrophobic teaching in the high school in Eldore. There were no social and cultural activities. Many white scientists and engineers migrated to other white-governed countries like Australia, South Africa and New Zealand. I found an opening in the Kenya Water Department where I became an expert in the assessment of water resources. Four years later I joined an international organization and migrated to Europe. My new position permitted me to help Kenya. Having lost roots in Kenya, I began to look for my roots in Jatpur.

At the start of my long stay in 2008 I toured Jatpur with Bhag in order to refresh my memory. I remembered a few Jatpurians, but many more knew me. That is how it is in any village. Everyone wanted to invite me.

We entered the dalit quarter. The village pond on the road to Pukhowal has shrunk to a cesspool. A refilled part of the pond and the old open cremation area form a sports stadium. Tall grass and bushes thriving in it indicate that it has not been used for some time. On the village side of the stadium stands a concrete-and-steel crematorium. Benches under a roof provide shelter for the grieving people watching the soul depart in flames.

A familiar face greeted us. It was Janak, my classmate from more than sixty years ago. His white beard did not change his round face. We embraced like long-lost brothers. Janak has retired from the Indian Revenue Service as a senior customs officer in Mumbai. He exuded the air of a rich and comfortable life. Gurdial was our common friend. We studied and played together and often I slept at

Gurdial's house. I peeped through the slightly open door. A woman I had never met before got up from a charpoy and invited me in.

"Come in, come in, and sit down. I'll make tea for you", she insisted. From her appearance I gathered she was Gurdial's daughter.

"Look, I'm sorry, I did not want to disturb you. I just wanted to see the room where I used to play and sleep in when I was nine," I explained.

"You might not know us, but we know you" she said. "I'm Harban's sister, you met him in Canada in spring this year. First sit down. Everyone has migrated to America and Canada. We live here and look after the house."

"I'm really happy meeting you. I'll come another day."

The last stop was Harnek's house. He is two years older than I am. He was reading a prayer book when I entered.

"Come in, come in, sit down," he said, putting the book aside. He pulled out two chairs and made us sit at the table.

"First, what will you have?" Tall and straight, Harnek wore clean white clothes supporting a neat white turban. From the kitchen he came up with an apple and a knife cut it into eight slices.

"I always think of you, Inder" said Harnek. "Our situations are similar. Like you, since my wife died life is not the same. Without one's partner life has shortened a little." He knew nothing of my life. Soon we were talking about the good old schooldays.

"We used to walk five kilometres each way from Litran, often barefoot under the scalding sun, running from the shade of one rosewood tree to the next," Harnek recalled.

"Our headmaster, Ajmer Singh, with a crooked little finger, was very clever" I said.

"He is still alive. His younger brother Harbhajan was also our teacher."

"The other short one with a scanty beard, Ajit I think, treated an infected sore protruding from my elbow. He took me to his little office, opened a small box, pulled out a scalpel and before I could resist he cut the sore level with the skin. He did not give me time to scream. He put some red powder on it and bandaged my elbow."

Harnek continued, "After school I joined the army and became a truck driver. I often met your uncle Colonel Vakil, who encouraged me a lot. I'm alone now. There are many old people in the village who are in fairly good health but poor."

"I'll come again, you tell me village stories. It's getting dark now, so please give us leave."

It is my first night in the village. At four-thirty on a Saturday morning the two gurdwaras became alive. Prayers started pouring out of the loudspeakers. I could not understand anything, for they made a veritable cacophony.

At six, I walked to the Khangura wing Sikh temple where Bhag was singing the last hymns of Assa di Var, an ode in Raag (a musical scale) Assa. Assa also means hope in common Punjabi. I like this ode. It's full of practical advice, condemning rituals and outdated traditions. It's a guide to a happy and a righteous life. Bhag and his companions sang it melodiously like a mantra expecting the power of Book-guru to correct all wrongs in the world. The preacher read the randomly selected hymn of the day from it. Bhag touched me on the shoulder, bringing me out of my reverie.

"My next engagement is at the Ravidas Sikh gurdwara. Do you want to come?"

"Of course, it might be different, I might find salvation there," I laughed. I was looking forward to seeing the dalits' temple.

"Let's have tea first."

We sat down on a mat outside and sipped hot tea served in metal glasses. From childhood I know how to manage a hot glass: hold it gently with the tips of the fingers of both hands above the level of tea and continuously pretend to play a piano on its rim.

Ten minutes later I was listening to Bhag singing the same hymns and melodies at the dalits' temple.

"Do you think these people really pray in order to attain nirvana?" I asked Bhag.

"The truth is, our prayer is a ritual. My routine performance cannot guide anybody to genuine meditation. You saw some swaying their heads as if in a trance. I sing without having to think and walk out as if nothing has happened. I assure you that most of the devotees wait impatiently for the end. You will see a special performance next week."

"What's happening next week?" I asked.

"It's the birth anniversary of Guru Nanak, the first Master, the messenger of love and peace."

The festival started with the uninterrupted reading of Book-guru in all three gurdwaras broadcast through loudspeakers. We sat on the charpoy sniffing aroma of parathas floating from the open-air kitchen. "Bhag, you can recite the entire Book-guru from memory. Can you make out what they are conveying to me now?"

"No one wants to follow the Word. It's a blind faith. People are convinced that just the sound of the mega potent verses can solve all problems and ailments. It's the mantra of holy cacophony." He laughed.

"You know the legend when Nanak died: Hindus wanted to cremate the body and Muslims demanded its burial." I paused. "When they lifted the white sheet the corpse was not there, it had simply disappeared. I wish the Muslims had succeeded in burying Nanak, he would be truly twisting and turning in his grave now."

Bhag burst out laughing. "Like Jesus Christ, he would have a good chance of being resurrected to save the Sikhs."

"Uncle, don't expect Baba Nanak to be resurrected. He lives in Book-guru, and we take good care of him," Bhola mocked. He rarely goes to the gurdwara. In every village, the gurdwaras compete to organise nagar kirtan, a procession of hymn-singing. The three gurdwaras of Jatpur hold their processions on different days or on alternate occasions."

"You say that few people benefit from the Word being transmitted through loudspeakers" I replied. "I have read that animals and plants do. Could that be the reason for the increased crop yield in the Punjab?"

"It's the fertilisers and uncontrolled spraying," said Bhola.

"Why don't you use your morning sermon to tell people what we are talking about?" I said. "You know everyone in the village. Talk to them."

Bhola was quick to respond. "He sees the same devotees each morning, a dozen from seven hundred houses."

"Not long ago you told me there were four hundred."

"Have you seen the number of new houses on the road to Raikot? Many are new, owned by people from the lower class. They form a very powerful group. Without its support, no one can be elected to the Panchayat, the village council. The election campaign is a miniaturized version of a national election in India or America with all the fanfare. Each candidate promises that he will clean the streets, remove roadside dung and garbage heaps, install sanitation systems, repair the water supply lines and organize sports for children. He must have at least one hundred thousand rupees available to offer gifts to each house. A bottle of whisky and some electronic device are a must. Many take from all parties. In Jatpur, candidates do not go to four or five houses knowing that their vote cannot be bought. After elections nothing happens, all promises are forgotten. They do not come to our house, they cannot buy our votes," proclaimed Bhola proudly.

Bhag is nearing eighty and with his son Bhola he runs a small sawmill and a flourmill in Raikot. They earn just enough to feed the family. Bhag's father Santa had considerable technical experience, which he had acquired in Kenya. Neither he nor his descendants have taken any initiative to improve the trade. While Punjab is rapidly changing economically and socially, Bhag is running a mill equipped with one bandsaw and one flour grinder.

"Have you thought of the future of the family?" I asked Bhag and Bhola.

"There isn't much we can do", Bhag replied.

"Bhola's two graduate sons haven't yet found a job. Teaching seems the only option. I'm sure you are looking for girls for them. Where will they live? You have sold all your farmland."

On my side, I'm the only one who knows our extended family in India. I feel nostalgic at the thought that at some point our children and grandchildren will shear off our roots completely. I wanted to safeguard my ancestral roots in Jatpur for future inquisitive descendants.

CHAPTER 9

GETTING LOST

❧

A palace in the wheat fields

Retiring was not a problem for me. Whereas many of my colleagues hated the thought of being lonely in retirement, I was elated. On my last day at work I walked out of the office with a spring in my step. There was so much to do, so many things I hadn't had time to do when I was employed.

My strongest wish was to see Malika. But where was she, in England, the USA or India? I didn't know. Our stars might cross in the motherland. Deep inside I wanted to lose myself in India, backpacking. My daughter Atima protested. She did not want to be left alone, having not fully recovered from the shock of the road accident in Kenya.

The minute I arrived home the phone was ringing. I dumped my briefcase on the floor and in quick strides reached the phone in the hallway.

"Inder, book your flight. You must be in Jullundur on 10 March," Davi said without any greetings. Davi Taman is a childhood friend settled in London.

"But why?" I asked at this sudden command.

"You promised that you would come to India when my house was built," he answered.

It was a promise I had forgotten, but one I was eager to fulfill now.
"Come prepared to sing," Davi added.

On my flight to India, I sat next to a clean-shaven Sikh Jat, Surjit,
leading a team of social workers from Manchester to Jullundur in the
Punjab to build a temple in a village.

"Is there a shortage of temples in India?" I asked, curious because
I had found it difficult to reduce the number of temples on my
itinerary. I had labelled my itinerary 'getting lost' because that's exactly
what I wanted to do – just hanging out footloose whichever way the
wind blew.

"Our project is different. It is with funds collected in the UK in
memory of Baba Balak Nathji."

"There must be a few temples in that village?"

Avoiding my question, he continued, "We want to use it as a centre
for social work, in particular to help widows. We also want to ensure
that our children in Manchester remain in contact with their roots. So
we bring our families to the village every year. The centre will be our
base."

When I told him that I was also going to Jullundur, he invited me
to his village. No way. No temples for me.

It was a cool morning when we landed in Delhi. I made my way
to the railway station and boarded the Shatabdi Express train to
Jullundur, four hundred kilometres north. At Jullundur station I walked
out carrying my backpack, wearing jeans and Reeboks and showing
off a neatly-trimmed white beard. I suddenly felt odd standing among
people of my own type: the first time feeling. Davi was nowhere to be
seen. I scrutinized the dusty traffic of two, three and four-wheeled
vehicles and warded off taxi drivers: "No, someone is coming to meet
me." Nobody appeared. I began to feel crestfallen. Then I saw Davi.

"Davi," I shouted. Walking beside him was Soma, also an ex-Eldore
friend.

"Where were you? We've looked for you everywhere in the train and on the platform," he demanded, giving me a bear-hug.

"Isn't this the main gate where you asked me to wait?"

"We entered through this gate. I told Soma to go to the left and I went to right to ensure that you did not escape," said Davi with his usual air of competency.

"You left the middle unguarded. Don't you know that great persons alight from the centre coach?"

We huddled together, five adults in a little Maruti, the Indian saloon car. The car squeezed through the narrow gaps between loaded bullock carts full of steel rods, bicycles, three-wheelers, scooters, ten-ton Tata trucks and people - this was 'Incredible India'.

The Maruti nose-dived northward on Pathankot road, which links Kashmir with the rest of India. The road is deeply potholed. Even tanks avoid it. Trucks do better, they can manoeuvre around the holes. We drove past villages and across lush green wheat fields bursting with seed. In the middle of one field, Davi pointed to a solitary white mansion with a red-tiled roof. "That's Taman Palace," he announced proudly. It was enclosed by a high wall, and no other house or hut was to be seen near it. Davi obviously saw his village as a good long-term investment to build a house in Punjab that was transforming rapidly economically and socially.

The following day was Sunday. I wanted to sleep longer but was woken by an ear-splitting voice when the sun was struggling to lift its head. It came from the adjoining first-floor lobby where Book-guru was being read for three days continuously. The loudspeaker, I felt, was to ensure that the holy words penetrated even the deaf. The spiritual, rather religious, phase of the inauguration ceremony had begun. The tradition requires that the end-pages be read slowly and deliberately. I dressed hurriedly and joined the small congregation. I noticed that the reader next in line was getting edgy, he forcibly pushed away the priest who was chanting - it was so embarrassingly laughable. Each one wanted to be paid for the time spent reading the holy book.

We stood up for the final prayer. The preacher sought forgiveness for any errors whilst reading Book-guru. The gathering moved to the spacious ground floor where Diwana, an ex-Kenya preacher I knew well, led the singing of hymns melodiously. Listening to him I felt that I had paid my homage to the Golden Temple of Amritsar. I dropped the idea of making the pilgrimage there in person.

Towards midday, everyone moved to an enormous tent put up in the compound the night before. Young men in jeans danced the Bhangra, the Punjabi folk dance, to the beat of deafening live music and singing.

"In my younger days such dancing was rarely seen," I reflected aloud. "I recall pre-monsoon folk dancing exclusively by women."

"Now no social function is complete without Bhangra. Look carefully, they are all turbanless Sikhs, high on drugs," said Jote, Davi's Gujarati wife.

"They look normal to me," I remarked. "See those girls sitting with their glum parents. Why aren't they dancing? In Britain the girls are the first to take to the floor."

"In villages, parents associate dancing with prostitutes" Jote explained. "Girls dare not dance in public".

"Listen to the lyrics, they undress pretty Punjabi girls," I said.

"Punjabis do not like to be described as dull humourless people. They claim to be world's most fun-loving people. Have you looked behind the tent?"

"Yes, the happy ones are sitting round a bottle of local whisky which I gladly shared," I replied.

I followed Earl Davi and his Gujarati Baroness, Jote, to the front gate, which was decked with heavy garlands of marigolds to receive the poor countrywomen and gypsies. News of such events does not require publicity through radio, TV or internet. Word of mouth through mobile phones travels fast. The women were showering them with flattery and wishing them happiness in the kothi (mansion), long life, more wealth, many sons and grandsons to the present family clan and to all future clans.

The rhetoric stopped only when the royal couple handed the women money; food alone did not satisfy them. The previous evening when jogging on the dusty tracks I had seen men decorating an elephant in a farm shed. In the morning the decorated elephant walked on the freshly-laid walkway to the kothi. It took money, food and heavyweight persuasion to see the men and the elephant off.

Davi stopped the car at the far end of the station road. "I'm not going to drive through that mess again" he said. He got out and called a cycle rickshaw, loaded me with my backpack on it and firmly instructed the rickshawala to take me to the rail station. I passed through the tortuous street with no barrier between my lungs and the exhaust pipes of trucks belching smoke on my face.

The second-class train ticket to Ludhiana, an industrial town – the Manchester of India - was less than a dollar, one-fiftieth of the price in Switzerland. Entering the compartment I greeted the four passengers. The turbanned and the shaven men ignored me and continued with their conversation. The two snobs disembarked at Phagwara station. The young man on the opposite bench seat wanted to talk but did not seem to have the courage.

"Where are you going?" I asked him in Hindi.

"Uttar Pradesh."

"What's your name?"

"Sita Ram."

"Are you visiting Punjab?"

"No, I was an assistant nurse in a big hospital in Jullundur for six years."

"You look so young. How old are you?"

"I'm twenty-eight."

"Are you going on your annual leave?"

"No, I'm returning home. I miss my family too much."

"Have you got a job waiting?"

"No."

"What will you do then?"

"I've finally decided to set up my allopathic practice in my village near Ajodhya."

Shortage of labour in Punjab attracts migrants from poorer states. This has changed Punjab. Turbanless bhaiyas, mainly from Bihar and Orissa, have replaced turbanned farmers. Factories in Jullandhar and Ludhiana depend on them. Punjab cannot progress without them.

"Where do you live?" Sita Ram asked.

"Where do you think?"

"I know you are pura [full] Indian, but from the way you speak good Hindi you must be from overseas."

The village pond

Feeling surer in Ludhiana, my home territory, than I had been in Jullandhar, I hired a three-wheeler that took me through the crowded narrow and dusty streets to the house of Melo, my niece. It was midday. As soon as I arrived, I was surrounded by family. Melo lives in an extended family of grandparents, uncles, aunts, in-laws and out-laws, nieces and nephews and grandchildren. They all knew me, or rather of me. I spent the afternoon getting to know them and in no time, I felt as if I had never lived elsewhere. I looked back at my thirty years of comfortable life in Europe and still felt a foreigner there. It must be something to do with culture. Melo's husband with his three brothers operates a small engineering workshop. They live in the workshop compound. Some twenty years earlier they transferred the workshop from rural Jagraon to Ludhiana, now a sprawling dangerously polluted industrial-rural city. Cut-throat competition and lack of initiative have not permitted them to expand much. However they all look contented.

Their two charming daughters were doing university degrees from home, gave private tuition to students and helped in a school across the street. The younger one, eighteen years old, amazed me: she could recite from memory nearly two thousand verses of Sukhmani, the Ode of Peace, as well as the five long daily prayers. The parents were stubbornly convinced that attending university full-time was not good for girls, it spoils them, they reasoned. I remained silent on this issue, knowing that in the Punjab there are more and better graduate girls than boys. Girls are breaking away from dependence on males, beginning a social revolution.

After dinner the family thronged into a small bed-cum-sitting room. Someone produced a harmonium and a dholak (drum). We sang until midnight. I shared the same room with three others sleeping on a sheet spread on the floor – it's good for my back.

Next morning the car that was going to take me to Jatpur was needed for delivering products. I took the time to explore the narrow street, its dusty, unsanitary drains, pollution and smells. Human, bicycle and scooter traffic respectfully accommodated children playing cricket in the middle of the street. Opposite the workshop I saw a neatly-painted signboard: Florence Nightingale Public School. Did it train nurses? I was curious. I pushed the corrugated-iron gate. Before it was even open a foot, a woman guard challenged me in Hindi, "What do you want?" Before I could answer, a gorgeous young woman wearing an off-white blue sari came towards me and greeted me with the customary joined hands and a knowing smile. She directed me to her office.

"I'm the principal of this primary school. I heard that you are around. I am related to Melo. Welcome."

Melo's daughters were at school too and they came running to show me around. I do not know why the school is named after

Florence Nightingale. We Punjabis like to choose exotic names for small establishments, easy publicity. The principal owns the school. The two-storey building stands on the periphery of a five hundred square metre plot, leaving a small courtyard in the middle. Children sit on bench-desks in pairs. When I entered the class, they did not stand up as we used to in order to show respect. Like normal children, they were excited, wearing broad smiles, and quite well disciplined, not shy to answer questions. Since then the school has bought two neighbouring buildings and put up bigger modern buildings and grown into a high school with nearly eight hundred pupils. Back in the office, the principal was telling me about the acute shortage of good schools and how parents sacrifice to educate their children when a parent came to see her. I decided to leave.

I left for Jatpur, my ancestral village, some forty kilometres to the south east of Ludhiana. Six years earlier my uncle Santa died at the age of ninety-six, survived by four sons and their numerous offspring. Dozens of them rushed out to greet me. All my cousins are older than I am. The men were into small-scale saw milling, flour milling, farming, mechanical-engineering workshops, building construction and providing technical services to farmers and others. They are honest people and for over fifty years they have selflessly looked after my interests in India, not a common trait in these changing times. I still have a small house in the village that I keep as my heritage should my European and American-based children and grandchildren desire to come here in search of their roots. However, the chances look slim.

On the next day I walked to Kishangarh to see Sobha. His wife, Joti, is the chairperson of the Panchayat, the village committee, of Kishangarh. She is in her late thirties and living with three lovely children in a house that from outside looks like any other in the village. Entering the corrugated iron gate and walking across the courtyard, I entered a modern house, furnished in the Canadian style, discreetly camouflaged in the old one. A four-wheel-drive Tata

Commando – a rustic version of the Mercedes M Class - was parked in the drive.

For decades, our families have shared a common destiny. Our grandparents migrated to Kenya in the early 1930s. They lived in Eldore, sometimes under the same roof. Now Sobha's parents live in Vancouver with his elder brother, Guma. His uncle Satti migrated from Kenya to Perth, Western Australia, so has my nephew, from Kenya to Melbourne. Here I was in one of the smallest villages of Punjab, which does not even boast a post office yet communicates easily with the world thanks to modern technology.

Next to the house is a gurdwara on the edge of an old pond. Images of me walking from Jatpur to the temple with my mother came to me – the two of us on the dusty path through fields and me jumping over irrigation drains, invariably getting wet. This was in 1941 when I was four. While the adults sang hymns inside and listened to discourses on spiritual life, we played under the huge banyan trees whose branches hung over the pond. Sometimes we joined the water buffaloes in it. I also remember the priest, sant Kirpal Singh, coming to bless our home in Jatpur. I remember a black car covered with a white sheet in the temple compound. It was the priest's car. Did it enhance his spiritual popularity? Or did his spiritual popularity earn him the car? That's a long time ago when I could not discern such issues.

My mind turns to the ninety Rolls Royces of Rajneesh Osho, an Indian mystic and spiritual guru who attracted disciples from the whole world. He opposed institutionalized religions and advocated sexual freedom. In India, his provocative lectures and permissive approach created tension. So he settled in Oregon, USA, in the early 1980s. His popularity enabled him to purchase a Rolls.

The pond has become a cesspool, a breeding ground for mosquitoes which pollutes the groundwater, the source of drinking water. The board chairman of the surrounding villages sought the villagers' cooperation to fill up half the pond. The villagers came out with their trucks and tractor-drawn carts and by evening, when I was there, over nine hundred loads of soil had been dumped to fill the pond. To celebrate the occasion the Board chairman arranged a dinner at Hotel Friendship in Raikot. I was invited. We drank beer, ate good food and talked. It was a fantastic evening, but Punjab is still a male-dominated world. There was not a single woman to brighten the evening, not even Joti, the village chairperson.

Back at Sabha's house, I opened the window and got into a comfortable bed, pulling a soft quilt over me. But at four in the morning my sleep was shattered by the morning prayers recited over the loud speaker again. Joti served hot stuffed parathas (shallow-fried chapattis) with home-made yogurt, standard in the village but a treat for me. To digest the heavy meal I walked to my old house in Jatpur.

Two old men, the white-bearded one with parched wrinkled face and the other, Jagar, my childhood friend, with glowing rosy cheeks, sat on the traditional woven bed as if in meditation in front of the house, their silhouettes hallowed by the soft sunlight. It was a picture of pure simplicity, something that I was chasing by losing myself. We hugged each other.

Ganga Yogi

Getting lost was my way of celebrating the end of the millennium. It's not easy to escape from the Punjabi ambience. I must go to Chandigarh, the main city in Punjab, to sort out a few things. Against Melo's advice, I boarded a regular bus in Ludhiana. Every part of the bus rattled, the engine the loudest. The bus shuddered out of the station and halted ten metres away. It did not seem to have a clutch. The hefty Sikh driver raced the engine and pushed the thick gear lever into gear with great difficulty. It made discomforting metallic noises. The bus shuddered again and lurched forward. Absolutely sure that the bus would break down, I drew pictures in my mind of horrific accidents. But none of the passengers seemed bothered. We eventually reached Chandigarh, amazingly only half an hour late.

After Chandigarh, I flew into Varanasi, popularly known as Benares. A rusty Ambassador driven by a Muslim chauffeur carried me to Hotel Barahdari. President Clinton was also in India, to be precise in New Delhi. An unsmiling man in reception checked me in.

The phone was ringing when I entered my room. I answered it, surprised that I should get a call so soon and hoping it was not an emergency. Somebody on the other side wanted to speak to someone in room 59. The minute I hung up, there was another call and after ten minutes of non-stop calls, I dialled reception.

"For some reason all incoming phone calls come to this room," I complained.

The answer from the receptionist: "Don't place the receiver back on the phone."

It was lunchtime. I went into the dining room, where I had two white boys and a girl at the table on my left and a white couple on my right. The girl was holding her belly and looked pale. I was sure she had the runs - Indian jelly-belly. This backpackers' medium comfort hotel is advertised as 'Two-star hotel with five star facilities'. Looking at the grey unhygienic atmosphere of the dining room I began to doubt the wisdom of undertaking such a trip. Then I reflected, "If they can, I can."

To be on the safe side, I ordered fried eggs and toast. The waiter's white clothes were as grey as the well-greased napkin he was using to clean tabletops, cheap metal cutlery and cracked crockery. What should one expect for twelve US dollars for a room with AC and TV, I consoled myself. It did not take long before I discovered that I was staying in luxury. I returned to my room and switched on the TV. I was surprised to find it worked. Clinton was being garlanded by a beautiful Indian girl who seemed to resemble Monica Lewinsky. Was it an accident or planned, or just my imagination? Her affair with the United States President was still hot news.

Equipped with a bottle of mineral water and a tourist map, I plunged into the crowded streets of Kotwali and headed towards the sacred Ganga Ghats (stepped embankment), Varanasi's world-famous attraction. Many shops were closed. People were celebrating the Holi festival, the day when people spray coloured water and powder on each other to celebrate spring. I passed youngsters carrying loaded plastic pumps. Either they did not find me an attractive target or they had spent all their ammunition, for I was saved from being showered with coloured spray.

An inconspicuous signboard pointing to 'Vishwanath Temple' led me into a metre-wide lane. Inevitably the sacred mother cow and dogs shared it. The lane to the holiest spiritual focal point of Hindus is far from sacred. The street was full of rubbish being burnt in the middle of the street, giving off nauseating smoke. Small temples on each side of the street offered solutions to all sorts of physical and spiritual malfunctions. On the left I hardly noticed the obscure entrance to Vishwanath Temple, which was built in 1776 by Ahalya Bai of Indore and dedicated to Shiva, the lord of the universe. Maharaja Ranjit Singh, who ruled over greater Punjab from 1801 to 1839, donated gold to plate its domes. Was it left over from the Golden Temple of the Sikhs in Amritsar? Or was it a political strategy? For Ranjit Singh was a very shrewd guy. I guess he donated the gold to gain the support of Hindu rajas against the British waiting to grab the prosperous Punjab, the last truly Indian stronghold.

The temple is small. Its shining golden domes are hidden between the street and the Great Mosque behind it. It is pointless to question why a mosque had to be built over a bigger and older temple. The space between the small temple and the derelict mosque is just enough to accommodate policemen and a steel barrier.

A little further eastward I found myself looking at the sacred Ganga, the Ganges, just below the Manikarnika Ghat. Seven main ghats are north of this point and the other ninety in the south. At this time of the year the river level is low. I walked over two kilometres southwards along the bank up to the last main ghat of Asi and photographed people bathing to purify themselves, buffaloes taking their afternoon nap in the warm sand and of course some sadhus. One body had just been cremated and a Pandit flung an earthen pot over his head, thus sending the soul of the defunct to paradise. Cremation of the next one was being negotiated. The price of his ticket to hell or heaven was in question. I walked over concrete platforms, zigzagged around river bank structures and jumped over smelly feeders from the city. Every niche in the ghat walls is a urinal producing a stench nullifying holiness and purity. I was not going to bathe in the river in case I polluted it further with my spiritual muck.

A yogi-dog in a dug-out grotto in the sandbank sat perfectly composed, eyes closed as if in another sphere. I took my camera near its nose to preset it for the light inside the grotto. He remained absolutely composed, undisturbed by my touristy antics. The little yogi projected the air of bliss I was seeking.

Looking back, the view of the riverbank with its boats and dilapidated ghats is indeed spectacular. What made this site sacred? What attracted the Maharajas and their Maharanis to build their palatial ghats here? There is the Rana Ghat, Jai Singh Ghat, Scindia Ghat, Raja Man Singh Ghat and Ahalya Bai Ghat, to name only a few. These are old versions of modern hotels for the rich tourists who now clog the beaches of Goa in India and numerous others in the world.

Climbing to the street that runs behind the ghats, I headed north. Because of the Holi festival the street was empty, unusual in India. People were at home eating the Holi meal. A naked woman, old, frail and mentally retarded, failed to attract anybody's attention.

"Let me take you on my rickshaw where you go. I am cheap," said a young rikshawala. I tried to ignore him. As he paddled alongside me he talked about his family, educating his children and his daily income. "If you don't hire me how can I earn more?" he said politely and cycled off leaving me struggling with the question: "What makes the Ganges so sacred at Varanasi?"

My mind trekked to primeval times, when the raised green wooded west bank was still in virgin state, no huts, only holiness manifested in the natural beauty of the site. I imagined looking across the apex of the gentle river curve, watching the sun rising and pouring out a flood of gold onto the river water. It was paradise. No wonder naked yogis had replaced the heavenly green patches of soft grass with shacks. They had planted signposts inviting the living and the dead to be taken to heaven. Since then Varanasi has been irrevocably emptied of its godliness.

Early next morning, crossing over the railway bridge to Mughal Sarai railway station, I stopped to watch the sunrise and erase the negative souvenir of acrid smell of urine along the ghats. Instead I was confronted by a sickly sun which was having great difficulty emitting its radiance through a cloud of polluted fog hanging over the river. I could see only a hazy outline of the Ganges and the ghats which had looked so picturesque the day before. I thought of the yogis and sadhus I met, but my opaque soul did not receive any holy signals from them.

Muslim brahmin

I shared the first class cabin with six others on the day of the spring equinox on the morning train from Mughal Serai station to Patna. The train was an hour late arriving in Patna. Loaded with my backpack, I disembarked from the train. Following my guidebook, I checked into Hotel President. It was lunchtime and I descended to the dining room, which was dimly lit. I could hardly read the scanty menu. Was the dimness intended to stop people looking at other men's wives, I wondered? Or was it to conceal the gaping holes in the tattered carpet? Or was it to mask the quality of food being served complete with the insects that might have fallen in it? A cold beer helped me put aside all those questions and I ate the half-cooked rice and lentils. The tandoori chicken was unchewable.

Lord Buddha had predicted in 500BC that Patna city, under its old name of Pataliputra, would become the capital of India. Two centuries later it did. Ashoka the Great, who exceptionally did not belong to the high Kashatrya or Brahmin caste, made it his first city. From there he spread his reign over the entire subcontinent except the south. I expected to see edifices like those in Angkor, Athens and Rome. I walked back to the rail station and hired a three-wheeler to take me eastward to Kumrahar, the site of the Pataliputra excavations. I was disappointed. There must be much more than the few unearthed foundations.

I had another mission to accomplish in Patna. My uncle Vakil in Chandigarh gave me his new book to donate to Patna Sahib gurdwara library. It is the fourth and last volume containing the verbatim sermons and commentaries of a well known Sikh saint transcribed from cassettes recorded in the nineteen fifties and sixties. The white marble temple built by Maharaja Ranjit Singh pleases the eye, especially its clean compound. The pot-bellied manager received me courteously and honoured me with a scarf just as the Dalai Lama does, and parsad, a sweet bun made of crushed leftover chapattis from the communal kitchen. Outside the clean confines of the temple, I stepped into the dirty and smelly main street. Being an expert in water resources, I was disconcerted by the human folly in ruining the environment. Why isn't the wealth amassed by this temple and other bigger ones such as that in Amritsar used to clean up its neighbourhood, I wondered wistfully. I conjured up a project:

First year: Mark out a ten to twenty-metre area from the temple boundary. With technical help from the local administration and the cooperation of residents, the temple managers would:

- Rebuild and cover open drains,

- Provide each household with a piped or pumped water supply and a toilet connected to the existing sewerage system,

- Train the residents how to use and keep them clean, and supervise until the residents form a habit.

Second year: Extend the project boundary to cover the next ten to twenty metres and so on. Gurus would be pleased to see their Sikhs venturing out and genuinely serving the community beyond the temple kitchen and extend their humility beyond wiping the shoes of devotees.

West of the Gandhi Maidan I climbed the one hundred and forty-two steps to the top of beehive-shaped Golghar, a British granary constructed by the Ganges in 1786. To reach the riverbank, I crossed a compound with a strange-looking unfinished concrete construction standing in the middle. It looked like a wartime bunker. A young man on site told me that the late Mrs Gandhi had ordered its construction. Now it accommodates local policemen. He could not explain why it was built like a bunker. Did she make provision for hiding, should dire days befall?

It was dark when I returned to my room with its worn-out curtains and stained wall paint. I switched on the TV to see what Clinton was up to in India. Who did he see instead? Was it Ram Godoomal, a Sindhi friend who once lived in Geneva ten years ago working for a multinational? Why was Gidoomal on TV? He had moved to London to run a Christian charity and welfare society. The BBC was interviewing him because he was running for election as Mayor of London against Ken Livingstone. Not content with the vagueness of Hindu religious ways, especially with respect to social welfare, he became a Christian and made rapid advances in church affairs. A few times I had attended his church services. What a coincidence seeing him for a brief moment in such a remote place on the globe.

Early next morning I visited Khuda Bakhsh Oriental Library and saw the books that survived the sacking of the Moorish University of Cordoba in Spain. I was keen to see the entire Quran inscribed in a book only twenty-five millimetres wide. The lone guard guided me to the manager, who received me courteously but would not show me the Quran. Instead he narrated a fascinating story in Urdu.

Bakhsh was a lawyer born in 1842. His foster mother was a Brahmin woman, who breast-fed him. In recognition of her love, he never ate beef, which was permitted in Islam but not in Hinduism. His son Khuda followed his father's example. Bakhsh, an intellectual, was keenly interested in collecting and preserving manuscripts and works of art. He greatly valued the need for archives and reading facilities for all people. In 1876, his last wish to his son, Khuda, was that he should collect manuscripts and publications and set up a multicultural library. Khuda engaged people for fifty rupees a month and sent them to Syria, Iraq, Persia, Spain and North Africa. They brought back some rare and unique Arabic and Persian manuscripts, including a book on surgery from Cordoba, Spain. It details surgical instruments which are still in use.

Khuda, also a lawyer, launched a similar campaign within India. He paid the cost of the return journey and the price of the manuscript handed to him. One of the most famous he acquired was Tarikh-e Khandan-e Timuria (Timur Nama), a stupendously illustrated history of the Timur family from Uzbekistan down to Akbar in India. Akbar had requisitioned its preparation. It is a priceless work of art. Sometimes he even bought manuscripts which he knew had been stolen from his own collection. He spent all his savings on this pursuit and died a poor sick man. The Government, then British, loaned him eight thousand rupees to get medical treatment. Now the library is well staffed, funded by the Federal Government and complemented with fifty thousand rupees from the State Government. Catalogues are being scanned to put on the internet. A quarterly journal publishes good quality articles in English and Urdu. Patna might not be a great tourist attraction, but I departed a more cultured person carrying a booklet containing twelve reproductions from Timur Nama.

Kali's black lamb

I was to fly to Delhi. "Go to Calcutta," insisted Bharat, a close friend. "My father would love to see you. He wants to take you to his tea estates in Orissa." I wanted to take a train south across Bihar to Bhubaneswar and Puri on the eastern coast of Orissa. There is no easy short cut, the quickest route is through Calcutta. Hesitantly I phoned Bharat's father, Basu. I needed a place to stay in Calcutta.

"There is the Oberoi Hotel, walking distance from here. The rate is about seven thousand rupees, bed and breakfast," Basu said.

"Didn't Bharat tell you that I'm backpacking using the Lonely Planet Guide? Please find a hotel that matches my status."

Basu booked me into the Lytton Hotel on Sudder Street at two thousand rupees including luxury tax. This was about five times the highest rate I paid elsewhere during the entire trip. The following day, I flew on the new Sahara Air to Calcutta, now Kolkata. I felt uncomfortable with the formality and cleanliness of the hotel. I wished I had cut out Calcutta. Six years earlier, returning from Kathmandu, I had toured Calcutta and walked in throngs of people during the evening rush, reminding me of the film City of Joy. Mother Theresa's mission did not attract me. It was early evening and I was hungry. I could not contact Basu. My guidebook had Khwaja and Khalsa restaurants listed on Sudder Street.

Just then Basu phoned. "Dinner is waiting," he announced with pomp. "Take the back street to the main road, Jawaharlal Nehru Road. Then turn right to Humayun Place, you cannot miss it."

Fifteen minutes later, walking in the warm evening, though it was cold for the Bengalis, who were wearing sweaters, I was in front of an old colonial office-cum-residential building. An elderly caretaker operating a rickety lift brought me to the apartment bearing two very prestigious-looking signboards. I crossed a wide office buzzing with fax machines and computers to Basu's residential quarters. The interior decor recalls British colonial times.

"Welcome. I hope you did not have difficulty finding this place," said Basu shaking hands, quite formally. Our dinner was frequently interrupted by phone calls and clerks seeking Basu's attention and signatures. After dinner, we agreed to meet the following evening. He was not taking me to see his tea estates. He reminded me, "The temple of Kali is a must." This Hindu goddess represents time and death, commonly in the form of a terrifying statue with a long bloody tongue, standing on the body of her consort, Lord Shiva. Her statue in the Kali Temple of Kolkata is the most famous. Early next morning I walked into the Maidan, the Hyde Park of the city, engulfed in a thick morning haze. A group of boys were playing a full-scale cricket match. On the way back I tried to get into Fort William, but an army guard abruptly put his gun across my chest. Since the British rebuilt it in 1781, the fort has remained in the hands of the Army, and the surrounding area is out of bounds. Sweating profusely, I had a relaxing shower, followed by a copious English-Bengali buffet breakfast, and felt strong enough to confront the terrifying Kali Mata. Kolkata is known for its numerous Sikh taxi drivers. "Where do you come from in the Punjab?" I asked the turbanned driver.

"My village is Mohi near Mulapur."

"That is not far from Jatpur, my village."

At Kalighat Mandir he cautioned, "Watch out for the pundits. They will ask you for big money for Kali Devi's darshan".

Seeing a big crowd trying to enter the temple, I decided to walk round it, though I was barefoot – shoes in temples are not allowed. At the back, I saw a hefty man enter a quaint fenced square carrying under his arm a lovely black lamb. Its soft pelt glimmered, even in the dull sun. The devotee must have bathed it for the sacrifice. Its eyes emanated pure innocence. The image is imprinted in my mind. What a contrast to the flaming eyes of Kali. The man sprinkled holy water on the lamb's forehead and in a flicker of the eyelid he placed its neck between two stakes and chopped off its godly head, offering his bloody finger to touch foreheads of worshippers and spectators.

One wonders how so much innocence has been sacrificed and yet goddess Kali's lust for blood has not been quenched. According to Hindu mythology, Shiva's first wife, Shakti, had transgressed. Was it adultery? It seems unlikely, because none of the wives of these gods bore them children. Were the god's impotent? No, invariably these gods impregnated other earthly damsels they encountered and produced many children. Nevertheless, Shakti was punished. Her body was strewn over India. One of her fingers fell at Kalighat. Her yoni fell at Gawahati in Assam, where in mid-year Hindus celebrate the end of the earth's menstrual cycle. The menstrual blood is taken from lamb sacrifice. Why don't they chop off human lingas, phalluses, instead?

To quell my anti-Kali sentiments I decided not to see her at all. Instead I went to the world famous Hawrah Bridge. I walked at a leisurely pace through the bazaar towards Hooghly River. A huge tractor was shovelling a three-metre high pyramid of rubbish into a truck. How long it had been accumulating only the seagulls picking maggots from it could tell. Crossing the railway line I reached the flower market. Strings of fresh marigolds look immensely better than in the photo I took. The view of the half-kilometre long single-span Howrah Bridge from the popular bathing ghat is spectacular. I was tired, but could not resist the temptation of walking across it to see the world's most frequently-crossed bridge. I'm glad I did it, otherwise I would have missed talking to the men and women carrying farm produce and other merchandise balanced on their heads: humanity, rather than humanness, on the move.

I just watched and watched, and then walked limply to the equally famous Howrah railway station. Inside the station, sitting on a railing, I pulled out the bun or the prasad from Patna Gurdwara from my mini backpack. It was big, not too sweet and tasted heavenly. In the hall and on the platforms, peasants sat on the floor in groups waiting for their train. Others shuffled from one platform to another looking confused. College boys and girls sat just close enough to each other not to be noticed, romantically sharing lunch. An hour passed. Walking out through the riverside gate, I joined people lined up to board a ferry on the Hoogly back to the Strand at Babu Ghat.

Back at the hotel, I had a refreshing shower and headed towards Basu's residence. I had time to spare and dropped in at the Indian Museum. Its huge galleries display the finest collection of enormous fossil tree trunks, archaeological, historical, cultural, and natural history artefacts. When I arrived at Basu's, the sahib was playing tennis, the cook informed me.

It was a blessing in disguise. I rested for an hour before Basu showed up. He was pouring whiskies when a charming lady in a bright green sari and matching jewellery walked in. "My husband is busy so I have come alone. I'm Shuna Bose, I'll have a gin and tonic" she said, shaking hands with me.

"Are you related to India's famous independence hero, Sobash Bose?" I inquired.

"Bose is a common Bengali family name. I deny any blood link with the hero." She gave the feminine touch that the evening needed. We traversed the whole of Indian history, in particular the British Raj. We talked about the clash of Indian culture with that of the Occident. Basu, sitting in his high-backed colonial chair, portrayed the Raj, and Shuna charmed us with her literary knowledge and talk of modern times and trends in India and abroad. Bengalis are a cultured people, and she exemplified them.

Lady with a handbag

Puri is one of the four most sacred centres of Hindu pilgrimage, the others are Badrinath, Rameswaram and Dwarka. Like most Sikhs I know Puri from a story I have heard countless times. Could it be that Nanak Dev, the first Guru of Sikhs, reached Puri in the first quarter of 1509 on Friday 24 March, coinciding with my visit on the same day centuries apart? How many months did Nanak take to walk the length of the subcontinent? Putting a date to such events is hazardous. Indian travellers shunned keeping a diary. The story goes like this: The pundits of Jaganath temple were performing Aarti, the evening worship . It involved walking round the statue of Jagannath, Lord of the universe, accompanied by singing, lighting lamps in platters, ringing bells, burning incense and offering flowers. Nanak was supposed to join but he stayed outside, blissfully attuned with nature. The angry pundits confronted Nanak. To appease them Nanak sang his famous song that many Sikhs recite before going to sleep.

In the platter of sky, the sun and the moon are the lamps.
Constellations of stars seem like pearls in it.
The warm air from Malai sandalwood forest is the incense,
And the breeze whisks over.
The whole realm of flora offers Him flowers.
What wonderful lamp-lit worship of Destroyer of Fear is taking place!
The heavenly music is the beating of temple drums, etc.

With this image in mind I headed for Puri after midday in a Hindustan car hired at Bhubaneswar airport for five hundred rupees.

Midway the young driver convinced me that for another two hundred rupees he would take me to the famous Konark Sun temple, which is the eastern apex of the sacred triangle formed with Bhubaneswar and Puri about sixty kilometres apart. Four centuries ago the Bay of Bengal washed the temple walls. Of the many beautifully-carved erotic carvings, my guide directed my attention to a woman with a trendy handbag. It is difficult to imagine the splendour of a thousand years ago. The Muslim invaders in the fourteenth century could not tolerate the religious music and erotic dances staged morning and evening with the sun's rays illuminating the performance. They tried to destroy the temple. Heavy granite blocks resisted them. Not long after them came the Portuguese Catholic sailors, who found it even more repugnant for their religious mores. The ignorant sailors did not know that at the same time back in Europe their Borgia popes had fathered many children and participated in sex orgies. They tied their ships to the temple domes with ropes, put sails at full mast and toppled them, joyously destroying an invaluable work of human heritage. Ironically what is left attracts a lot of Christian tourists.

A few weeks earlier a tropical cyclone had devastated Konrak town and its surroundings, I saw the houses swept down and coconut palms flattened to the ground as far as the eye could see.

Tanuja family guesthouse in Puri is about a hundred metres from the beach. The young host, Robby, offered to take me on his scooter to the Seventh Beach Festival. The festival, usually held in February, was postponed to March because of the cyclone. There were many stalls selling local artefacts and food. Young artists were absorbed in a sand sculpture competition. Two pretty girls attracted more spectators than others. The State Governor and other VIPs came to open the festival. They took more than an hour to say nothing. Tired, I dozed in a metal chair. I had read about the local disorder known as Puri paralysis, which manifests as a state of inertia. Was I becoming prey to it? Glamorous enchanting Oriya dances kept me awake until nine, when I decided to head back. Seeing a young woman operating an open-air roadside eating place, I hesitantly ordered my dinner. All she had was a gas stove, a tray of eggs, bread and two small rickety benches, dimly lit by a distant neon light. Sitting on the ground, she started to prepare two fried egg sandwiches. Two other men were sitting on the opposite bench.

"Are you a visitor?" asked the younger one in perfect English.

"Yes," I replied. "You have a very nice town here. Your people are very artistic and appreciate cultural activities. It's not like that in some other parts of India."

The young one introduced himself. "My name is Vijay Patnaik. I'm a local journalist. I recommend you visit Jagannath Temple."

"Yes, that's what I intend to do, although I have tried to avoid visiting temples, they are everywhere," I complained.

"I can show you around," volunteered Vijay.

I took up the offer. The following morning I rode Robby's old bicycle. My legs felt weak. Vijay was not at the kiosk. I ventured alone and entered the crowded temple. My friend, Bharat, was once refused entry on the ostensible basis that the Lord was ill. Apparently, this happens from time to time, occasions on which He goes to visit His sister who feeds him a special yoghurt-based preparation and khichri, which is cooked rice and green lentils. Inside the temple, I watched devotees perform rituals and prayers, inhaling air thick with incense and smoke from the burning of purified butter. I returned to the guesthouse before lunch feeling feverish and weak. Feeling unwell is not only Lord Jagannath's prerogative. Guided by Robby, I cycled to Dr N. Pandit's clinic near the railway station. I did not have to wait long.

"Where do you live in Europe?" he asked. "I have been to your city. I lived in Paris for a few years."

"You must speak French fluently."

"I haven't spoken French for ten years."

Unfortunately for me, the doctor was more interested in practising his French than treating me. While conversing he diagnosed, "You have a viral infection."

"Is it the infamous Puri Paralysis?"

"A form of it."

"But I arrived here only yesterday!"

I bought the antibiotics while he prescribed a diet of Britannia Arrowroot biscuits, apple juice, bananas, coconut, weak tea and Khichri, the food of god Jagannath, for me. Afraid of getting sicker by eating in none-too-clean eating places, I asked my host if I could eat with his family.

I still had to deliver my uncle's book to Puri Sikh Temple. I found the temple in a derelict building composed of two small rooms, one housing the Sikh Book-guru and the other on the left displaying Lord Jagannath's idol. The Udasi, non-Sikh, caretaker told me a story that I had not heard before: Nanak went into such a deep Samadhi (meditative trance), that on the third day Lord Jagannath got worried about losing his status. Jagannath himself walked from his temple to meet Nanak. That is why his idol sits next to Book-guru.

The caretaker showed me the steps descending deep to a Baoli (well). It was quite dark, so I did not test the sweetness of its water. The legend goes like this: One morning Guru Nanak went for a stroll on the long sandy beach. There were many people bathing, just as the pilgrims do now, fully attired. As is common in many miraculous legends associated with Nanak's travels, it's Mardana, his companion, who falls into some trouble or trap. He is thirsty. The salty or brackish water all around was undrinkable. I cannot resist any more. My tongue has become like dry wood. Surely I'll die, pleaded Mardana, a name that means one who cannot die. With his walking staff Nanak struck the sand and out gushed a spring of cool sweet drinking water. Quenching his thirst, Mardana survived and remained true to his name.

Did Mardana ever die? According to the legend, Nanak gave him that name after saving him from death. How could fresh water suddenly appear on the beach? The well is likely on or near an underground stream emptying into the sea. The simple caretaker would not know all these things. He did not know what to do with the book I handed him. Should I have taken it to the other gurdwara known as Mangu Math, near the Jagannath temple?

Next morning I walked to the sandy beach two blocks behind Tanuja Guest House. From far away the beach looked wide and long. Nanak must have trod the same long beach. I started to jog to the fishing village. Unfortunately, a few strides away there was human excreta everywhere. Was the beach fouled like this when Nanak walked here? I am unable to erase the scatological imprints left in my mind, nor can I forget the well-dressed handsome man taking off his trousers, neatly folding and placed them by a tree trunk. Then he wrapped a white cloth around his waist and I assumed that he was out for his morning swim. But the handsome young man looked around to see if anyone was there, lifted the cloth over his knees and squatted down to enjoy his toilet not far from the track.

Robby's family lives in a house by the guest house. He invited me for dinner. It was simple – plain rice and lentils, not spiced too much but tasty. The children loved the bar of Swiss chocolate I offered in return. Not long ago, the family had migrated to Puri from the countryside near Chilka Lake. Two brothers and their families and the young widow of the third live in three congested rooms under the supervision of the old father. The widow runs a small grocery shop and an eating-place. She sleeps on the floor behind the counter.

I left for Bhubaneswar on the nine o'clock morning train. My first visit was to the famous Lingaraja Mandir, an impressive temple surrounded by a high wall and dedicated to Bhubaneswar, the lord of three worlds. It does not require an expert eye to notice pundits manipulating pilgrims. Non-Hindus cannot enter the temple, but no one stopped me. I must look like a Hindu. Two priests holding trays for receiving toll money guarded the entry to the linga-yoni statue carved out of granite. I watched the devotees going round it, taking a sip of milk and coconut water previously poured over the linga and flowing around it inside the labia of the yoni. A priest led a handsome well-dressed young couple to the statue. After making an offering of a coconut and fruit they stood with folded hands and eyes closed while the priest recited Sanskrit verses with his eyes mechanically rolling in all directions watching other visitors. Did he deliver the couple's prayer to its destination? Pondering on this issue I walked back to the station.

Temples and buns

The 8.47 Coromandel Express screamed out grudgingly on time for a twenty-hour journey to Chennai, old Madras. Just when I was beginning to relax in an airy compartment a family of six poured in: a young man of about thirty with his wife, baby son, sister and elderly parents. They all looked serious and talked little. I felt like an undesirable. I decided to break the ice with the young man. "I'm Inder," I introduced myself.

"My name is Dev," he replied. He told me the family was going on a pilgrimage to Rameswaram.

"That's far. You have plenty of holy places here."

"Rameswaram is different. There God Ram crossed over to Sri Lanka walking on a bridge he built with floating rocks."

"He killed Ravan, the mighty king of Sri Lanka, and freed his wife Sita. Yes, I know the story," I mused. "You speak English very well, are you working in a multinational?"

"No, I'm a geographical information systems expert with the Orissa Government."

"Amazing! Your government is already into GIS when it is in its infancy in Europe. Are you able to obtain all the data you need? GIS is a useful tool for planning and developmental purposes. Are you using it for a specific project?" I poured out the questions.

"At present nothing is happening. The civil service is inefficient, salaries are low and initiative is lacking."

A train attendant appeared at the door and distributed rust-coloured bedding. The waiter came to take the dinner orders. The family declined. I ordered fried eggs, toast and a bottle of water. For breakfast I ate soggy pre-jammed toast and drank tea from a mini-flask. The family started to sort themselves out for the long day ahead.

I took off to explore the train. The kitchen wagon was filthy. If I had seen it earlier, I probably wouldn't have ordered anything. Next to it was an empty staff cabin with wooden benches and fresh air blowing in from the open window. I sat down there and watched the land roll by, occasionally getting a glimpse of the sea. A young Moslem man joined me. Originally from Hyderabad, he now lived in Calcutta. He was in charge of maintaining the train's air conditioning system, which was subject to frequent breakdown. He earned about six thousand rupees per month, just enough for the family. He was happy living in Calcutta and he did not experience any religious tension there.

The train crawled into Chennai's Egmore Station on time at 5.35 pm I checked into the Hotel Pandian nearby. Realizing that there was so much to see in and around Chennai, I booked a fifty-rupee guided tour of Tirumala and Tirupathi. The bus departed at five in the morning. On average one hundred thousand pilgrims flock daily to Tirupathi, to pay respect to the world's busiest and the richest temple of Venkateshwara, an avatar of Vishnu. My fifty-rupee ticket allowed me to have a special Darshan (meeting) with the god, and priority over ordinary souls who had paid nothing. One had to creep for many hours in the claustrophobic steel serpentine tunnel for a darshan. God, the businessman, fixes the price according to demand:

to secure a position of no waiting one has to pay considerably more than fifty rupees. Luckily it was one of the less crowded days.

I was expectantly nearing the famous statue. From afar I saw garlands covering the carver's artistic accomplishment deep inside the temple. Then I saw vertical bands of white cloth covering the middle of each eye.

"Why are his eyes covered? I asked a devotee.

"His gaze is more powerful than a laser beam. It would scorch the onlooker."

A smart pilgrim behind me was looking through her binoculars. After nearly two hours at a slow crawl I was still too far to see the idol properly. Suddenly two hefty women guards pushed me forward, ensuring that no one stopped too long and got scorched. This was my viewing of Venkateshwara.

Several temple workers in their priestly white dhotis (loin cloths) came out of the temple carrying heavy trays piled with sweet buns the size of a grapefruit balanced on their heads. This was the prasad, freshly blessed by the Lord. As I emerged from the temple, I received prasad in exchange for my fifty-rupee bus ticket: two big buns with plenty of whole green cardamoms. A hungry-looking boy of about seven extended his hand for money. I handed him one bun. The boy ran away looking extremely happy. My Indian co-travellers stood wide-mouthed and one of them exclaimed, "You gave away prasad, just like that!"

That evening back in the hotel I ate part of the bun for dessert. It tasted so good that I regretted having parted with the other. But the memory of the boy's delight made up for it. It is believed that the idol of Venkateshwara grants any wish made in front of him. From my experience one had to be very quick to ask for the wish before the two big women pushed you on. So, I should have come prepared. For best results, go there with a clean-shaven head, the blessing penetrates the skull better. I saw many pilgrims, mainly white, with heads shaved, good business for the temple barbers.

Kanchipuram boasts one thousand temples, of which two hundred are still standing. I was relieved when the guide said that time allowed me to see only one. I had befriended a British-born honeymooning couple. Nitin was a Gujarati and Rajni a Punjabi from Nottingham. As three foreign Indians, we stuck together. Kanchi rivals Varanasi and Mysore for its fine silk. In the silk handloom factory Rajni bought a beautiful sari. I had no intention of buying, but ended up spending a few thousand rupees on one. Was I buying it for Malika? I did not know.

After lunch we visited the nearby seashore temples and magnificent Mahabalipuram elephants carved out of huge rocks on the coast. At three in the afternoon I broke off from the tour and boarded a rickety local bus to the old French enclave of Pondicherry.

Ashram to Ooty

Descending from the bus, drooping with heat and humidity, I walked a few kilometres across Pondicherry to Sri Aurobindo Ashram Park Guesthouse at its eastern end by the seashore. The evening sea breeze revived me. The guesthouse is for visiting devotees. As there was no meeting that week, I got a superb large clean room with a private bath and a spacious balcony overlooking a well-manicured garden along the rock-lined sea shore with a spectacular view of the sea. Big waves crashed on the rocks. I could not resist going out. The Beach Road was crowded.

One cannot see Pondicherry without visiting Aurobindo Ashram. I walked to the Ashram before the morning crowd. In the courtyard were two samadhis (tombs), one holding the ashes of Aurobindo, the venerated sage of modern times and the other of his successor, the Mother. Aurobindo, an erudite and prolific writer, synthesized yoga and science. At one time he became very popular among westerners. In the courtyard a dozen people meditated in perfect silence. One sad-looking young man sat embracing the tomb itself with his head placed on the cold stone as if listening to the sage's spiritual message emanating from inside. Adorning the background was an old black car, a Humber of considerable antique value.

I took a bus back to Chennai the next day. From my schooldays I remembered Robert Clive of the British East India Company and Fort St. George of Madras. I strolled along the outer wall of the Fort, now housing a museum. It was built in 1653 by the BEA. In the porches of the dilapidated outer wall live poor craftsmen and workers. I walked out over a trashy and smelly path. Looking at the tourist map, the Kuvam River appears to be the city's main natural attraction. It's probably why Madras was founded at that spot. I backtracked to the city centre and crossed over to the riverbank to satisfy my hydro-geographical curiosity. Langs Garden Road, which runs along the river, was filthy, but the river was filthier. Turning a blind eye to the slums on the opposite bank and the trash floating in the placid river, I closed my nose to the stench and instead pictured the intrinsic beauty of the sick river.

It was Friday, the last day of March. I was on the train to Bangalore, speeding across a plateau dotted with clumps of eucalyptus trees interspersed with tawny grass and granite boulders, reminding me of Kenya. The train was about to stop at Bangalore Cantt Station. I spotted a turban, I knew the face in it, but the beard had greyed. My last meeting with my cousin Harman had been thirteen years ago.

"Daddy from Punjab and brother from Delhi have phoned many times to find out if I had heard from you he complained. "Daddy is quite worried. I was expecting a confirmation from you."

"I told them not to worry if they did not hear of me. They know I am out to lose myself" I replied.

Harman is a senior research engineer at MICO, the Bosch of India. The first time we met was when he visited Switzerland in 1983 on his way back from Germany.

"Where are those British buildings I saw in 1971?" I asked. "What has happened to those clean roads winding around big green parks, manicured gardens, colonial hotels, and neat shops?"

"They are all there," Harman laughed. "They are hidden behind the new tall buildings. I'll take you there. What you saw were a few defence-related telecommunications and engineering industries. Unknowingly they sowed the Silicon Valley seed ."

Bangalore's moderate climate and colonial facilities in a beautiful setting, similar to those in Kenya, attracted many Punjabis from Kenya in the late sixties and early seventies when many Indians looked for greener grass, especially from Great Britain. They have not regretted relocating here.

"You see those big estates with ultra-modern buildings? They belong to national and multinational companies. Behind them are multi-storey housing complexes. It's like this for kilometres. The city is mushrooming in all directions. Roads and sanitary systems are almost non-existent. You see litter everywhere. No one is bothered about air pollution."

I had stopped in Bangalore to visit my aunt, Harman's mother, who was recovering from a stroke. She is the one who raised my younger brother Mohi after our mother died in 1941. I was glad she recognized me. She would take a few months before recovering her memory. Meeting her gave me much emotional motherly comfort.

Having had enough of eating at bus stops, in trains and at roadside kitchens, I took my cousin and his wife out to dinner at Caesar's, one of the original posh colonial restaurants housed in a large villa. A valet opened the car doors with utmost courtesy. A waiter in a black suit and bow tie showed us to our table. It had been a popular restaurant with a lovely bar for tourists before the metro works messed up the MG road in front. The waiter took the order and promptly served me a scotch, a cold beer for Harman and a Coke for his wife and son. We raised our glasses to the happy reunion.

CHAPTER NINE

Assuming that food would be mildly spiced in this five-star place, I ordered a spicy masala fish. The term mild is relative. It was so hot that even the whisky was not potent enough to soothe my burning mouth.

The eight-hour bus trip to the Nilgiri Hills the following day was a nightmare. Eating only bananas, fresh oranges and biscuits pacified my stomach. Yogis associate such ailments with the state of mind. A student nurse, Shani, studying in Bangalore, sat beside me. Talking to her helped me forget the discomfort. She disembarked at a small hill village before Ooty. From there the bus growled through the steep forested hills. I looked for wild game, forgetting that this was not Africa. I had to content myself with the monkeys and birds.

Over two thousand metres above sea level, Ooty, short for Ootacamund, is chilly in the evenings. Karnataka Tourist Guest House was on Fern Hill, four kilometres from the town centre. The three-wheeler brought me there and back to town. A century ago, Ooty was made the summer capital of the Madras government. Ooty is a small town, now called Udagamandalam. Surrounded by rolling green hills, lakes, forests and plantations with hillside bungalows, cottages, tearooms, gardens, and churches, it reminds one of southern England. Its centre now resembles any overburdened provincial Indian town. Ooty is undeniably charming, but the roadside filth hurts the eye.

At nine o'clock the following morning I boarded a crowded bus to Sandynulla reservoir with my tall Tamil guide. The bus turned off the main road into another stunning green panorama and dropped us in front of a roadside hut. Trekking towards the lake, we reached a Toda tribal village. Today only a thousand Toda people are left. Some ethnologists think that they are one of the indigenous pre-Aryan people of India, having linguistic and cultural kinship with many other tribes in Afghanistan and Iran. However their language has Dravidian roots. Yet they take pride in claiming to be direct descendants of Aryan Pandavas of Mahabharta, caretakers of the soil. Cultivating land is against their culture. They worship the buffalo. While men take care of buffalo herds, women embroider shawls. They still maintain round igloo-like wooden houses, now mainly a showpiece for tourists.

An old lady invited me into her half-barrel house. I crawled into it on my knees. The inside was very clean. She made coffee on an open hearth in thick buffalo milk. Sitting on an earthen bench watching the smoky flames while waiting for the coffee to brew would excite many a western tourist. The show did not mean much to me, but I displayed a tourist's interest. It was the sugar that made the coffee taste good. A similar hut nearby served as a place of buffalo worship.

"Women are not allowed to go in," said the guide. "They must stand outside at a certain distance, while men pray for them." Then he announced, "I'm going to bathe at the village watering point. You take that track, it will take you to the Pykhara River Dam and the lake it holds back."

Trekking through mainly eucalyptus forest for an hour I saw a truck collecting dry cattle dung. Across the blue reservoir I saw a herd of wild buffaloes waddling in the mud and water. Even though the lake level was low, its blue water was fringed with a forest, providing a spectacular view. Human activity in the area surrounding the lake is restricted in order to safeguard the reservoir from pollution. I was not surprised to see a boating club by the dam. A lonely woman was gathering dry eucalyptus leaves to sell at the local oil mill to supplement the family income. I ambled through the forest for two hours, hoping to see gaur, sambar, flying squirrel, langur, antelope and elephant.

"For that you need more time to go to Mukurthi National Park, which is only a few kilometres further upstream towards Nilgiri and Mukurthi peaks," said the guide, standing next to a very pretty and well-dressed young girl. Sensing my curiosity, he introduced her.

"This is Asha."

She greeted me with a Namaste with hands joined, not shy at all.

"She speaks Hindi and English."

"Where did you learn English, Asha?" I asked her.

"I understand English but I cannot speak it," she replied in Hindi.

The guide intervened, "Recently she had hole-in-the-heart operation funded by some overseas benevolent person."

"How old are you?"

"Eighteen" she replied. "And I am in university," she continued before I could ask her.

During the return bus journey, the guide complained about an elderly European friend from whom he had inherited one hundred and forty thousand Swiss francs, saying the Swiss bank holding the money would not accept his documents. Reaching Ooty in the evening, I still had strength to walk in the Botanical Garden, which is paradise for a botanist. A burger at the popular Hot Bread tasted better than a multi-course dinner.

I discovered, much to my dismay, that to travel from Ooty to Mangalore, then northwards along the West Coast to Goa, would take many days. So I returned to Bangalore. "No Indian meals for me for a few days," I told Harman. The family had gone to Punjab and so he took me to Koshy's Parade Café in St. Mark's Street. It was still very British.

"I used to frequent this place before I got married," recalled Harman. We ordered fish and chips followed by butter chicken, which we chased down with cold beer. It was the most satisfying meal I had in India, and so cheap.

Vasco to Bhagwan

The tourist map of Goa shows a beautiful blue Vasco Bay with a sandy beach at walking distance from the centre of the coastal town of Vasco da Gama, not far from Goa's Dabolim airport. To pay respect to the famous Portuguese sailor, I chose to stay in this town and not in Panjim, the capital, twenty-five kilometres further to the north. Vasco da Gama, the first European to sail round southern Africa, with the help of an Indian pilot hired from Malindi in Kenya, reached Goa in 1497. I recalled his monument overlooking Malindi's silver beach in Kenya.

The Citadel hotel is close to the beach. After a quick lunch I asked at reception for directions to Vasco beach.

"You must not go to that beach. It's not good. To walk or swim you go to Bogmalo," the young receptionist advised. For five rupees, a rickety minibus took me to Bogmalo, eight kilometres from Vasco. The people in the bus were friendly, spoke softly and freely. There's a five-star Park Plaza Resort at the clean sandy sea front. There are no public toilets and changing facilities. Resisting the temptation to go to the hotel, I entered an ordinary beach restaurant and changed in a tiny bathroom at the back. The roof was so low that I could not stand straight. The floor was wet and muddy. I kept my eyes focused on a well-stocked live insectarium. After a refreshing swim I walked to the other end of the beach, where a young soldier stopped me. "You cannot go further, go back," he told me in Hindi.

"Why?"

"This is the boundary of the Naval Centre." I chatted with him for a while. He complained about life in the army and his village. Like most young people in India, he wanted to live in a foreign country.

Before going to bed that night, I decided to combine my morning jog with solving the mystery of Vasco beach.

I woke up suddenly at four in the morning. I felt my bed sliding headwards and then footwards. The morning paper confirmed that the area had experienced a mini earthquake.

At daybreak I jogged towards the rail station. A well-trodden dirt path took me to an old rusty steel footbridge over the railway yard. On the other side I climbed down into a poor area. The small food shops were opening and owners were sprinkling water in front to keep the dust down. I was at Vasco beach. The emerald seawater gently splashing a welcoming white sand beach must have captivated Vasco da Gama. I surveyed the broad stretch on my left and saw rows of men squatting with their bottoms exposed, occasionally moving forward a short step like penguins having made their first scatological imprint. That image is indelible – I have seen people do that before, but not so many in so charming a place.

I took a guided minibus tour at the main bus station. Sightseers were packed like sardines in it. Since I was alone, the controller asked me to sit on the engine cover while waiting for more passengers. One and a half hours later, the claustrophobic heat and humidity became unbearable. Children began to cry. The controller-owner announced, "We are waiting for some more people. Anyway, this bus will not go to Old Goa because strikers are blocking the roads."

Visiting sea resorts on the northern coast full of European tourists did not interest me. I had not yet paid for the ticket, and abandoned the bus. The bus owner standing outside frowned, "We have to earn our meal as well".

My destiny took me instead to a local bus. As if it had been waiting for me, it drove off the moment I stepped in. At the main bus station outside Vasco, I caught the Panjim bus to Old Goa. In half an hour I was walking on the side of a wide road with numerous churches and historical buildings, reminding me of the Iberian Peninsula. Of the churches, Basilica of Bom Jesus is fascinating, especially the silver casket containing the body of St Francis Xavier perched high in a vault between intricately carved pillars. I returned to Panjim - some call it Panaji - in the late afternoon and walked to the Government Tourist Office to buy a ticket for a sunset boat cruise on Mandovi River. I talked about Vasco Beach to an officer, who expressed keen interest and took me to meet the Deputy Director.

"We know the situation," he told me. "We constructed a line of public toilets and tried to educate the people in the area. You see, it is difficult to break the habit of using the beach. The problem is complicated by the continuous inflow from a rural population not familiar with the toilet system. A bigger problem is the narrow-minded intransigence of the local politicians."

Panjim is an attractive city, especially parts of Fontainas, which remind one of houses in Portugal. I visited a number of art galleries and attended a church service in the Chapel of St Sebastian. The church was full. The evening boat cruise wasn't as spectacular as I expected. Local tourists looked satisfied watching folk dances on the deck. My eyes remained riveted to the glorious view of the sun sinking into the Indian Ocean. In the last bus at midnight to Vasco, I met the couple and their small child who did not get off the tour bus in the morning.

"You did the wise thing. We were very hot and uncomfortable the whole day, and there wasn't much to see," said the man, an Indian Army officer holidaying at the coast.

Checking out of the hotel, I mentioned to the manager my meeting with the Deputy Director of Tourism regarding Vasco Beach.

"You should talk to the owner of this hotel. She is the Chairperson of Vasco Municipality," he said. "Look, she's coming."

Carrying a briefcase which she handed to an attendant, she ushered me aside to listen to my concerns.

"That is a red-light zone, you should not go there", she advised. "We have a serious problem of drugs and AIDS there. We have built six public toilets, but no one uses them. Decisions taken by the council cannot be implemented because local politicians do not co-operate. They demand that water and electricity be provided free of charge to the slum dwellers and to maintain the toilets. Educating the people in personal and public hygiene is not easy because most of them are poor and are afraid of paying for a water supply and sanitary services. The authorities are conscious of the problem and keen to bring about changes, but progress is very slow."

"The next time I come to Vasco I expect to sunbathe and jog on Vasco beach and swim in the bay. Vasco da Gama would turn in his grave with joy!" I joked with her as I hurried to leave.

Harman's niece, Cheeru, and her husband, Praful, received me with broad smiles at Pune airport. Eight years earlier I had met them in Hong Kong on my way to China. Cheeru, a Punjabi Sikh and Praful, a Maharashtra Hindu, fell in love studying hotel management in Pune. Cheeru got a job with Cathay Pacific as chief of flight catering. Praful joined her and worked as a stockbroker. I savoured their culinary art in their Hong Kong apartment. When China got Hong Kong back, the couple had to return to India. In Pune they started a neat little restaurant called Malaka Spice specializing in Indonesian and Malaysian cooking. Located quite near the Osho Commune International - Ashram of the famous Bhagwan Rajneesh - it attracts Osho's devotees especially when they are tired of eating from the Ashram kitchen, run mainly by Germans, Italians and Japanese.

I was not lost any more. It was my last day in India and it turned out to be exceptional. I enjoyed a refreshing early morning walk with Praful's father at the foot of the sacred hill with Kali's temple at the top. It sharpened my appetite and I devoured a breakfast of hot parathas with yoghurt. The drive through Pune City was unlike my 1968 visit. Like Bangalore, Pune is mushrooming in every way. It has become a rich dormitory of crowded Mumbai. At Malaka Spice, Cheeru catered for my special request for noodles cooked with vegetables in the Indonesian style - simple and delicious.

"Let's visit the Osho Ashram, because I have not been there yet. The white devotees always turn up here and I hear all these stories of the ashram. It's like living in the dark shadow at the foot of a world-illuminating candle," said Praful.

"I like the idea, although I had not planned to go there," I replied.

I was familiar with Osho's books – the impressive and convincing work of an intellectual. People remember him for sexual freedom. And his Rolls Royces.

"As you are casual visitors and do not wish to meditate, you do not have to buy and wear long maroon togas nor prove that you are HIV-negative," the guide informed us at the entrance. "We have on-the-spot test facilities."

An ultra modern reception desk and computerised system reminded me of a Club Med Resort with added spirituality.

"My uncle would like to visit the Nalla Park also, is it possible?" Praful inquired.

The soft-spoken receptionist said, "A senior member of the Commune must recommend you." As luck would have it, just then a rich Indian friend wearing a maroon toga greeted Praful. Permission was granted and immediately the park caretaker was alerted by telephone. The guide requested us to observe complete silence during the tour. The moment our group of seven entered the inner yard, there was loud psychedelic disco-music. In an open hall walled with transparent curtains a big crowd of mostly white devotees were dancing in a trance. Nalla Park was a short walking distance away.

"The tiny nalla (stream) used to be filthy with industrial and domestic waste. It was unsightly and its putrid smell spread through the holy Commune," the new guide explained. "Osho failed to convince the local authorities that polluting influents must be stopped and the stream cleaned. With great difficulty, Osho managed to buy a stretch of the stream. He engaged sanitary and environmental experts and got the stream cleaned. At the same time he educated the riparian residents. Now you see clean water tumbling over stones, although not totally odourless. I wish you an enjoyable walk."

We walked in the balmy, humid, well-maintained growth of tropical plants and trees covering both banks. Osho's model should be emulated by numerous filthy-rich religious institutions in Tirupathy and Patna.

That evening I caught a train to Mumbai and sat next to an Italian, one of Osho's devotees and a frequent visitor to the ashram. He was also a fan of Malaka Spice.

"What attracts you to Osho?" I asked curiously.

"My main objective is to learn to cook all the vegetable dishes served in the ashram so that I can introduce some of them in my restaurant in Italy."

I burst out into an uncontrollable laugh at his honesty, devoid of any spiritual pretensions.

CHAPTER 10

JOURNEY TOWARDS LOVE

～

Married life is like skateboarding. You skate, sweep across the trench, twist and turn in the air and land smoothly. If you miss one you crash, and break your nose or neck. I celebrated New Year with my daughter and her husband, who live in California. Two days later their skateboards missed a manoeuvre and suffered a painful fall. To allow them time to recover I took off to Los Angeles to spend a few days with Chand, a university professor of hydro-sciences. He was my fellow hydrologist in Kenya until the late 1960s. He's married to Gita, a lovely open-hearted woman. Chand and I have remained friends even though we live on different continents.

Chand, as usual, has a field trip lined up. Twenty years ago, we drove to Mojave Desert University Research Center at Zzyzx, on the shore of Soda Dry Lake near Baker. Researchers and students from many universities, army and various US departments come here to look into every aspect of the desert environment and habitat ranging from archaeological sites of early man to migration of animals, defence, volcanism, dry land management and crop production. Chand briefed me on the hydro-geologic model and water budget studies being undertaken by some of his students.

"Zzyzx is unusual, is it an Indian word?" I asked Chand.

"The story of Soda Springs is fascinating, almost a legend. At first, the springs became a stopping point on the historic Mojave Road in the middle of the Mojave Desert for all the tired and thirsty trekkers and their animals. It is also the gateway to Death Valley. In the early forties an enthusiastic self-claimed religious minister built a spa with nine pools in the shape of a cross. He wanted to give it a name with no vowels that sounded like sleep, and so 'Zzyzx' came into being. He offered through his own radio station miraculous cures. The elderly spent their life savings to holiday in its shabby rooms and to relax in the mineral waters. Springer was arrested for violation of law. Our University took it over and made it into the Desert Studies Center."

We reached the Center at sunset. The temperature quickly dropped to freezing at night and I spent one of the coldest nights of my life in the unheated room with my knees curled up to my chin. It was quite dark when we drove to Las Vegas for dinner and tried our luck at the casinos, gambling as everybody does in this town, with nothing gained or lost at the tables but a lot of fun.

On another occasion I joined Chand's university team evaluating the ecological impact of chemical pollution on Laguna Niguel in Long Beach. This time we trekked a snow-covered trail up Mount Baldy, part of the San Gabriel Mountains. Driving back, I recognized the name of a suburb, Linda Yorba.

"You know Malika lives somewhere here. I heard that she is not keeping well. She does not want to meet me, yet I would like to meet her once, just one more time," I wished aloud.

"You have her address?"

"Yes," I replied looking in my diary. I read out the address.
Chand exclaimed.

"We are actually there. It will take us two minutes to reach her house. Do you want to pass by?" Chand asked excitedly.

My heart was beating fast. The thought of being so close to her suddenly left me breathless.

"Don't you think it's risky? She might be standing in the front garden."

"We'll go, it's exciting."

He took the next exit into the suburb. Like all streets in America, one sees rows of pretty houses but rarely a soul. I felt like we were two white-haired Romeos behaving like teenagers.

"There on the left is her number," I pointed. We turned back at the cul-de-sac and passed the house again and saw no sign of life.

Suddenly, I felt empty. Was I hoping to see her? And then what?

Ten minutes later back home, Chand was raving like a teenager about the drive to Malika's house, sipping hot tea and relishing a warm chocolate muffin.

"Men will never grow up," Gita shook her head. "Inder, don't let him entice you away. Chand is like that around women. Malika doesn't want to meet you, so leave her alone".

"She is not well and she might have changed her mind", Chand said. "Inder, I've just finished reading this book by Elizabeth Gilbert, *Eat, Pray, Love*. I'm sure you'll like it. Take it and read it on the plane. It's real-life story about… " Gita interrupted, "You want me to read it as well, so I don't want to hear about it."

Flying over the Atlantic, I began the book, not knowing I was going to follow the author's footsteps within days of returning home, first to Italy and then to India. My journey to love in Indonesia remained a mystery.

A few days later I received a message from Roshan. "Malika is coming to stay with me for two weeks. Come join us."

Should I go? I ran a mile to understand my emotions. Was I scared? What was there to be scared of now? I called Roshan, "OK, I'll come," I stated simply.

"I'm delighted. You will arrive at the same time as Malika," gushed Roshan.

Then Malika herself phoned. "Are you coming?"

"Am I expected? I've just returned from India."

"You can still come."

"I'll try. It looks difficult to get flights at such short notice. Do you want me to come? Do you really want to see me?"

"Why do you think I'm going there? It's obvious."

What had changed her, her illness? Was she unable to fill the gap left by unfulfilled love? Bridge the fifty-year blank? Her plea did not mirror what was going on in her mind.

Silence.

"Please come, it's probably our last chance to meet," her voice was soft on the other end.

I landed in New Mexico half an hour before Malika. Roshan was there.

"What does she look like?" I asked Roshan, trying to stay calm.

"You're asking me? I haven't seen her in fourteen years. Other than the four-year-old photo that she allowed me to send you I have no idea. The illness might have changed her."

"The picture you sent cannot replace the image of the young and svelte Malika imprinted in my mind. I wonder if seeing her today would replace that image."

I was in for a shock.

The luggage carousel started to grind. I caught sight of a grey-haired woman walking towards Roshan. It was Malika.

I stood frozen, staring. Finally.

The two walked up to me, Malika with the same smile, just older, with grey hair. She seemed relaxed, more in control of her emotions than me, as if she was meeting me after a recent coffee date. She simply placed her head on my shoulder, no words spoken.

Malika looked tired. I took her bags. In our own worlds, we are lost for words. She smiled. "How have you been?" 50 years later.

The Malika of my youth and the Malika of now are two different women. The Malika of my youthful love was the ever-cheerful Malika, forever active. . This was another Malika.

We walked to the car and I opened the door for her. We stood by it for a few moments looking at each other, trying to bridge a gap of fifty years. She shook her head and placed her hand on mine.

"Thank you for coming" she said.

"Thank you for inviting me" I replied. "I had to catch up with you."

Roshan drove out with me in the back seat trying to fathom my emotions. To tell the truth, I was dazed. Dazed at how Malika had changed. And she seemed more talkative.

"It was difficult for me to make any plans to get out of town," Malika was telling Roshan, oblivious to me in the back seat. "The oncologist ordered a body scan and a bone density test. She is concerned about the new pain in my rib-cage area. I wanted to have both these tests done on the same day to avoid the long drive to the cancer centre. You can't imagine how hard it is waiting for weeks for the test results. It was like dying before death."

"I was worried about you, so I thought it was a good idea for you to get away from it all," said Roshan.

"I try not to worry. Thanks for keeping me in your prayers. I was so happy when most of the results showed negative for the spread. I immediately booked my flight to Santa Fe to celebrate with you and Inder."

Hearing my name from her lips broke me out of my thoughts. She reminds me of her father, Shera. After the cruel separation inflicted upon us by him, I had erased him from my memory. Strangely, I now see less of the Malika I loved and more of her father. Short and stubby, he had plenty to say on everything in every discussion, not always unreasonable. Full of humour, he was quick at twisting words and ideas and he loved having people around him.

We reached Roshan's house quite late at night. Seeing Malika in the flesh was like meeting another person. She noticed.

"I've shortened a lot. I used to be taller than Roshan. Now look at me," she said defensively. "It's anti-cancer medication and pills against my hip pain. To reduce the side effects of these strong drugs I take more pills. I have put on a lot of weight."

She looked visibly exhausted by now. Roshan showed her to her bedroom.

That night I did not sleep much, my brain was trying hard to accommodate the new Malika. I heard a door creak and found Roshan in the kitchen preparing brunch. A little later Malika walked in and greeted us animatedly. "Good morning. How are you? Inder, you have grown more handsome now," she exclaimed, sizing me up.

"You are in good spirits," said Roshan. "Sit down anywhere. You must be very hungry, last night you didn't eat anything. Inder is rolling parathas and has a few more to go."

"Actually, it's the smell of cooking that woke me up," said Malika, placing her transparent pill box on the dining table. "Pills have become an essential part my breakfast."

She pointed at the pills sorted into compartments - one for each day of the week. She seemed to enjoy displaying her medicine box. I placed a paratha straight from the frying pan on to her plate. "Especially made for you, with love," I teased.

Malika lopped a heaped spoon of butter on her paratha, another in her daal, pulses. I wondered about her cholesterol.

"I take my tea brewed in the colonial style," she said. "Have you heated the teapot?" She walked to the kitchen counter, picked up the kettle, poured a little boiling water into the teapot, rotated it to make the hot water swirl inside, and handed it to Roshan. "Pour it into the sink. Now put in tea bags."

Roshan put three bags and filled the pot with boiling water.

"Please warm the tea mugs in the same way before you pour the tea. I like hot milk in my tea."

Roshan obeyed, wanting her friend to feel at home. The flow of

Malika's unsolicited suggestions and advice on cooking was quite amusing. We have changed, I thought to myself. We have little in common other than talking about our bygone youthful days. Roshan's quick eye contact with me seemed to be on the same wavelength.

"My children and grandchildren love my cooking. You know, when I was in school my mother would not let me cook. Making dough was an ordeal for me. I hated it sticking to my fingers. So I never learnt to cook like a normal Indian girl."

Malika kept up her solo banter. "My younger brother was like me. We always found some excuse to avoid doing housework. Going to school for me was having fun. I never had a desire to study. Yet I did as well as the best in our class. Kanti was an exception, he only studied and did nothing else."

She talked endlessly about her two years in a women's teacher training college in Nairobi. Roshan brought out her old photo album. We looked at the many group photos of our schooldays, trying to recognize who was who. I held a group picture of teachers taken in early 1959.

"Malika, you're missing. India..." I let the words trail. "I came to see you off at the station, do you remember?" I asked after a pause.

"Vaguely, I was drugged. There is a blank in my memory. A few years are missing. I remember nothing", replied Malika.

"I can't believe I'm with you fifty years later. How do you feel?"

"I don't know, I can't put it into words what I feel."

We were alone. I wanted to know if she had any feelings from our penthouse meeting. What was I looking for?

Roshan and I have met over the years. We spent a week in Andalucía in Spain and Tuscany eating pasta and drinking Italian wine. I was at her daughter's wedding in the NATO-bombed Novisad in Serbia. A woman from the local administration attended the wedding reception and performed the civil marriage in a chatty way, making everyone laugh. The boy, who lived also in Santa Fe, wanted to celebrate the marriage in Novisad with his large family and relatives, none of whom could go to the USA. After the dinner offered by the boy's family and cutting the wedding cake, we danced late into the night. In return Roshan and a few of her family decided to entertain the hosts with an Indian dinner the next day in the boy's house. She depended on my cooking skills. We planned a simple menu of tandoori chicken, daal (lentils) and chapattis for one hundred and fifty people. With the help of the boy's mother we managed to get most of the groceries we needed. In a small apartment where we met every day I put three persons to prepare and marinate chicken in three huge saucepans.

Roshan and I struggled with making the dough and chapattis until five in the evening. Exhausted, we transported the food to the house on a farm on the edge of the city. Not knowing the Serb customs, we waited for the guests to arrive and sit down at the tables. They trickled in, had their dinner and went away.

Standing behind an inadequate grill, I could not turn out roasted chicken at the required speed. Nearly three hundred guests turned up. There was no food left. While Roshan was feeling quite embarrassed, it did not bother the Serbs. The boy's mother pulled out a mega-size bag of sausages from somewhere. That saved the day.

Malika talked much about her children and grandchildren. She showed me their photos, but not a word about her husband. She avoided being alone with me. Every time I invited her to join me in the garden she had an excuse, "It's too cold for me". She couldn't walk a lot because of her weight, or her weak state. I felt they were excuses – she had let herself go. She was convinced that cancer was the cause of her overweight. She spent hours in front of the internet forwarding jokes and colourful aphorisms about life. I reminded her of her email 'Life is a train' that she had forwarded.

"That was five months ago. You caught me off balance when you said you wanted to meet me" she admitted for the first time. I was silent, unsure what to say.

"You know Malika, old wounds don't hurt me any more. I was happily married and have children, but I never stopped thinking of you. I always felt that I was dangling at one end of a cord trying to catch you on the other end. I wanted very much to tie up the ends, complete the circle. In my mind I always see you sitting in the front row of the group photo, slim and classy."

She kept her lips tight. Half a century is too wide a time gap to bridge. The period of courting was too brief. We really did not know each other. Reliving old memories is exciting. Any new relationship will have to start with new values, the schooldays are over.

"It was sweet of you to phone the next morning," Malika said.

"I wanted to be with you to share your worry. Longing to meet you became painful. I wanted to see the real person I'd been talking to."

"Just keep me in your thoughts and prayers and keep your shoulders strong for me to lean on. I know you are hurting for me. It's OK for you to grieve for me, but only for a while. But I want you to be strong for me when I need to place my head on your shoulder."

"Here, my shoulder is for you always, place your head on it any time. My hand is waiting to caress it."

"Your soothing words comfort me. There is so much to say, yet words run short."

I told Malika of the photograph Roshan had sent me. I was restless after seeing it.

"You are sitting with your handsome husband on the steps holding your grandchildren. You looked beautiful, like a queen. Your name, Malika, queen, fits you perfectly. I should behave more respectfully towards you!"

I remember that day. Seeing Malika's picture after so many years left me yearning for her. Does one fall out of love half a century later?

I jogged on a twisted path in the woods along the Rhône for an hour. It didn't help. Later I went to see a Voodoo performance by a Haitian group. The community hall was full when I entered. Expectantly I waited to see people falling into a trance and making supernatural pronouncements, something we see in films. But the presenter announced that it was cancelled. Instead an Afro group put on a dance performance - two young guys dancing, or rather jumping, to a rhythmic tempo and women dancing with them. In a trance, I joined the jumping group. Before going to sleep, I phoned Malika.

"You have been so kind and caring," said Malika. "Talking to you over the phone and reading your emails have given me much pleasure, hope and comfort. When my grandchildren come to see me I count them as God-sent, precious gifts. Wishes are never ending. I do wish that some other loved ones who are dear to me lived close by too."

That was the most she opened up to me. Malika claims she is not afraid any more. The cancer has not spread. But her neurosis manifests in fatigue, body pains and feigning loss of memory. Is she afraid of dying? She is acting brave.

CHAPTER 11

THE TWIST

Dado is my sister. Not my real sister, but we grew up together in Eldore and share a bond like siblings. Dado has a thin face and a sharp tongue. She's very lovable and playful and unashamedly teasing. When I returned to Eldore after four years at university she didn't waste time with trivialities.

"Why didn't you and Malika run away?" she said then. "You know, like in the movies – elope?"

"You're telling me now. Where were you four years ago?" I asked, angry at her for offering advice so late in the day.

"Malika is married, she has a son," continued Dado, oblivious to my query.

"Where is she now?" I asked eagerly.

"England. You should have eloped," repeated Dado. Dado, in her occasional letters, did not reveal that Malika had migrated to Britain in case I tried to meet her there. Was she protecting Malika or me or hiding her fear of losing me?

"That would have upset our families. You belong to her clan" I replied, not convinced myself if it would have made any difference as time went by.

"Who cares now?" she asked looking at me as if I were an idiot.

I pondered. "We had been too idealistic – Malika and I, young and hot blooded. We wanted to prove to the Sikh community that our families were following the doctrine of our Gurus. That there were no castes, that we were all equal."

"Malika didn't think like you," goaded Dado.

"Huh... she was even more convinced than me that we should marry with our parents' blessings. She wasn't going to elope."

"You idiots, I should have given you a good beating for giving in."

"Ah well, it's too late now," I replied.

Now Dado lives in Leicester, United Kingdom with her husband, Mitu. After Kenya's independence, Indians were marginalised in the push for Africanisation. Many of my generation suddenly found themselves with no jobs. Like Dado, they migrated to various countries.

I visited Dado in 2008 after a long break. She was alone and waiting expectantly. We hugged. "Where is your left hand?" I asked jokingly.

"He's gone to collect hot pukorras (potato fried fritters) especially for you." Dado, like many of her generation, referred to her husband in the third person, following the old fashioned tradition of not calling a husband by his name.

"Just for me?" I looked at her quizzically because I knew Dado loved fried stuff.

"Stop the small talk and tell me if you have spoken to Malika." Trust Dado to be direct. She had sent her poor husband on an errand about the time I was arriving so we could talk about Malika.

Then she broke the bad news.

"Malika has been diagnosed with cancer, a nasty one."

I did not want her to know that I had contacted Malika a few months before. Malika does not want anybody to know about it, especially Dado. I asked, "How is she?"

"Not good – well, most of the time. She needs our support and love. You should talk to her."

"But I haven't seen her for years. I don't even know what she looks like now. I wonder if she wants to see me?"

"Yes, she wants to see you, Inder. Very much. She lives with her husband, but their relationship broke down years ago."

All these years I blocked everything to do with Malika. I didn't want to know anything about her. Now I was being given updates at a time when she was unwell.

"Malika was the breadwinner of the family and worked very hard to bring up her three children. She needs comfort from someone close to her heart," said Dado.

"How bad is she?"

"The breast cancer has spread to her bones. She wanted to talk to you but didn't want to bring the past out."

"I have nothing much else to talk about, only the past."

Malika, like me, has crossed seven decades. An old friend told me that she lives a double life: the one she wanted to have and the one she lives. She has started to recall her younger days.

"She doesn't say it, Inder. But you were her first and only love. She cannot forget you. Speak to her. I'll call her."

I wanted to laugh now. We were in our seventies and behaving like teenagers arranging dates.

At that moment Mitu walked in.

"There you are at last!" Mitu exclaimed, dropping the paper bag on the table to hug me.

Dado went on with her single track. "Just have faith in the Guru Granth, everything will be OK."

"Have you been quarrelling again?" asked Mitu for he knew that we were forever bickering.

"That's the only way she knows to express her love for me, by arguing," I replied trying to look hurt. Mitu laughed and said "Inder, don't mind her. That's her way of showing she cares about us."

"Where was your Guru Granth when I wanted to marry the girl I loved?"

She remained silent.

When I turned fifteen, I was assigned to read the Guru Granth for two hours as protocol during the continuous reading of it. Dado does not like me calling it Book-guru. I could only manage thirty pages an hour compared to Malika and Dado, who read up to forty.

"You read fast because the female tongue is more nimble," I'd teased Malika and Dado at which Dado would hit out at me playfully. Malika would come and sit in front of Book-guru on the pretext of listening to the Word while I read during the day. I liked her being there and would do the same when it was her turn. Now I laugh at those memories.

Dado, Malika and I had numerous discussions and arguments about religion while growing up. I was strongly opinionated.

"Book-guru directs us to the Sikh way. To be a true Sikh we only need to follow its simple teachings and not follow a religion blindly," I often stated with satisfied ego.

Dado was quick to react, "Don't forget, Book-guru promotes democracy, freedom of speech, human rights, brotherhood of all human beings regardless of race, religion, caste, creed and status. Only our Book-guru says that women are equal in every respect to men. That is religion. I do not understand what's troubling your twisted brain," Dado argued.

"We use those words to find faults with other religions. What we practise is different. The Sikh way of life requires us to do nam, dan, ishnan – reflecting on the Name, charity and purity of heart."

"You have not even taken a dip in the sacred pool in Amritsar and you are talking about ishnan," she said, ignoring all else I had said.

For me religion represents a human institution, nothing to do with any purity. Malika was forcibly taken away from me and married off to someone in far-away India. Had she resisted further, she would have become the victim of an honour killing.

"These twists in the turban made me take off the turban," I stated now to Dado. She was getting frustrated with me.

"I'll continue saying my daily prayers," she asserted.

The following morning I sneaked out for a short jog near Dado's house .

"Where have you been?" she demanded when I returned.

"I went out to sharpen my appetite for your parathas. No toast."

"Why don't you get a wife who can feed you properly?"

"Find one for me if you're so concerned," I retorted.

"When did you last see Malika?" Dado pursued as soon as her husband walked out.

"I told you I never met her after our parting."

"Years ago I invited you both to come and stay with me but you didn't reply. Why?

"You know my answer. I want to meet her. But it was her – she did not reply."

"It's a God-given opportunity, to love someone the way you two did. This world is cruel," Dado shook her head.

After a few minutes' silence, Dado continued.

"Malika broke up with her husband years ago. I think she is embarrassed to meet you because she has put on a lot of weight and has become quite slow. You know more than anyone else how beautiful she was: slim and smart. She has seen your photos looking so fit and still handsome. Malika, I think, became depressed after her marriage. Food and little exercise is what caused her to become fat. The last time I met her, she opened up for the first time. All that pain hidden behind her smiles and laughter made me cry, and she cried too. Life did not treat her well."

In Dado's kitchen hangs a sepia photograph that I hadn't noticed before by the side of the door. I got up to look at it. It is of a group of youngsters. The year scribbled on it – 1954. It's me wearing white shorts, Roshan, Malika, about ten of us on our last day in high school. All very fresh-faced and innocent.

"If Malika wants to meet me again, I will return," I stated looking away from the picture.

On my flight back, memories returned. I used to spend many weekends with Dado's family, the only family I knew. It was my family. Her parents, like most Indian parents at the time, discouraged contact between adolescent boys and girls. To tease me Dado would contrive some excuse to be near me. At her elder brother's wedding I was sorting dinner plates on the floor when Dado walked in, pretending to look for something from the shelf above me. She dug her knee into my back and remained there for a good moment until someone noticed and scolded her.

When my love for Malika became public and we were not allowed to meet, Dado offered to pass messages between us. She's still trying to do the same. I smiled at the thought. Then I remembered the long argument about the power of Book-guru. I argued that for the followers it's Book-guru that matters, but I am concerned about what people practise. Book-guru is words, on their own powerless and ineffective, but revered and kept in silks. If I say this loudly some extremist's bullet might make me a martyr, the first for defending Book-guru's ideals. Book-guru's follower will be the executioners - a beautiful martyrdom!

Once, when I was in my teens, I was allotted a two-hour shift starting at two in the morning to read Book-guru. I had to keep my voice low not to disturb some souls, including my support person sleeping on the floor. It's the most difficult hour. The shroud of sleep started wrapping me. Varying my rhythm and tone failed to keep me alert. My reading turned into mumbling; for how long I cannot tell. My incoherent noise awoke the support person, Hey, what are you saying? The shock alerted me. I started reading again, feeling shamed and guilty. At the end-prayer we seek Book-guru's forgiveness for all reading mistakes. But I felt that my dereliction of duty was unpardonable. I might be making a mountain out of a molehill, but it left an impact, another twist added in my turban. I realized that followers of Book-guru just follow; they are not students, learners and disciples: not Sikhs, like becoming a medical doctor by worshiping a book on medicine. Does Book-guru need followers? Leaders need followers.

"You have a twisted brain," Dado taunted once.

"I do not know how you hide these twists in your head-scarf," I laughed.

I'm convinced, what is written in Book-guru does not make a religion, what people practise makes religion. I am not disparaging great Book-guru. It's not like other Holy Scriptures, it does not contain absurdities. It talks about the evolution of life on Earth and other planets after the Big Bang. However, its followers have created many other twists. Their number varies from one turban to another depending on the size and shape of the head, the texture and amount of hair, the size and texture of the material - starched or not, its colour, the style of tying, and the whim of the person at the moment of tying.

"You said something about 'ishnan'. Do you know what it means?" I asked Dado.

"It's obvious: A true Sikh must take a dip in the sarover, the sacred pool of the Golden Temple."

"That's not what Book-guru says. Ishnan is purity of heart and not bathing in holy places. We often sing that saying waheguru once is like visiting the sixty-eight most holy places of India. Pilgrimage has become the Gordian knot in the twisted turban and we need an Alexander the Great to cut it with his mighty sword. The tenth Guru, Gobind Singh, said that he who utters the divine Word without understanding gains nothing."

"Don't tell me that I have been wasting my time reading Book-guru."

"It's not my job to judge you. In your eyes I'm a Sikh only if I wear a turban, even though I might not obey his thousand and one other instructions. Can you untie this knot?"

"Guru Nanak will take care of it."

"Wait a minute, he or Guru Gobind Singh cannot take care of you, they are not God. You know very well what the latter has said, I was ordained to establish a brotherhood and lay down its rules, but whosoever regards me as God shall be damned and destroyed. Let there be no doubt, I am but a slave to God, as other men are: a beholder of the wonders of creation. Whoever would worship him or any other guru as God and seek favours would surely go to hell."

"You still remember all that? I seek his favours every day. At the end of my daily prayer I sing: The one who holds the double-edged sword and a plume adorns his head, may the plumed protector of the world that is Guru Gobind Singh, protect us all. Am I sending myself to hell?"

"You are lining up behind millions of others!" I laughed.

Human laziness has no limits. It's much easier to confide in the visible Book-guru than learn its teachings. Reciting and singing hymns is pleasing, satisfying – an excellent auto-psychotherapy. We need it. Few have time to take the next step of understanding and putting to practice what we recite. It is so easy for me to bow down in front of the Book-guru, place a pound coin and hire him as my agent who would do everything for me, just ask. Treading through the tangles of life's dark jungle the shroud covering my brain lifted a little, letting in some light that revealed the way through nature's beauty. For a long time my twisted turban and groomed beard formed the badge of my spiritual exclusiveness covering up my real character. With a false air of superiority I was a person apart, from another world.

CHAPTER 12

LIFE IS A RIVER - 1

⁓

When I walked into the kitchen, Malika was at the table munching cornflakes. Roshan was by the kitchen counter emptying the dishwasher.

"Roshan, have you heated the teapot? Cups as well? Also please heat a little milk in the micro, half a minute, I like my tea blistering hot."

"Yes, my Malika," Roshan curtsied as if to a queen. "I haven't made tea that way since our college days. Some people never shed the British colonial yolk, even in hot California."

I sensed a touch of sarcasm in Roshan's voice. I joined Malika at the table.

"Good morning. Looks like you slept well," I said to her.

"Yes," she replied, busy eating.

Nonchalantly I continued. "I woke up dreaming of being in a train. I've been trying to figure out the train journey half the night."

Roshan brought the tea to the table and joined us.

"I think everyone does, now you try and figure out what the dream is about," said Roshan.

"I know, I liked that website 'Life is a Train' you forwarded a few months ago," I said to Malika. "How do you find such sites that make me dream?"

"I have friends and time. Did you like it?" Malika suddenly brightened up.

"Your train analogy reminds me of the train you took in Eldore. You left me stranded at the platform."

Malika put on a wry smile. Roshan took over the conversation. "I read your article on your website about life."

"Life," I repeated. "Yes we think about it."

The more I ponder about life the more I know that life is more than human life. We are only a minuscule speck in the total flow of life on Earth and even smaller in the universe. A spadefull of garden soil contains more organisms than there are people on Earth. Just because we reason better than other beings, we've pushed aside the main flow of life and stupidly believe that ours is the only flow of life, the rest does not count.

"I found the eight sketches of your image of God in your website interesting," continued Roshan. You say 'The Flow is love and our destiny, object of spirituality', or something like that."

"Did you get time to read it?" I asked Malika, curious.

"I will when my mind is ready for it. The tests and waiting for results have made me sicker than the disease itself."

"Stop talking like that. You're perfectly fine", said Roshan encouragingly.

"But the ordeal is killing me. You can imagine how relieved I was last week when I was told that the cancer has not spread. I'll read your Big Bang story when I'm at home. It looks very erudite, probably beyond me."

"I don't think you should have any problem," I replied. "You're intelligent."

"How did you get onto the issue of spirituality?" asked Roshan.

"Seven years ago, some guys - people regard them as wise men - held a discourse on the benefits of investing in spirituality. At the first meeting I appeared to be the only one who did not understand what spirituality meant. At the following meeting I dared to present a flow diagram split into eight visions."

"Can you do the flow chart again now?" Roshan asked, intrigued by the topic.

"Yes I can," I said with vigour, because Roshan seemed so interested and I wanted to impress Malika. She looked indifferent, but followed us to Roshan's computer.

"You see things in another light, different from what our traditions have implanted in our brains," Roshan continued.

The flow diagram appeared on the screen, showing the first slide, labelled Vision One.

"May I ask you a question?" I started.

"Shoot", retorted Malika. I wondered if she was bored.

"What image do you have in your mind when you pray?"

A pause.

"I've never thought about it but I think it is the portrait of Nanak," said Malika. "But it varies. Sometimes it's the image of the Guru Granth or the Ek onkar sign [God is One]."

"No image for me", said Roshan. "The sky, emptiness, His Highness the Aga Khan."

"Well," I said. "I have received answers to this question varying not only according to different faiths but also within the same faith: a light, Jesus on the cross, the Bible, the Universe, the temple, Ganesh, flowers, Sai Baba, Krishna, Virgin Mary, the Ka'bah, and so on. In short, a global common image of an entity to which we address prayer does not exist".

"Why did you decide to write about this?" asked Malika.

"Because the discussion group could not explain to me why I should invest in spirituality," I responded. "You see, I didn't know what spirituality was. I know a little about Nestlé, Toyota, Microsoft and Google, they are real companies and I would not hesitate investing in their shares. But how does one invest in spirituality?"

Malika and Roshan looked at me, waiting for me to continue my discourse.

"We Indians find it difficult to accept spirituality being explained with sketches" I went on. "We expect to see some guru or swami in an ascetic ochre toga propounding abstruse metaphysics in Sanskrit.

"So I confronted the investors in spirituality with the eight transparencies. The red explosion represents the Big Bang. It's the beginning of a flux that I call Flow. My eight visions show the evolution of this one Flow. The beauty of these visions is that they are predisposed to change and improve at every moment, even now discussing it with you. Your comments will surely enlighten my brain with more information and knowledge, and my vision will change. Every person experiences or perceives a change in what we call God in proportion to the change in himself. Here I assume that God does not change. This should please all peoples of the Book!"

"What Book?" Malika interrupted.

"Muslims are people of the Book, the Bible, as well as Jews and Christians."

"We have The Adi Granth."

"That is true. We are also people of the book, a different one. If you don't mind I'll call it Book-guru, without the definte article. Granth means book. We consider it to be the embodiment of the gurus and therefore living, a person. As you know it better than other religious books, I'll quote whatever I can remember from it to see how it fits the Flow concept."

Roshan stretched. Malika smiled as I stopped for a breath.

"For centuries, many famous thinkers have used this concept. The important point I want to illustrate is that in the context of the Flow, religions of the world are only tools, often tools of contention, fooling their own followers and fighting others to prove their superiority. Once I was at the European Organization for Nuclear Research (CERN) complex with a group of scientists. The nuclear research centre stretches over many kilometres across the France-Switzerland border, mostly underground. The first thing our physicist-guide said was that there is no difference between us and this rock. Everything has the same basic structure: the atom composed of electrons turning round the nucleus held by an electromagnetic force. It means that for everything the origin is the same: The Big Bang. Do you know Book-guru also describes the Big Bang?"

"Never heard of it, Malika replied.

I recited a part of the poem in Punjabi, the language of the Sikhs:

Through uncountable ages, complete darkness pervaded
Over utter emptiness,
There were no worlds, no firmaments.
The infinite Will alone reigned.
There was neither day nor night, nor sun nor moon,
But only a multidimensional Force,
Forming a perpetual, unstoppable, unfathomable flow in incessant trance.

"Amazing!" exclaimed Malika.. "Is the Big Bang our God?"

"Wait. What astonished me more is when the guide said that before our Big Bang there was information or energy."

Malika was intrigued. "The Guru Granth calls it Shabad and Bani," she said excitedly. I did not expect her to call it Book-guru, which is the exact translation of Guru Granth.

"Exactly!"

Roshan added, "The Bible says that when all things began, the Word already was."

"Are you saying that God is the word, information and energy?" queried Malika.

"Well, science has helped to pull us out of one delusion, that God is not a long-bearded superman sitting on a throne in the sky and manipulating everything. Many philosophers reach the same basic concept by using terms like thought, idea, dream, vision, intellect, sensation, breath and wind."

"Who decided that this phenomenal energy must condense to the size of a pinhead and make it explode with an unimaginable force, producing our cosmos of millions of galaxies?" Roshan inquired.

"How many Big Bangs have occurred before ours? This is beyond imagination and scientific theory. Ours is not the only universe; there are megaverses and multiverses, says the Book-guru: Millions of universes above and below. Our universe is expanding and at some stage will collapse again and cause another Big Bang. This cycle runs on a time and space scale beyond our imagination and calculations. Nobody decides; it happens. Our earth is like a minute dust particle that we see floating in a beam of sunlight projected into a dusty room. What our Big Bang has produced is one unique eternal supreme force, an everlasting reality of conscious spirit-energy, all-powerful creator, fearless, without enmity, of timeless image, not begotten, and being of his own being.

"That is the Preamble of the Guru Granth. I never looked at it in that way", said Malika.

"Have you noted that in this fundamental statement, Book-guru does not use names like Brahma, God, Allah, Bhagwan, Krishna or Ram?"

"Why?"

"These names do not convey the image of the unstoppable River Flow."

"I see that in your Vision Two."

"The Big Bang started our Flow, which is made up of information or energy, indivisible, infinite, dimensionless, unstoppable and timeless. Book-guru says:

"With the graceful walk of an elephant
You walk unperturbed absorbed in your own self."

"I have heard this song before", said Malika.

"You must have, very sexy," I joked. "The raagi [musician] sings it when the bride enters the gurdwara and walks towards Book-guru and sits next to her husband to be. She does not know that he addresses her as an elephant." We all laughed.

"The Flow is perpetually in equilibrium. It's cellular-atomic in structure, be it macroscopic with planets playing sehaj dhun, heavenly music, harmoniously going around their suns or microscopic with electrons and protons revolving round their nucleus. An intelligent force or vital energy fills all space and holds these physical elements together. What we think is emptiness is filled with the missing element of Higg's equation, which we call the Higgs boson."

I stopped for a moment to take a sip of coffee. "This force gives birth to molecules. Again, the scientists and Book-guru agree that the origin of everything is Ek Onkar, One Unique Force, which continues to flow eternally or until the apocalypse in the unknown future. Everything has a common birth. Everything, rocks, animals, insects, birds, plants and human beings, is subject to the laws of nature."

I clicked on Vision Three.

"We have already covered this one. Book-guru frequently expresses the idea of the Flow as a river. *Tu daryao sabh tujh he mahen, jujh bin dooja koi nae*: You are the River and everything is in you and nothing outside. *Tu daryao dana bina*. For you Roshan, in Farsi, *Man kmeen kamtreen, tu daryao khuday*. In Earth's miasma many types of molecules came into being. One of these molecules evolved into a human being. Was it an accident or deliberate will or creation? I let people fight it out."

Turning to Vision Four, I continue, "Here you see a balance or weighing scale at the top reminding us that the dynamics of the Flow containing the entire universe and all its traits stay in perpetual equilibrium as far as we know."

"But where is God in all this?" asked Roshan.

"I often say that whatever we do not know is God. When we claim that God is unknowable, unfathomable, etc, what we are saying is that ignorance or non-knowledge is God. Aren't we? Actually, what we are admitting is that we cannot comprehend the enormous scale and complexity of the Flow."

"What you mean is that human beings invented God and we now know much more about him. But, followers of religions do not want to admit it," Roshan stated.

"Thank you, you have said what I found difficult to explain. To sidetrack people from the Flow, we have devised attributes such as the Truth, Reality, Satya, Active Intellect, Light, God, Bhagwan, Allah, Waheguru [giver of wonderful light], all words and symbols, yet reality is beyond us. Astrophysicists talk about cosmic breath: the universe and the flux breathing with a certain rhythm. Films on space have reproduced this effect with a deep howling sound in emptiness."

"Are all our prophets wrong? How do their revelations fit into this Flow?" Roshan asked.

"They all fit in beautifully, but we human beings have twisted them. We are concerned only with the love-hate relationship between us. We ignore the total environment, the Flow, the true God."

"I like the idea of Flow," Malika said. "It allows me to link what religious and other ancient scripts say with the knowledge we have acquired since the beginning of time. If we rewrote the old books by inserting our findings many problems of the world would be solved."

"I fully agree with you. Human beings especially like your American shamans who loved and lived with nature, were conscious of the force of the Flow even at the dawn of humanity. It gave life and took it away. I am told that the first wise persons were women, the spring of human life. They had time to look deeply into the spiritual and physical mysteries of the Flow. They saw the living and the dead, plants and animals and everything around them in the state of being on the same space and time scale. This enabled them to draw solutions to problems directly from nature itself, even look into the future. They did not need temples, churches, gurdwaras and mosques. At some point in the course of evolution human beings settled down in villages tending their farms instead of hunting and collecting fruit and berries. Through intrigue and corruption man assumed all these functions, and managed them badly. He has held that power since then. We read about emperors, kings, dictators, prophets, gurus, avatars, rishis, popes, all men.

"Let me digress a little. Up to the present, none of the religious gods has been able to stop the collapse of a society. Every time a community mistreated its environment, in simple terms, it did not dip in the Flow and did not appreciate the embrace of the vital energy (yogis call it lifetrons). Hatred consumed it."

I stopped for another sip of tea while the women tried to absorb my viewpoint.

"You should read Jared Diamond's book *Collapse*, where he writes about religious practices and prayers which could not stop their apocalypse. In school we have learnt of the collapse of communities that ignored their environment: Mesopotamia and Indus. Diamond describes what happened to Easter Islands, Anasazi, Mayas, and Scandinavian settlers in Greenland. However, we did not know that a community of a thousand persons living on a tiny island of Tikopia survived because it took measures to adjust itself and live within the meagre means that its environment offered, thus expressing its respect and love of that minute part of the Flow that envelops it. Like the Tikopians, we must understand and respect our environment and habitat in order to give meaning and dimension to human love. In short, the Flow is love and our destiny."

"I see that you have defined spirituality here," Malika pointed at the middle of the flow chart.

"Yes, it's knowing the Flow and flowing with it, something

concrete, tangible, real, actual - something pragmatic and non-abstract. Hence, I can invest in it. Many a wise person has tried to define interrelations within the Flow with terms like Om, Kalma, Jump, Holy Spirit, Lao, Naad, Sarosha, Silence, and Voice. Book-guru expresses the ensemble of the Flow, information, interaction and interdependence in equilibrium with the word Nam, literally 'Name', neumena in Greek and naman in Sanskrit. All He has created is Nam, there is no place without Nam, writes Nanak. You see the prophets knew that all elements are intimately linked – the universe, planets, ecology, nature, animals, humans, the supernatural, the natural and the divine. In the river of time the entire history of everything is eternally flowing in front our eyes, transforming, adjusting, enveloping, mixing, dying, resurrecting, rejuvenating and changing. The mist of our ignorance obscures the view of the flowing river. The Flow is carrying with it the past along with the information and wisdom that we call knowledge. It displays the future downstream, hidden by smoke that our ordinary eyes are unable to penetrate. But it's all there, only some can see it."

"You're a poet and you make sense", Malika said. "I've been reading the Guru Granth blindly."

"You are not alone."

"So how can I invest in spirituality?" Roshan asked.

"At the very start after the Preamble, Book-guru tells us Abide by His order, all information (that is in the Flow) is also in you. Luke also says in the Bible that the kingdom of God is within you."

"Doesn't it mean that we should know the River and its Flow?" asked Roshan.

"Yes, it does. God is in the information, information is God. Nam that includes knowledge is power, and with it man can perform miraculous godlike tasks. Few know that nature is God, even though Book-guru says so. Few know its awesome power. People have kept it hidden behind a veil of absurd religious rituals and symbols. Book-guru holds the doors open which we refuse to enter. It expresses the Flow-River also as a Force and often as Guru. Guru means anything that gives light and removes darkness. I do not recall who said: I want to stay away from temples, preachers and sacred books. The silent contemplation of nature is my yoga, prayer and link with God."

"So the Flow is my best Guru," Malika concluded.

"That is exactly what our Book-guru says."

"But what about nam japo, meditate on Nam?" Malika inquired.

"It is definitely not closing your eyes and falling into a trance when the beauty of the Flow surrounds you. In the first poem, Book-guru says that you must know and understand this Flow, accept it and then see what and where you are in this totality and live accordingly. Then you will be as good as any prophet. You could be the first ever woman prophet in human history," I joked.

"Yes, Malika, you would be a good prophet," Roshan laughed.

We were off for a drive to the mountains and Roshan wanted to leave before it got too cloudy.

"We have our new prophet, we need not worry about clouds", I said logging off the computer.

CHAPTER 13

AMERICAN YOGI

The three days passed in a flash. We walked and talked about old times and friends as Roshan showed us the city. Getting used to Malika's presence was a delicate business.

Close to Roshan's house was a lake. It was windy and the water rough. Except for a pair of eagles in the sky, it was deserted. The city crowd finds time to flock to the lake only on weekends.

"You two can walk along the leeward shore, it's less windy there," Roshan pointed towards the lake. "I want to clean the car and will join you later."

I led Malika towards the path. Three joggers passed us. I was tempted to join them. Malika stopped and leaned against a rock to rest. I looked into her dark brown eyes with the hope that she would say something that would awaken my dormant emotions. I felt as if I was riding a wave. Memories of her leaving in the train and myself climbing Mount Kenya to kill my pain resurfaced.

"Why are you looking at me?"

"I'm trying to penetrate your soul. Am I there?

"You cannot. My soul does not exist." She fixed her eyes on the lake.

"Don't turn your eyes away. They are the same as I knew. Let's travel together into the past."

She shook her head and pointed at the trail, as if she had not heard me.

"I cannot believe that I'm walking with you."

She said nothing.

"We'll go to the end of the lake. Hold my hand, I'll support you."

"I'm too heavy for you. I do not know how far I can go. It's OK like this. I should walk for at least fifteen minutes, but I cannot," she lamented.

"You wanted to meet me, here I am. What next?"

She remained silent.

"Malika, I feel that we knew each other before we were born. My reason for coming here is to take a trip with you back into the past. Where did we go wrong? When we met on this earth a dark cloud separated us. Why? I'm here to seek answers with your help, on my own I'm lost."

Malika remained silent. She shifted her eyes towards the lake, but seeing nothing, she was emotionless. Eventually she replied, "Since I left Eldore I do not know if I really exist. Something happened on the train. I was not sure of myself any more. I have lived a good life after that, but soulless. The world is not fair. Living soulless is worse than death. We should have returned together to the other sphere." I realized she was referring to her failed attempt to take her life and I had tried to follow her to prove that I was one with her.

"Destiny has brought us together again," I said.

"Yes, but for how long?"

"Are we going to part without freeing our unfulfilled love?" I asked looking into her eyes.

"I see no solution to it. With time I have changed, my values and priorities have changed. No desire, even less passion. I wanted to meet you, that's all."

I felt like a schoolboy – it's true what they say, that age is just a number.

"It's strange, my wife was obsessed with a premonition that she would not live long and she didn't. She used to say that she would wait for me on the other side. She did not want anyone else. In this world she seemed to feel that my soul was with you all the time, although she never mentioned it."

"Maybe we are together again in order to liberate your soul."

"I do not believe in parallel worlds. Everything is here. The railway platform of Eldore is still there. It continues to haunt me."

Malika avoided my eyes. She started to walk. Two hundred yards on, she said, "I'm tired, let's go back."

We returned and sat down at a picnic table facing each other. Malika likes to talk, but not about us or about me.

"I need to speak with you" I said. "Can I visit you and your family as a friend and share your joy and grief?"

"I have told you before, I do not want to remember the past. The more I slide downwards, the more I feel attached to my children and grandchildren. That is all that counts. All this has nothing to do with the past actions.

"Being together is a new experience. Let's make the best of it."

I was rambling, talking to myself. Malika was elsewhere. I recalled our first kiss. I have never felt the same passion since. Sidetracking my questions, she talked about her brothers and sisters and their children.

"One of my nephews is a follower of Bhajan Yogi. Have you met our American Yogi?"

"I have heard of him. I met his lady followers, both white. One of them, a lawyer from California, came expressly to spread Yogi's message in our city. The two wore white dresses over leg-tight white trousers and straight untwisted white turbans adorned with a shining Khanda, the Khalsa crest – two celestial houris descended from paradise."

"Yes, they do look smart."

"The lawyer called a meeting of selected people in the five-star Beau Rivage Hotel. After introductory words about her Yogi master she talked on the virtues of meditation combined with breathing through one or the other nostril to attain spiritual bliss and treat illnesses. Then she turned to the important role of sexual intercourse in meditation. If practised in the yogic way it enhances sexual pleasure and mental peace."

"I have written this with Yogi's guidance," she said, showing to the audience a book with a colourful cover depicting a couple in a blissful posture copulating in a flower. I was tempted to invite her to give me a practical lesson." I laughed.

"You really have become very naughty," Malika said smiling nevertheless. "My nephew wants me to join but I stay away from such cults. I met Bhajan Yogi once and was suspicious of him. He's a handsome and learned man. He emigrated to the USA from India, where he was a senior Revenue Officer. His long flowing beard attracts people and his way of taking Nanak's message to Caucasian Americans draws a large following in California. His followers are mostly whites, just like Osho's. They organize functions meticulously in a businesslike manner. The Sikh gurdwaras can learn from them. He trained my young nephew to sing hymns. He gives hope to the young whites. In his mysticism and his message of peace, I also saw his violent side. Do you have the patience to listen to it?"

"I love listening to you," I answered. Finally Malika was talking to me.

"A Sikh general in the Indian Army visited Los Angeles. I've forgotten his name. He was in California trying to explain his involvement in the 1984 Operation Blue Star to chase away armed extremists from the Golden Temple in Amritsar. A big crowd turned up to listen to him. The General came on the stage to deliver his address. I saw Bhajan Yogi stand up, roll up his shirtsleeves and shout abuse at the General in the foulest language: 'You're a traitor to the

Sikh nation, a party to Sikh genocide'. Suddenly, with his fists raised, he rushed at the General. The security men stopped him before he could attack him. He and his yelling followers were forcibly ushered out of the assembly. He continued his barrage of insults outside."

"It's unbelievable, I thought he was a man of peace. When was that?"

"Quite a few years ago. He died in October 2004. You know the U.S. Congress passed a bipartisan resolution honouring Yogi Bhajan's life and work listing him with distinguished people like Dr Martin Luther King Junior, Mother Theresa and Pope John Paul II."

"That is amazing, people barely know him in India. Yet in this country such people get recognition," I said with awe.

"Recently, New Mexico Highway 106 that passes through here was renamed Yogi Bhajan Memorial Highway."

I saw Roshan returning from her solitary walk.

"Were you guys able to do some soul searching?" Roshan inquired.

"She told me a fascinating story of her encounter with some famous people."

Malika gave me a playful slap on my arm. I laughed.

"It's getting chilly. Let's indulge ourselves with tea and American pastry at a countryside coffee shop on the other side of the lake. "

"I hope it will have apple pies and tarts," I said smacking my lips.

Roshan understands what we must be going through trying to synchronize our lives. She has been through a similar experience. When she was studying in England she met her soulmate. He was not of her religion. Her family never let them marry, leaving a permanent vacuum in her spirit.

CHAPTER 14

LIFE IS A RIVER (2)

❧

"I'm so stuffed," I whined, holding the car door open for Malika. "Roshan, you should have warned me about the servings in America. They are enormous. Do you want me to become obese like your countrymen?"

"You were just being greedy. You didn't have to eat everything," retorted Malika. "You'll get only soup for dinner."

"Fine with me, I'm not sure about you," I replied playfully.

Malika gave me a glare pretending to be angry. I smiled.

"I so want to have a siesta. But then I won't be able to sleep tonight," said Roshan, stifling a yawn. "So let's finish your Big Bang theory. It'll keep me awake."

We took our seats by the computer.

"Let's see. Where were we?" I said, browsing the page. "Yes, we talked about the coming of human beings on Earth."

Roshan interrupted. "I read that a virus from another planet travelled through space and reached our Earth. It then evolved into human beings."

"That is most improbable. It would have been burnt out by the time it got to Earth," chirped in Malika reminding me of her father.

"I accept Darwin, who said that we are a result of genetic combinations that evolved voluntarily, adapting to changes in climate," I answered. "It was a question of survival and facing environmental hurdles. Evolution was fastest when the struggle to survive was severest. You can see what we have done to animal and plant life. We must have evolved from an urge to outdo all other animals in order to eat them."

Roshan and Malika burst out laughing. I shrugged my shoulders.

"Texan fillet steak tomorrow," Roshan announced after we quietened down. I continued.

"Whatever the origin, like everything else living or non-living, human beings are an element of the universe. The molecule that evolved or incarnated into a human carries sparks or bits of all information. Hindus call it karma, scientists have named it genes. All living beings have a similar genetic code. It happened that humans acquired an exceptional capability to observe, reflect, imagine, comprehend, communicate and question."

I looked at Malika. "You should know Book-guru's song on evolution. It goes like this:

For many births, you were a worm and an insect, an elephant, a fish and a deer.

For many births, you became a bird and a snake, a draught-ox and a horse.

After a long period, you got this body.

Now is the time to meet the Master of the Universe.

For many births, you were rocks and mountains, and you sifted through the womb;

For many births, you evolved as trees and you wandered through millions of species."

"My turn is coming soon. Can you figure out what I will reincarnate as?" Malika inquired.

"You'll join Hanuman, the Hindu monkey god's army," I laughed. .

"In Eldore, the preachers frightened me when they told me that I would become a dog in my next life because I had lied about some minor misdeed. The hymn talks about the past and about rocks and mountains. It does not conform to the karmic logic of reincarnation. So I'm convinced that Book-guru is talking about evolution, the atom and the molecule and not reincarnation."

"I think you should make Darwin your guru" Roshan said.

"If he were born in India he would not be a guru or prophet but God. Haven't you noticed that our preachers try their utmost to prove that what Darwin has said is already in their sacred books? What they do not want to admit is that Darwin has enabled us to know our God better than their books have done. Look at Vision Five," I said.

"I see that humans have pushed the main Flow out of the way and set up their own as the dominant central feature," Roshan remarked. "That proves your point that we would do anything to outwit anyone, even God."

"Exactly, we are suppressing the Flow, the real God. Human beings are deluded by their intelligence. They forget that according to Book-guru their intelligence includes five wicked attributes or capital sins: greed, lust, pride, anger and jealousy. The Bible adds gluttony and laziness, that makes seven. Like intelligence, these bad traits have also evolved most among us. Unashamedly we have appointed ourselves as the master of the Flow".

"The Flow has been made for us", said Malika raising a clenched fist over her head. "I'm the master, dictator, abuser and devastator of Nature."

I paused for a sip of water while Malika stretched in her chair, raising her arms above her head.

"It's only recently we have begun to realise that we have created an insurmountable problem. To console ourselves we have humanized the Flow by naming it God, Dieu in French, Dev, Ram, Ishvara, Lord, sitting high up like an emperor. I'll skip Vision Six, which shows that the chronic cause of human separation from the

Flow is his ego, self, or anthropocentricism, what Book-guru calls maya and non-knowledge, and figuratively often advises us to cross this river of maya and join the Flow."

"That makes sense", Malika said standing up. "I can see it, the Flow is our God. It is so simple, just join the Flow."

"Then, what will the priests, mullahs and pundits do?" Roshan asked.

"As long as those capital sins are part of us, nothing will change," I continued. "Prophets, gurus, messiahs and lamas will continue to come and go, temples, churches, mosques, synagogues and gurdwaras will continue to be built, preachers will continue earning their living and religious institutions will go on getting richer. Living simply is considered negative, anti-progress."

"Why can't we use our new knowledge and science to fathom facets of the Flow and to better understand the true laws of nature?" asked Roshan.

"Religious leaders are not interested in science because it has exposed the hollowness of their God, whereas the Flow is unique and self contained," I said, trying not to sound like a teacher. "Book-guru clearly alludes to this way of thinking when it uses the Arabic word 'kudrat', which means power, art, nature, manifestation or an extraordinary drama. It says your kudrat is what we see and hear. Its fear is the root of our happiness. It operates the universe. Whatever we see is Your extraordinary drama. The Vedas, Puranas, (Semitic) books and all thinking are your art as well as eating, drinking and all love. Your power pervades and manifests in castes and races of different colours, in world's living things, good and bad deeds, respect and pride, air, water, fire, earth and soil. You run and maintain all these according to Your law and You actually reside in them." I emphasized the last words.

"This is a poetic way of saying that nature in its universal sense is God and God is nature – the Flow. At the start of the evening prayer we Sikhs recite: *Balihari kudrat vaseya, tera ant na jai lakheya* - I am sacrifice to you who pervades nature, Your limits cannot be known. God in the form of nature is perceptible to our senses and we can feel something concrete.

Now here's Vision Seven. Some genetically gifted humans have access to the information in the Flow. Such persons become our spiritual guides. They help us unite with the Flow. These guides are the prophets, avatars, messiahs, gurus, ascetics, yogis and innumerable others - less known or not known. The true or perfect Guru is the Flow itself. Do you remember the definition of spirituality?" I asked Malika.

"Of course", said Malika. "It's something practical and not abstract, yes, it is to know the Flow and have access to its information, energy, and light-speed".

"Wonderful, the message has been passed!" I exclaimed with joy.

Roshan, pointing to the Flow Chart, remarked, "Sacred books such as Vedas, Torah, Upanishads, the Gita, Bible, Koran and Book-guru are our guides that show us the way to rejoin the Flow. We have turned these books into inflexible idols, often contravening them. We have turned them into awkward, rigid religions."

"The tragedy is that religions never stop fighting each other with faked politeness as well as in open confrontation, each trying to prove its supremacy," I added. "After every political or commercial war or conflict, no matter how ghastly, there is always a treaty leading to peace and cooperation. Have you heard of any such treaty between two religions?"

"The anger and the fatwas against those who criticise religious texts and prophets are a camouflage of flaws in human behaviour," I continued. "Religion practised by one group is never equated or merged with that of another. The others are labelled kafirs, infidels, and godless. Crusades, jihads, conquistadores, inquisitions and colonization have engendered inter-and intra-religion cruelty, genocides and hateful divisions. This type of religious antagonism takes us further away from the Flow."

"Who advances towards the Flow?" Malika asked.

"Many individuals who love nature and pray; they live within the context of the Flow".

"Where is the science in all this?" Malika asked.

This was the old Malika, engaging with me like in the old days when we discussed community issues.

"Sorry, in my zeal I overlooked science. Its role and place is shown in an earlier Vision we skipped. Science brings exact knowledge and information. It does not create divisions. In that sense, environmentalists and ecologists are our new emissaries of God. Uniting with the Flow through them is nirvana or enlightenment."

A bird chirped at the window. The late afternoon sun was slinking into the horizon. Outside Roshan's garden was filled with early summer flowers in every colour. Deep violet fuchsias and red roses mixed with white magnolias. The trees were in leaf and a squirrel scampered up. We were all looking out, taking in the long discourse.

"Vision Eight is interesting," Malika remarked looking at the screen. "Let me see if I can interpret what you want to say. The Flow always advances, goes forward. Nothing can stop it. The priests, monks and gurus continue to urge people to return to the past Vedic, biblical and Koranic times. This is impossible."

"That is exactly it," I patted her shoulder. Malika's hand touched mine and I felt an electric shock. I was 70, a year older than she. Does love always stay, I wondered. I left my hand on her shoulder and continued.

"The only option for us is to rejoin the Flow and move forward within it. For that we have to be simple, use our consciences to obtain information on interactions and interdependence that envelope us.

We will become one with the Flow, a perfect state of bliss. Book-guru expresses that state very succinctly: You are I and I am You. The Bible also says that God created man in his own image, implying that the human is equal to God."

I paused to take a sip of water.

"We do not only merge with the Flow, we also find our relative place and role in the Flow. We live and act in the context of our total environment and not only our relationship with fellow human beings." I looked at Roshan. "Do you remember Ibn Arabi's poem from his Interpreter of Ardent Desires that we picked up in Cordoba at the Roman Tower? Look, its here".

Roshan bent forward and recited it from the screen.

My heart has become capable of every form:
It is a pasture for gazelles,
And a convent for Christian monks,
And a temple for idols and the pilgrim's Ka'bah,
And the tables of the Torah, and the book of the Koran,
I follow the religion of love:
Whatever way love's camels take,
That is my religion and my faith.

"Isn't that beautiful?" remarked Roshan. "We do not need all these religions that divide us."

Malika was unusually quiet, thinking.

"Earlier you quoted from the evening prayer, 'You are the river and all things are in you and nothing outside'," she finally said. "I never viewed Nanak's idea in such a wide sense."

"Book-guru shows this vision very frequently. Its followers have failed to impart the idea that the Sikh way is the simple way:

God is a flowing River... God is Guru and Guru is God. Guru, the River, treasures the jewels of all knowledge. Guru is the ladder, our boat as well as boatman, and our sacred place of pilgrimage. Guru, the Flow, is Nam. It is the saviour of the drowning, those who do not recognize the River Flow are simply washed away. Life itself is a River, we have to become the River. If Guru is the ocean, his teachings are rivers. The human body is like an ocean full of jewels that one can find through guru's teachings."

"You must have been thrilled to find that the concept of Flow is so well upheld by the authors of Guru Granth," Malika remarked.

"All I have done is to merge the scriptures and new knowledge. I'm not the first one to use this way of expressing spirituality. Your Californian compatriot Deepak Chopra in his book *The Book of Secrets* says that spirituality is practical. He evokes the simultaneous interdependent co-arising: all living things are related to the Flow/Universe (Conscience). He tries to show the way to reunite humans with and live in the Flow."

"I equate the ten gurus and the Guru Granth with God. What's wrong with that?" Malika asked.

"Neither the gurus nor Book-guru are God, they are guides and teachers par excellence. Do you follow the guide or just worship him, adore him?" I asked. "I'm attracted to them because they were human beings. I try to follow the guides and avoid worshipping them. All gurus have presented themselves as slaves of the Flow, the true God. Divine reading of their teachings is an unpardonable sin and an insult to Book-guru and its authors. People have total faith in Book-guru as an idol. They are convinced that it knows our inner desires and automatically fulfils them. So why study Book-guru? Of all creatures, human beings mess up the equilibrium of the Flow. This reminds me of the marmorated stink bug. Have you heard of it?"

"No, never," both women shook their heads.

"It originated from Japan and is now found in China and parts of South East Asia. In Asia they are a choice meal of a wasp species. So, their population in Asia is under natural control and in some equilibrium or ecological balance. They are not a problem in Asia. However in America, where they have no predators, they are a menace. This applies to all species, including human beings. The global human species is, conceivably, the number one predator species, with little competition except from the microbial world. That poses an interesting question, namely: What's going to happen when all dominant species are predator species? Do physical conservation laws of energy, momentum, and mass apply?"

"Oh stop," said Malika suddenly. "This is getting too much for me to take in one sitting."

"Just a minute more, and I'm done," I persisted.

She sighed, looked at me with annoyance.

"Look, we have all become, so to speak, unchallenged predators of nature, the Flow, or our God itself. Will the equilibrium of the Flow go topsy-turvy? We do not realize that the Flow is too powerful to be disturbed by anthropocentric egoism. There is little doubt that we human beings are heading to a suicidal end. Neither the gods of religions nor prayers nor divine readings of sacred books are going to be able to help us. Whenever a people did not respect its living environment, it's the people that disappeared. If we wait for auto-adjustment of our way of doing things we are thinking of a genetic change, a slow process of evolution. We have the option of changing our minds, a faster process. But, will our egocentric brains agree to change?"

"I need a cup of coffee," said Roshan holding her head. "Inder, I'm optimistic that God will save us."

Malika giggled. "Don't look so serious, Inder. Loosen up." I had to laugh.

"I'm back," Roshan announced two seconds later. "Are you joining me for a sinful feast of cream cakes and coffee?"

"Yes," said Malika walking past me.

I followed, waiting to give the final word on the discourse.

"Wise people know the way. It's simple. Make work your worship. Love work and not your skin. Don't let the devil make his workshop in your empty mind. Take the initiative because it attracts the goddess and prosperity."

"Enough," interrupted Malika and Roshan, as each took a bite from the cream-laden coffee tarts and smiled to the heavens.

CHAPTER 15

MONGRELS AND ROBBERS

⌒

Malika walked into the lounge, and my heart skipped a beat. Her face was delicately done. Her pink lips matched her lilac outfit – a Punjabi ensemble of a salwar kameez, a tunic worn over loose pants with a long scarf draped over the shoulders. For me this is one of the most elegant dresses.

Standing in her high-heels, Malika looked tall, her loose kameez hiding her stoutness. Her pepper-grey hair was trimmed short. She looked attractive, like the Malika I knew. I would have picked her from a crowd even after all these years. Her eyes, her smile, her walk – years melted.

I stood up, my heart beating like a teenager's, my voice almost lost in the emotions welling inside me. Seeing my eyes wide open she smiled, "Are you OK?"

"You look fantastic," I replied.

We hugged. After all these years the suddenness of meeting a lost love is profound. It's a delicate moment. We did not kiss. For an eternal moment we were lost in the embrace.

She was the first to move away. "Let's sit, Roshan will be here soon," she said. I marvelled at her composure. After so many days together we sat down next to each other. Roshan's friends had invited us for tea. Where do you begin after a silence of five decades? I asked her how she was.

"I'm fine."

We smile, we laugh, we talk at the same time.

"What are you thinking?" she asks.

"I have been thinking of you all the time."

The silence again. Malika looks at me, her eyes trying to read something in mine.

"Destiny," she said the word barely audible. The pain of the parting is still fresh.

"I wonder why our destinies have kept us apart?" she asks, so many years later. "In Eldore, we were so close. Our families – my aunts, uncles, brothers and sisters - no blood relationship. Why were they against us marrying?

"It's the caste system. Even now it overrides everything in our society. Over the years I've learned more about it on my visits to our villages in India," I replied.

Malika looked at me, waiting for me to continue.

"A girl must be married outside the perimeter of a group of villages. She is the daughter of these villages - a sister or an aunt for everyone according to the age group. For example, because we were from the same perimeter, I am your brother, the caste or clan does not matter," I explained. "Your mother hailed from the village, which is three kilometres from Jatpur. So she is a sister to all the men of her age-group within that perimeter. This does not apply to your father from another perimeter near Ludhiana. This unwritten code is to safeguard people from sexual promiscuity."

I felt like a social anthropologist.

Malika smiled reminiscing the yesteryears. "When we were in school in Eldore I thought we were all related, uncles and aunts, cousins, brothers and sisters."

"That's the whole idea. To make us feel like we are one big family and so we must hold the honour of the clan," I replied. "But we broke the code. We became lovers."

We were silent for a while, unable to continue. I wanted to ask her about her marriage. Had she been happy marrying the man chosen by her family?

"I can't complain," smiled Malika. "He's been good to me and my three children."

"How old is your daughter?"

"She is 36."

"We prayed in the same gurdwara, celebrated all the weddings and festivals, ate together, and helped each other look for suitable girls and boys to marry. Why couldn't we get married?" she persisted.

"The caste," it came out as a vile word in a whisper.

"In Eldore," I continued "you recall how everyone struggled to make people accept that all Sikhs of all castes should be members of the only gurdwara in town. No one knew that a non-artisan could not become an official member of the temple, only a tarkhan [artisan] could subscribe to become its member and be elected to the committee."

"So you being a tarkhan meant that I from the jat [farmer] caste could not marry you," said Malika ruefully.

Silence again. "In my reading, I trace this caste system to the Vedic times some six or seven thousand years ago. There were three main castes: Brahmin (priest), Kshatrya (soldier) and Vaishya (administrators, merchants and producers). The jats and tarhkans belonged to the last category. Now there are numerous sub-castes based on occupations. Claims of superiority aroused competition and jealousy. In a given village jats are more numerous, many of them poor peasants with a few rich landowners. The jats have ascendancy over the tarkhan minority, who provide technical services and own small farms. Wealth, inheritance and work-related disparity reinforced endogamy, the practice of marrying within the clan. The two clans or sub-castes are interdependent, hence an intense love-hate relationship."

"We should have chucked out the hate and kept to love," smiled Malika nostalgically. "A few days ago my closest tarkhan friend asked me to look for a suitable boy for her daughter. She imposed a condition: not a jat boy. I was shocked. She said jats are arrogant and uncultured. Can you believe this, coming from an educated person living in California? Did she forget that she was talking to a jat?"

I thought we would have spoken about other things – I don't know what. But here we were, lovers from a bygone age talking about a social complexity like anthropologists.

"Well, you know Punjabis love insulting each other," I continued. "There is a common insult in Punjab: Sala, (brother-in-law, implying that I sleep with the other man's sister) *Changez Khan da khoon*, Jengiz Khan's blood."

"You mean Genghis Khan? Malika inquired. "Why him?"

"We behave like Mongol hordes. Calling each other names must be a karmic memory of the good old days when our ancestors roamed on horseback in the rolling hills of Moghulistan near the Issykul Lake."

"Didn't the Moghuls conquer India?"

"It's confusing. Genghis Khan split his empire among his many sons from his many wives. He also had a great many children with many other women." I made light of the story. "One of his sons got the Khanate of Moghulistan. He became a life-long enemy of the hub of the Mongol empire in the Samarkand region. Attacks on India originated from this power hub. Why Mongols in India are called Moguls is anybody's guess."

"What's wrong with our blood?"

"Nothing wrong with our blood. However there is a good probability that many of us have Genghis Khan's blood running in our veins".

"Aren't you going too far?"

"Hmm. Genetic studies reveal a lot about our blood. You see, Genghis Khan is the most prolific man on Earth. He had eight hundred thousand times the reproductive success of the average man of his age. This blacksmith's son, an artisan like me, conquered and ruled over the world's biggest contiguous empire early in the thirteenth century, extending from the Pacific Ocean to the Caspian Sea. His rampages and subsequent rule brought about cross-fertilization on a continental scale. Sixteen million living men carry his Y-chromosome. Researchers have traced this gene back a thousand years to Mongolia. His sons, who expanded the Mongol Empire towards India, sired many children. Researchers are frantically looking for his remains to find the missing link."

Malika suddenly looked at the clock on the wall and exclaimed, "What's happening to Roshan? Why is she is not here yet?"

"Let her take her time. She has things to arrange in the house. It gives us more time alone."

Malika smiled. "How do jats and tarkhans come into it?" she asked, curious.

"Jats and tarkhans originate from the Moghulistan region. The Punjabis remember Genghis Khan's formidable successor, Tamerlane, by the name of Temur Lang, the 'Sword of Islam'. Temur remained an Emir, one rung lower than a Khan. His wife was the daughter of the great Genghis. He expanded the empire up to Delhi by the end of the fourteenth century. For him Islam was a tool to justify many of his conquests. History shows that his sword mowed down more Muslims than people of other faiths."

"Where do we come in?" Malika persisted.

"Here's the shocker," I replied. "The term jat is not what you think, a farmer. It comes from the Mongol word 'jete'."

A pause. Malika is listening.

"Jete means robbers. They probably migrated into the Punjab

144

and at some stage they gave up the nomadic life of shepherds and settled in villages as farmers. However, their nomadic instinct and military skills are still evident in their behaviour. The Punjabis were the first in India to migrate to foreign lands, like you and me. In their own land they fought the invaders."

"Were they really robbers?"

"No. A section of the nomadic Mongols became rich agriculturists, merchants and administrators. They mixed with other people and settled in cities and towns like Samarkand and Bokhara, and later became Muslims. The aristocratic military, mainly of Moghulistan, shunned the cities and Islam. They stuck to pagan beliefs. They abhorred the settled life, scornfully calling them qurannas, bastards or mongrels. In return, the settlers called the nomads jete, robbers, or jats, like you. See, you stole my heart."

Malika laughed – a soft bitter-sweet chuckle.

"And you?"

"Just as you are not a robber, I'm not a tarkhan. It has to do with Genghis Khan who conferred the title tarkhan to the highest-ranking army officer. Under Temur, the tarkhan was allowed to keep everything he plundered and was immune from criminal prosecution. The link of artisans with these hordes comes in another way. Every time a city refused to accept the terms Genghis and later Temur offered, their armies slaughtered the entire population except for artisans and craftsmen, because they were needed to build new towns and manufacture weapons."

"Hmm – so you say we are genetically programmed to live together in a love-hate relationship," mused Malika.

"I guess so."

CHAPTER 16

FOOT IN THE MOUTH

Roshan was asleep in her easy chair in the patio. Malika was sitting opposite me. I wanted Malika to say something, but she said nothing. Did I want her to say something endearing as she had in our youth? My mind was wandering. Malika just sat there, like a statue frozen in time, expressionless. Surely meeting me, I thought, would recall something of the forgotten days. But it seemed to me that she could not or did not want to remember the past. She said her memory was blank from the time her father took her to India and forcibly married her to a farmer's son.

So as not to disturb Roshan, I whispered to Malika, "What are you thinking about?"

Malika remained glum. Then out of the blue she said, "I don't go to the gurdwara much. I feel uncomfortable there. I only go when there's a good preacher around. I feel something is seriously wrong, but I cannot put my finger on it."

Malika does not want to admit that she has a place for me in her heart, or else why would she have come?

"Malika, look, places of worship are usually centres of political and economic power. What's in your heart is important," I said, trying to lift her out of her glum mood.

"In Eldore you were so pious, always ready to sing hymns in the gurdwara. What has changed you?" Malika asked.

"I sang to impress you and other girls." I laughed at the memory. "And they were always hymns of love."

Suddenly Malika burst into one: "Fly O blackbird and take the message to my beloved and my heart is pierced by the Lord's arrow".

I was stunned.

"Who were you trying to hoodwink?" It was Malika laughing this time.

"You remember that," I blushed under my white beard.

"Yes, I do," she said with those sad eyes again.

Roshan awoke to the laughter.

"You guys, I'm glad you are talking about yourselves. Carry on, I'll brew some tea".

Malika looked at her friend fondly. "I have survived all these years because of Roshan's moral support," she said. Roshan waved her hand in denial.

"Roshan is special," I remarked. "She has total faith in her Imam and accepts his leadership without question. Yet she is open-minded and cultured." Roshan had disappeared into the kitchen.

I told Malika about a professor friend who doubted that I had written about the Big Bang and spirituality.

"I can imagine that. Our people expect such things to come from some swami or guru."

Roshan returned carrying a tray. "What are you on about?"

"I'm waiting for the light", I said. "We were just talking about my Big Bang idea."

Placing the tray on the sawn-off tree trunk that acted as a table, Roshan stated, "Your concept of an eternal, all-powerful flow or flux of vital energy and information is called God. But God is conceived differently in each faith."

She poured us tea, took a sip and continued. "People go to war to support their own God. That is how we humans function. I like the way you are striving to give a new image of God."

"Do you remember the life-size figurines of the four famous Andalusian thinkers in the Roman Tower in Cordoba?" I asked. "One of them was Maimonides. Someone asked him if God was merciful and vengeful. He replied that these attributes originate in the self-serving purpose of humans. Ancient texts explicitly state that the love of God is a function of knowledge. It is impossible to love something one does not know."

"You say narrow thinking is the source of evil," Roshan said. "Our Imam says the timely interpretation of Holy Scriptures remains at the centre of man's survival today. The foremost cause of contention between religious sects is the narrow interpretation of scriptures as lack of freedom of intellectual discourse regarding spirituality and knowledge. "

"Roshan, roshani – your name reflects the light and wisdom you radiate," Malika chipped in.

"I have another point," continued Roshan, placing her hand on Malika's shoulder. "Religions don't kill. The anti-gun control lobbyists' slogan says that guns don't kill, people do."

"Your analogy is attractive," I said, "Last night on the news we saw students gunned down in Virginia. If guns were inaccessible, there would not have been this killing. So in the same rationale, if there were no religion, fewer people would be killed."

"Did I put my foot in my mouth, with this slogan?" Roshan pretended to be aghast. "All I want is to show that humans are the perpetrators of evil."

Malika shivered. Roshan was too hyped up to stop.

"I have another question. Does the human being, after death, re-enter the Flow? Is there rebirth, and if so in what form? If there is no rebirth, what becomes of the vital energy that you claim is the human soul?"

"A short answer: according to the Flow-linked meaning of spirituality, a person, whether alive or dead, is always in the Flow.

Only the timing, place and form are different. The fear of death and desire to be reborn is a human artifice. The death of a human is no different from that of a plant or another animal. The vital energy encompasses all states of being or non-being. So let us not worry. When we meet in some other state, which is not too far, we will not remember this discussion."

"I have been thinking. Messing up the environment should be added to your list of seven sins," said Roshan.

"Brilliant. You have started to update the sacred writings. Keep going," I encouraged her.

"Hmm," Roshan looked at me squarely. "What will you do with faith?"

"Faith is complex," I said. "People have an inherent resistance to examining beliefs critically because these are rooted in faith and hence opposed to reason."

"Faith for me is the way, the path, the quest, the pursuit of an individual's search for reality through free inquiry and reason, as opposed to dogma and empty rituals," said Roshan.

"I did not know faith in that sense," I admitted.

Malika had finished her second cup of tea. She touched the teapot. "It's cold." Before Roshan could stand up to get more, Malika was on her feet. "All I want to say is that no other people show as much faith in their Holy Book as we Sikhs. We respect it, adore it, adorn it, try to feed it, put it to sleep, wake it up in the morning, request it to fulfil all our wishes and desires. No other faith can beat us on the number of uninterrupted divine readings of the Book-guru. Isn't that real faith?" Malika queried with a chuckle. "The most pious act is singing the praises of the Guru Granth and its authors. By doing this we can solve all personal, local and global problems. Can you beat that?"

"So with the same reasoning, if I want to become a medical doctor," I asked, "all I need is to sing the praises of medical doctors and books on medicine instead of spending six years in a medical school?"

We all laughed at this.

"How does one become a good person?" Roshan pondered.

"For that I need many gurus and guides, starting with parents and family, people and friends around me, teachers in school, professors in university, society and good companions," I replied.

I paused for a moment.

"If I decide not to work, all these gurus are worthless. The guides like Book-guru and men of wisdom are useful only if I follow their teachings. With my expanding knowledge and life experience I learn to benefit directly from the Flow, the ultimate supreme Guru manifest in nature and environment enveloping me, a perfect source of inspiration and therapy."

"I wish we had been guided by this reasoning when we were young," Malika remarked. "Even today parents are more concerned about education at school than the spiritual."

"I work with the needy in our community," Roshan intervened. "I can tell you this, spirituality is of little use to a hungry person."

"The Flow invokes universal oneness, no duality. The Flow conforms to thinking. It is not Christian, Jew, Hindu, Parsi, Moslem or Sikh, not of the East or of the West, of the land or of the sea. It brings the old and the new together. It's Tagore's clear stream of reason not having lost its way into the dreary desert sand of dead habit," I said.

"I suppose that is why people blindly accept faith-based scriptures, because that does not require much effort," Roshan commented.

"Inder, you have talked too much." Malika stretched. "Go and cook something now, something tasty, or else I will starve."

It was a timely end to our discourse about the Flow. Roshan happily opened a bottle of wine and insisted on doing dinner.

Turning around, I saw Malika staring at me and then look away. Was that look of sadness of our long-lost love? I will never know.

CHAPTER 17

AT THE STAKE

❧

Shashi, an old friend from Wisconsin, USA was in Geneva to deliver a keynote address at a conference on climate change. Shashi is short and thin and doesn't suffer fools. Joe, another old friend of ours who lived in Barbados, was also in town. Joe is calculating. With his Caribbean humour he is the only one who can handle Shashi's quick intellect. Tall with a thin greying moustache, he carries the air of a serious diplomat. This would be our first meeting since we retired.

I was the first to arrive at the Jardin Anglais at 5 pm, followed by Shashi.

"Joe came to my presentation. He looked tired from the long Caribbean flight. He should be here any moment."

We waited. It was a pleasant evening.

"Has Joe read your Big Bang write-up?" asked Shashi. Without waiting for my answer, he continued. "I'm amazed he has difficulty accepting evolution, him being a physicist-meteorologist."

"He is also a born-again Christian," I reminded Shashi .

"Personally, I like your catchy title and find your essay most inspiring. After reading it I did away with all the superstitions I believed in drowning them in Lake Geneva."

"You better drown with them because they will resurface", Joe's voice boomed from behind.

We spun around and the three of us hugged. There was a lot to catch up on. We walked over to Le Lacustre, a lakeside café near the Mont Blanc bridge, and ordered coffee and apple tarts.

"So you read the Big Bang theory," I said, eager to hear the comments of my learned friends.

Joe was the first to begin. "You embed faith as a driving point in your theory, but camouflage it to the outside reader as a subtlety."

This was Shashi's mercurial brain. "Spirituality has no meaning for me if it bars discussion," he continued. "Actions by people don't seem to support their proclamations. But it does appear to have special meaning on an individual basis, be it right or wrong. At the end of the day, it might not matter if the end result is non-destructive. The issue is quite simple. Consider a black-box (BB), a science term, to denote an entity, be it an individual or a community or a country. Now, consider how one is to decipher or define the characteristics of this BB stated, up front, as an unknown. One looks at the characteristics and/or performance of the BB with regard to the input and output functions."

Joe and I listened carefully to Shashi's analytical jargon.

"One cannot just conduct a single pass-through experiment. One has to look at the response to many variations of input and so on. This can take time. Eventually, one can specify the functional characteristics of the BB. Unfortunately, eventually it could also be infinity. But, the end result, the output of the BB, under varying input conditions, does quantify the BB in regard as to whether this is a constructive BB or a destructive one. And, it does not really matter what the philosophical foundation of BB is or was."

I quickly intervened, "My black box is transparent and luminous. Everyone – except for blind souls - can see the Flow streaming through it."

Joe, who had been quiet, now spoke. "Congratulations, I found your Big Bang theory most inspiring. However, before I say anything

I want to know your religious faith. To me your article will only be relevant against the background of faith. Mine is Christian, water baptized publicly at the edge of the ocean, born-again believer practising my faith in the Pentecostal Fellowship."

"Joe, I fear you will put me on the pillory or burn me at the stake if I reveal my faith," I joked. "Then I'm not holy enough to be crucified? For you I'm a pagan, infidel, or heretic. My faith changes the moment I get more information and my image of God changes with it."

"Nothing of the sort, Inder. I have no intention of placing you at the stake because of your faith, or lack of it, since I haven't really understood your definition. But what I did understand of it is enough to tell you how you can keep track of this bowl-of-spaghetti story."

"Having read my Big Bang article, can you not guess to which faith I belong?" I asked.

"Do you really want to know my first impression of you? You are a badly camouflaged Christian believer. I'm researching Saint Paul's spirituality. You not being holy enough to be crucified reminds me of the Apostle Peter when he was being martyred. He told the Christians that he was not worthy of being crucified, as was his Jesus. So he was crucified upside down."

I rolled my eyes at the thought of being crucified upside down.

"After I finished going through your spaghetti I was under the weather a bit. Then surfacing, I wondered whether the latter resulted from over-stressing my brain cells."

Shashi's habit took over, "How can you, when you have so few."
Joe ignored him.

"I'm proud of my faith," continued Joe very seriously. "I hold to the Genesis of the Holy Bible version which is neither a big nor a small bang – actually it has no bang. It's very simply a creation, all described therein. Incidentally I do find your eminent Francis Collins, who headed the human genome project, a bit ambidextrous in accepting the Big Bang and evolution. Ironically he explains their existence by the existence of a God."

Joe took a sip of coffee and continued. Shashi, unusual for him, was quiet.

"It is not procrastination that has kept me out of this arcane discussion," said Joe, "but your inconsistent questions trouble me. Your God has been on my mind, although it does not keep me awake at nights."

Shashi tried to appease Joe, "I am contemplating the issue of creation. Inder's eternal Flow, composed of vital energy that binds together all information and interdependences, is the same as all other flows that all people individually believe in. But each one thinks it's exclusive to his or her own belief system. I see no conflict here. Nevertheless, you have raised an interesting conundrum. Namely, how does one prove or disprove an intangible "X"? It is not clear to me that a mathematical solution to this problem exists"

"Hmm," went Shashi. He muttered while we sipped coffee, "The human brain cells or neurons are supposed to operate in a tertiary logic world if one were to apply Boolean algebra... I think we need to invoke String Theory. In this mathematical world of eleven plus dimensions, just about anything is possible. We are left with one instrument: the human brain in physical form. One may need to enter the metaphysical world to begin to explore a solution to the issue of X."

A waitress came to ask if we needed refills, a pretty Swiss girl – blonde and blue-eyed. We ordered more coffee. Shashi continued pondering. "The brain is multidimensional. We invoke the question of mind versus brain, versus spirit or soul. One could add an astral plane of existence. Bottom line, we need to escape from the physical entrapment of and by the multidimensional world. As regards proof or disproof of X, I have no idea."

Joe raised his hand, "Listen Mr Ghost, I don't pretend to understand these complexities, or rather your idiosyncrasies. But it occurs to me that meteorologists of our generation, at least those of us who were weather forecasters, undertook to do something that was impossible, because there is so much information in the state of the weather at any one instant and it changes in space and time. Nevertheless, we derived satisfaction from forecasting the weather well enough on relevant scales in relevant dimensions for our efforts to be sufficiently useful for people to keep coming back for more."

"Joe you are divine," I interrupted "You have given me a perfect example that I can use to explain exactly what I've been trying to tell everyone. We cannot cope with the immense amount of information on weather which is a minute pin-prick in the Flow. Imagine how much information is available on other elements, living and non-living, on the Earth and in the universe. You cannot estimate the amount of information on interactions in your little beach garden. What we do not know, we call it God. We know almost nothing that is in the Flow."

"Big Bang or no Bang, I recommend you read the interpretations of Genesis in the Hebrew and Mesopotamian texts in this regard. And, according to a multi-dimensional universe, all theories are equally possible or impossible," said Joe.

"I have read them all," Shashi claimed. "And, I agree with you about all other possible interpretations. As I said before there is no conflict in interpretations. The conflict is a human-created response to the notion of the absolute interpretation. Nothing wrong with this, as such. But, it is also the cause of wars between ideologies, countries, societies, tribes and individuals. Hence, one has to question the notion of the absolute."

Having exhausted the discussion for one day, we were quiet for a few moments till Joe announced, "I met our Italian colleague, Mario, at the conference today. He's representing the Holy See there."

"Ah, the Vatican. An interesting entity," commented Shashi. "Did you know that it has a high-level Science Advisory Committee whose members include Nobel Laureates and other notable names?"

"Is this Committee the same as mentioned in the DaVinci Code book?" I asked.

"Well, this committee simply exists. It has nothing to do with the DaVinci Code."

"What does it discuss?"

"Nobody has any idea, but I guess the Vatican wishes to know what science is talking about in case it needs to strategize on how to respond. The Dalai Lama has a different position altogether."

"I've heard the Dalai Lama speak at the university on this issue," I intervened. "He does not separate science from religion. He has interacted with the science community for several decades - it appears to be one of his interests. Recently he was the keynote speaker at a conference on neuroscience. His take on this is that science and meditation seek the same - the truth - and approach this via different pathways."

"This is akin to the seven varieties of Yoga which is religion neutral - you choose your own," noted Shashi. "The Dalai Lama made an interesting pronouncement at this conference. He said, If science proves the scriptures wrong, then the scriptural proclamations should be changed. I have never heard a head of any religion make such a statement. But, of course, he was referring to the Tibetan Buddhist scriptures. What the Dalai Lama wants to stress is that there are many pathways to enlightenment or knowledge or wisdom or whatever. They are religion-neutral. For him there is never any conflict between pathways. On the other hand, there are belief systems or religions of many kinds which lead to conflict. Yet this has nothing to do with the philosophical proclamations or the philosophical intent. It's to do with the human genome - genetics and its propensity to be predatory as opposed to seeking a balance.

The bottom line here is that human beings as a species really have no idea what they are doing and why they are doing it. That is bad news for the evolution of the planet. And time may not be on our side -too much damage is going on at an increasingly rapid pace."

It was my turn to speak now. "The egocentric flow that human beings have set up is separate from the main Flow and is overwhelmingly fuelled by the capital sins close to our heart. I do not see any God going to clean up the human heart or mind and get rid of these sins. Numerous spiritual leaders and thinkers have tried by looking into the similarities or commonalities of religious beliefs that clashed in various lands. The root cause of all turmoil and the most troublesome are the differences. Our solution lies in the knowledge of our commonalities as well as differences on the touchstone of the universal Flow. This includes the non-human component: animals, plants, land, air, water, the Earth, the solar system and beyond. We have to reject all that does not accord with the Flow. The religious scriptures, dictated by God or not, that do not treat and respect these non-human values at the same level as they value human souls are seriously defective, deficient, and anthropocentrically egoistic. Researchers have found that the animal and plant world communicate with the human world in some mysterious ways. Our selfishness has kept us opaque and blind."

"I like the way you have presented the anthropocentric flow with a positive ending showing how human beings can join the main Flow and save the world," said Shashi. "By synthesizing the ideas of diverse writers and subjects you have provided a new perspective. However, the Flow can be explained in simpler terms and made more accessible to the common reader."

Our discussion had taken us well into the evening. We had exhausted the Big Bang and the Flow for now. As a parting shot, Joe gave me a hug and said, "Keep the Flow flowing, even if Shashi does not know how to swim."

CHAPTER 18

THE DIGNITY OF NOT JOGGING

‿

In 2008 I returned to Jatpur after twenty-eight years. I was staying with my cousin Bhag in his new house. Having arrived late at night, I was fast asleep when an ear-shattering voice woke me. I almost stumbled out of bed. Looking at my watch, it was only five thirty in the morning.

It was the priest in the temple reciting the morning prayers, amplified though the loudspeaker. Times have changed. I recall as a child listening to the quiet aura in the temple, listening to the morning prayers recited by the priest sans the loudspeaker. Through the curtain-less window I saw the dawn sky. I was tired but unable to sleep, thanks to the loudspeaker. I got out of bed and looked through the window at the tiny miserable house I had inherited in the adjacent plot. My eyes stopped at the little kitchen, its open door facing me. I pictured my father sitting against the wall outside, brewing his morning tea nineteen years earlier. Then on the fateful morning, he died without much fanfare. He was found slumped against the wall a few minutes later.

My mind backtracked to my childhood living with my aunt in

a village called Thikriwal. My mother had died and my father had left for Kenya. Left alone, I missed my father. I could not stop thinking of him. I wondered why he did not write to me. Did he not miss me or had he forgotten me? Then I reasoned. He did not know how to read or write. I had just begun school and also did not know how to read or write. This was before the age of instant communication with cellphones and the internet. My father knew little about my childhood and sadly there was nothing to bridge the gap in later years. In my childhood innocence, I spoke to him from afar, hoping that he could hear my voice carried by some powerful force across the ocean. I hid behind a mask of silence, not allowing anyone to see the turmoil within me.

I remembered my village school teacher, the only one for the entire school, who doubled up as the village postmaster. One day he handed me a letter.

"It's from your father, from a foreign country. Does he not know that your name is not Joginder?" asked the teacher-cum-postmaster. Embarrassed, I took the envelope and did not know what to do with it. I wasn't even sure how to open it and much to my chagrin, I didn't know how to read. Ashamed, I hid it; I did not tell my aunt. I can't recall what happened to it. All I can say is that life went on. I lived in another world satisfied with the little I had. Love: I was attached to nobody. I adjusted to live with everybody. True love came late in youth. Why didn't it endure?

My reverie broke with the singing of The Ode of Assa, the morning hymn. It was not Bhag's voice. Had the other gurdwara acquired a new amplifier to outdo him? A young voice repeated the stanza and then sang a hymn in a Bollywoodian melody. It broke the monotony of the Ode. I returned to bed and dozed off. The broadcast ended just before seven with the reading of a randomly chosen hymn from Book-guru, which Sikhs consider as the command for the day.

My father spent his last years in Jatpur. As an elected member of the panchayat (village committee), he supervised the paving of the back street that had once served as the main road. On a cold February morning, he got the work started, and then went home to brew his tea. He asked Bhola's sister to bring the milk and sat down in the kitchen to light the kerosene pressure stove. She found him sitting where she had left him, leaning against the wall, dead. He was cremated the same day, as was the custom, at the village crematorium. I arrived a day after the cremation, just in time to catch my uncle, Santa and his son, Bhag at the bus stop. Bhag was carrying a white cloth bag containing my father's ashes and remains that could not be consumed by the fire.

"We are going to Kiratpur to immerse brother's ashes in the Sutlej River," Santa said. "I'm glad you caught us, now you can do it with your own hands." I was intensely moved and tears welled in my eyes. Hardly a minute had passed when the bus arrived and left without us. Was it a coincidence or God's hand?

The following day my younger brother Mohi and his wife, Arti arrived from Kenya to attend the final prayer. In our father's memory we donated five thousand rupees to the panchayat to build a school. The amount was enough in those days to build a big classroom. It took two years and Santa's considerable effort to make other villagers donate more money to build two additional classrooms and the first formal school in the village came into being. Later the government took over and added more buildings as well as upgrading it to a high school. Now all the children, regardless of their background, attend the school. The teachers earn good salaries, but the parents are furious and complain that they spend more time asking for higher salaries than on teaching in school. Many a time, the teachers are absent giving private tuitions.

Jas, Bhola's son, is a teacher in the village private school. Every morning at five thirty, half a dozen boys and girls come to him for extra tuition. After school, at four in the afternoon, there's another dozen. The teachers earn more by giving private tuitions. Teaching is good in expensive private schools in Raikot and other nearby towns. I asked Jas if I could visit his school. It wasn't a problem.

The private school occupied the village dharamsala (community house). It was flourishing in many ways other than teaching. Two classrooms held two hundred students. Jas received me in the middle of the big courtyard and led me to headmistress's small office equipped with one table and five chairs. It also served as a staff room. Twelve teachers, all women, were waiting. Jas was the only man and the only graduate. None of the others were qualified teachers. They did not know English, yet they taught it from a textbook. The pupils were mostly from poor families. For them education was expensive: the school fees ranged from eighty to a hundred rupees per month with extra expenses incurred like paying for registration and the examination fee, and buying books, notebooks and the school uniform from the school at a price higher than that in the market.

At the school I asked how all the classes - from the first to the tenth grade - were housed in two rooms. Most of the pupils were forced to sit under the trees in the courtyard for classes and abandon school on rainy days. The poor children also had to take private coaching, because the teachers were incompetent. India's main education system operates outside school hours.

Every morning I saw many minibuses bearing the school names on their flanks shuttle the rich children from the villages to the town schools. These families have sons and daughters living in Canada and California who send money home regularly. The town schools teach in English where the children speak good English. Jas gave me an insight into the private colleges where the professors coach the not so bright students in writing the answers to questions which appear in the exam papers, thus guaranteeing success. At a price, anyone can buy a university degree.

It took me considerable courage to jog the first time in Jatpur;

nobody jogs there. Men in the workshops stopped to look at me. Women milking the buffaloes turned their heads in surprise, and others came out and stood in the front door to watch this crazy old man jogging. They got used it after a few days. One evening I jogged to Kishangarh, a mile away, to see Sobha's family.

"You promised you would come today to see my new house. What happened"? I reproached Sobha.

"My whole day was wasted. You know uncle, our customs are a curse. I had to attend a young man's funeral. It took forever. You cannot even imagine how stupid some speakers are. One chap's speech went like this: The young man used to drink but he was very obedient. When I saw him riding his scooter after drinking, I would tell him to get off and he would listen. He died when he failed to stop at the stop sign and he fell and hit his head on the concrete. It burst like a melon. He died instantly.

"I could not restrain myself, I stood up and told him: 'If you do not have anything better to say, better sit down. We have come here to pray, not to hear gory accounts in this holy place'. He sat down and the gathering breathed a sigh of relief."

"Yesterday morning I jogged with Jas to Bheni and passed by your house. Just after the turning to the martyr's monument, we met a man walking. He had a well-groomed white beard, and wore a white long chemise over white pyjamas. His rosy cheeks glowed in the morning sun but he had a big potbelly. We were about to cross him when he raised his hand and said, "Hold on, are you from Jatpur?"

"Yes."

"I saw you running two days ago. I told all in my village that I saw an old man running with a young man. They were all amazed. I come out for a walk only."

"Walking is also good, it's better than doing nothing".

"But I walk very slowly. People here do not even walk. Running is good for your health, I think".

"It depends on how you walk. It's better to walk briskly, like this. You know, the difference between walking slowly and briskly is the same as the difference between my belly and yours."

Jas looked aghast but the man laughed heartily, his belly shaking.

"Baiji, how could you say that?"

"In my experience, people respond better when they see a real example," I replied to Jas. He still looked embarrassed.

"I know the man," Sobha said when I recounted the experience to him. He also laughed. "Exercise is not our culture. Most people in the villages are busy trying to earn a living and so there's little time left for exercise."

"I see that you have lost weight since I last saw you," I complimented Sobha. "I'm sure you feel good too."

"Uncleji, I follow your example. Everyone in the family has become health conscious. We have a treadmill, weight lifting bars and a pulling machine. But we are lazy, not regular. Tell me, uncle, do you jog every day?"

"Not really. Yesterday, I jogged and walked to Litran to see Kareeranwala High School. You know, I went to that school when I was nine. Your father in Canada jogs every day. I do not have to tell you how fit he is and he is five years older than me. Do you jog?"

"Nobody jogs here. People laugh at you. Jogging is considered beneath your dignity."

"I see a change," I said. "Do you remember the first time my niece, Melo, and her husband brought me here in their Jeep, a few years ago? You were standing in front of your house. When you saw me descend from the Jeep, you ran towards me and we hugged as if we had known each other for years. It felt so good."

"Yes, I cannot forget that moment."

"I had tea with you. It was the sixth one that afternoon, containing more milk than water and sweet like syrup. Feeling heavy in my stomach, I decided to jog the mile back to Jatpur. The proud Jeep owners grudgingly accepted my request to take their Jeep without me. Did I offend them or their Jeep? They got into the Jeep with downcast faces. Seeing their discomfort I said that I would not run, only walk."

It was a nice walk to Jatpur, with the fresh evening breeze over lush green wheat fields. I turned into the village main road. With two hundred metres to go, I saw the Jeep parked on the side off the road. Meekly, my niece's husband said: Uncleji, it is better to go in the car because it is not dignified to run in the village. What will people say?"

Sobha laughed, "You were downgrading your hosts jogging around in a respectable Punjabi village while they had a car. That was certainly not dignified."

CHAPTER 19

SOS GURU

With three days left to Guma's niece's wedding in San Francisco, everyone met at their house for one of the many pre-wedding ceremonies. It was a new house perched on Fremont Hill in a posh neighbourhood with stunning views of the South Bay. The downside however was that downtown was too far to walk for the old men, the grandfathers and great uncles of the family, and they were finding it difficult passing time. There was nothing for them to do, like meeting their friends at the mall where they spent hours sitting on the benches, chatting and checking people out. When they needed to stretch their legs, all they had to do was take a stroll in the mall.

The American wedding was unlike a wedding in a Punjabi village in India. There, everyone has something to do. No one is exactly in charge of anything. Only absolute flexibility governs. Nevertheless some logic is palpable in the operations. Everything happens as it should at the critical moment. The hired confectioner suddenly realizes he is running short of cooking oil or sugar. Someone is sent to the nearby town to buy more. Another person is dispatched to purchase more potatoes and cauliflower because more guests have turned up. No one escapes making errands. A gunny sack full of pea-pods is opened in the middle of a group of elderly people who, without being told, start shelling them. There is no panic save for the newcomer who is unfamiliar with the setup. Family honour requires that there are no snags or shortcomings. In California, what family and friends would do in India is contracted out to professional wedding planners, leaving a lot more time for the relatives to relax waiting for scheduled ceremonies to begin.

Driving a hired car from North Bay, I reached the palatial house before midday and parked by the front entrance. It was a bright winter day with a dazzling sun. I saw legs moving behind a half-raised gate of a double-car garage. I bent down and entered. The enormous garage had been converted into a kitchen-cum-breakfast room. The women were frying parathas, the Indian chappati heavy with ghee or butter, the usual breakfast of the Punjabis. The latecomers sat at the table for breakfast. My entry surprised many women, who hugged me. I felt elated. Satti from Australia almost lifted me off my feet in excitement. Grasping me by my hand, he led me to a huge marquee with enormous transparent window panels looking into Silicon Valley. Satti's elder brother, Guma's father, also gave me a bear hug. He then introduced me to five elderly men sitting quietly on plastic chairs round a big table. We knew of each other in our Indian network of extended families, but it was the first time we had met. "You said you will come on Monday, it's Friday" said Satti accusingly. "Where have you been for four days?"

"I'm here, that's what counts." I said in defence. I had done that on purpose, for had I arrived earlier, I would have been bored sitting around. Satti poured the whisky, the Sikh nectar of life to celebrate the reunion.

We, the guests had been checked in at the Holiday Inn, courtesy of the family. It was a short drive from the house. Every afternoon, the women gathered in the marquee to perform one of a series of pre-wedding ceremonies. The first one was the batna, the beautification ceremony involving women only. The girl getting married is made to bare herself as much as tradition allows. Her friends rub her with a yellowish paste prepared with fine flour, turmeric and aromatic oils. This symbolic beautification ceremony provides much fun, women sing folklore songs and tease the bride-to-be about the first night. Before beauty shops mushroomed in the Punjab countryside, batna was used as an exfoliator to make the skin soft and fair to please the bridegroom. The groom goes through a similar treatment by his family. Following this is the bangle ceremony in which the girl's maternal uncles adorn her arms with a set of red bangles until each is decked to the middle. Ceremoniously they hand her the wedding dress and other gifts.

Done with the bangle ceremony, someone announced lunch. The old men took their time sipping their last drop of whisky and unhurriedly made their way towards the lawn. There was tons to eat. Barbecued chicken and lamb, curried vegetables and daal (lentils), chapattis and nans (oven-baked chapatti), plain yogurt and raita (an Indian favourite, yoghurt mixed with grated cucumber) - everybody's taste was catered for. For dessert, we had a choice of hot jalebis (flour ringlets fried in ghee), barfi (Indian sweet toffee) and a variety of ice creams followed by cardamom tea. It went without saying that the bar was open till the last person left. The women occupied themselves with their wedding outfits while the men idled away their time with whisky and gossip.

Holding a cup of tea, I walked into the lounge with Mitu, Dado's husband from England. This British, turbanned, non blood-related cousin asked me the question he has asked many times: "Why have you cut your hair and stopped wearing a turban? You used to be so religious."

I was in no mood for a discourse on anything to do with religion. I just wanted to have fun at the wedding. So, to cut him short, I flippantly replied, "Sikhs are more stupid than people of other faiths. That's why I cut my hair."

I had forgotten about the militant Dado being in the same room.

Her voice shot through the crowd. "How can you say that?" she demanded, shocked at my remark. Small as she is with greying hair tied in a bun, she's a devil to reckon with. She pulled up a chair beside me. I buried my head in my hands. I didn't want to take on Dado.

"My dear brother," she began. "Since our school days, I have known that you have a cracked brain. Unfortunately, you have not changed with time. I thought you'd get wise with age, but no. Are you trying to set up your own religion? What do you think you are, a prophet?"

Her sharp tongue attracted a few in the lounge and they closed in. "Where is Bali?" shouted someone. "Call her, she'd like this." Bali turned up a few minutes later. She was an attractive lady with a short crop of hair and dressed in a smart suit. Sitting around the table, all the men, save for me wore turbans. They were the archetypal believers in Waheguru, God the great illuminator, who they believe wrote Book-guru. For them every verse, every word and every sign in it is sacred and infallible. A reader must pronounce each word or letter as written.

Dado's eyes bored into mine, waiting for some response. I took a deep breath and announced. "We Sikhs do not like to be left behind. The Jews, Christians and Muslims are called peoples of the Book. They believe that God wrote and conferred the Torah, the Bible and the Koran. We have also become a people of Book-guru."

"But our Granth Sahib is unique," chipped in Satti. "It's universal, for the entire humanity. It has no dogma, no doctrine, no religious differences, and no castes. So..." Before Satti could finish, Dado interrupted, "Let him tell us what's so special in the Big Bang Yoga article he has written."

Satti finished his sentence, ignoring Dado. "You can achieve anything, all you need is complete faith in the Guru Granth."

"History shows that faith in a religion has turned perfectly normal people into tyrants, launching holy wars, killing thousands of innocent people in the name of God. It frightens me. According to our faith I must wear a turban to prove that I am a true Sikh. But Book-guru does not say that. It actually condemns a thousand and one times symbols and the wearing of religious garbs," I replied.

This disturbed a nest of wasps. Few would have appreciated the idea that the evolution of living things and religious thought are closely interlinked. I persisted. "Sikhs believe that Book-guru contains all that a human being needs, that learning sciences is a waste of time, that other religious books are incomplete. Just seeing Book-guru is supposed to wash all our sins and bring happiness. We are offended when told that we worship Book-guru.

There was silence. I grabbed the moment to continue.

"I admit, ritual worship has considerable psychotherapeutic value, but our ritual has gone too far. It has coaxed us away from studying, analysing and understanding what Book-guru says. This narrow approach has choked its rational spirit."

"We are not extremists like the Muslims," someone interjected.

"Are you moderates?"

"We accept all," said another.

"Then why do we need a separate religion?" I asked.

"Actually Sikhism is not a religion," Mitu stated.

"Then why do you want me to keep long hair and wear a turban? We are the most confused people in the world, neither here nor there. We are so caught up in rituals that we are unable to contribute to human welfare as Book-guru requires of us."

"We do not have any dogma," Dado claimed.

"Forcing people to wear symbols is a dogma," I retorted.

"What I want to say is that we've twisted Book-guru's universal rational principles into a blind, dumb and deaf faith. We know these shortcomings yet we allow crafty, half-educated preachers to lead people towards the worship of Book-guru and to impose symbols and rituals. We are lucky: Book-guru's message is not like that of the

Torah, the Bible and the Koran. Its authors did not prescribe laws and punishments such as chopping off hands and heads, stoning women to death or eliminating infidels from the face of the Earth. Nor does it offer virgins to male martyrs or handsome men to women martyrs."

I turned to Dado. "Don't try to become a martyr, Dado, because there will be no virgin men waiting for you." Dado's face reddened as everyone burst out laughing.

"We're not fanatic," retorted Satti.

"Well what about the hotbloods who blew up the Air India plane over the Irish Sea? Their justification: the Khalsa will rule the world."

I was not going to let go of this discourse now that we had come this far. "Luckily," I continued, "this slogan does not come from Book-guru."

"Sikhs condemn such cowardly acts," argued Satti. "We confront and fight tyranny and injustice fearlessly. That incident is an ugly black spot on our image."

"I do not doubt that. But can someone explain to me how setting up Khalistan conforms to the Sikh way laid out in Book-guru? During the peak days of struggle in the early eighties I visited the Indian Punjab a number of times. The Sikh countryside sympathized with the Khalistani fighters, Pakistan supported them openly. I flew into Lahore. I stood in the Diplomat line for immigration with Others on my left and Nationals and Foreigners on my right. A dozen Sikh youths made up the Others line. They were empty-handed, while we all held our passports. They looked perfectly serene and happy. A tall moustached man appeared behind the immigration officers and said in Punjabi, "These are our special diplomats, let them in". The youngsters were escorted through the crowd, while I waited half an hour to be closely scrutinized. Were they Khalistani fighters returning after accomplishing their mission? Or were they illegal immigrants who had paid through their noses their passage to Europe and America? To me they looked more like Khalistani fighters.

"Sikhs were promised their own independent homeland in 1947. Hindus cheated us," said Satti.

"Are we not mixing religion and politics? Indians do not know the fact that the Sikh movement and forming the Khalsa brotherhood saved Hindu dharma in northern India. Without it the border of Pakistan would have passed south of Delhi. Now we want to separate from those we saved. Assume that Khalistan is set up with its own religion. Pak in Persian and Khalis in Arabic - the two words mean sacred and pure. The theocratic Khalistan would scare away Hindus and Muslims. Poor Book-guru and its universality will fall into a political trap. Many non-Sikhs the world over are attracted to the values of Book-guru but the enforcement of symbols and rituals repels them."

"So, you accept that the Guru Granth and the Sikh religion are for the entire humanity?" Satti said.

"Not the Sikh religion as we commonly practise it, but the Sikh way as described in Book-guru. I wish it had laid down clear rules or enacted strict laws. They would have formed the basis of the modern human rights laws."

"Don't you see the laws of life in it? It has all that you need."

"But not in the manner that permits us to build our society," I argued, "Or its institutions and political strategy. It says how to become a good Muslim, it condemns certain practices but it does not touch their awful dogmas. Certain malpractices were unknown. For example, Book-guru says: Why do you practise male circumcision, how do you do that for women? The practice of excision of the clitoris was not known. Transplanting practices and beliefs particular to the Punjab in another culture and environment is often unnatural and confusing. As we are unable to adapt our ways to the new conditions the Sikh way is sliding into the abyss of religious dogma and fundamentalism. Fortunately the Sikh moderates and intellectuals are not silent; they continuously raise their voices to stem the slide. The bottom line is that nobody will respect the beliefs of others as long as each religious community continues to proclaim that only its way is the best." I was trying to end the discussion. Dado's voice rose sharply above all others again.

"What is written in the Guru Granth is nothing but the truth."

"You might be right, and I think you are. But my concern is not what is written in it but what we practise and what the world sees. What the world sees is that the Sikhs follow a very orthodox religion, similar to the Russian Orthodox Church run by long-bearded priests. I know it is not true. Book-guru has helped many to achieve a high level of open-mindedness, even among the less educated."

"It allows us to choose our own way of life" said Dado, eyes flashing. "There are no hidden or binding laws in it. There is no possibility of twisting its interpretation. In many ways it is very scientific, for it accepts the concept of the universe and the evolution of life on earth. We do not require specialists like you to interpret it, just a little effort."

"I always knew you were smart," I joked, giving her a pat on the back. It reminded me of our arguing days as youngsters. "What you have just said is what I say in the Big Bang yoga. Human beings have acquired more knowledge, or at least more detailed analytical knowledge which reinforces the general concepts prescribed in various sacred books, in particular Book-guru. My idea is to connect the two – Big Bang representing science and yoga representing spirituality - and use the new information to reinterpret these books so that they become more palatable and relevant in the present."

"What you mean is that the Guru Granth is not the final word," said Satti.

"That is exact. Many Christians and Muslims do not accept that there is anything beyond their books. They continue to waste astronomical amount of resources to defend unscientific assertions, such as the Earth being the centre of the universe and the sun revolving round it."

"And that Jesus was born of a virgin and Archangel Gabriel dictated the Koran," Bali intervened for the first time.

I had forgotten about her. We all turned around to face her.

"Exactly, the trouble with the Sikhs is they continue to introduce old Hindu and Muslim myths in their rituals and teachings," I continued.

"We don't fight," Bali stated as I stopped for a breath. "We do not kill or even argue if someone does not accept what the Guru Granth says about eighty-four hundred thousand forms of life that a condemned evil person must transmigrate before being reborn in the human form. We accept what science tells us. We endorse the theory of evolution of life as confirmed by genetic studies."

Bali had impressed everyone.

"We have acquired a new fetish or obsession," I added. "To show that we are modern in the western way, our preachers try hard to present the Sikh way in the Christian style. Like Jesus, Nanak has been upgraded to the status of God."

"All one needs is faith," Satti repeated stubbornly.

"In what?" I asked.

"In the Creator, Waheguru."

"Do you know him or her?"

"You have to find him."

"If you tell me where he is, it will save me a lot of time and effort. You know, I'm a busy man."

"He is in your heart."

"I do not see him or her. Why should I have faith in someone invisible? I know that the world and the nature exist, only God knows if God exists."

There was murmuring again in the room. Some were purely disgusted with my sentiments on Sikhism and God. Others purely bored. They moved away from us.

"Human beings have set up numerous fabulous gods who have

failed to help anybody. God is our tool to justify unrelenting destruction of our habitat and killing each other. Satti, you are a jat. Can you work your field without oxen or tractors? I'm a tarkhan [artisan]. It is impossible for me to build a palace or the Twin Towers again overnight. Nothing comes without labour and yet we live under the power of holy men, saints, fairies, miracles, myths, legends and magic. With them we have been wiping out a God that manifests itself in nature in innumerable shapes and colours: air, water, rocks, soil, animals, and plants. Nothing can live without them. They must be God."

Bali clapped. I acknowledged my lone supporter with a nod.

"I'm a minuscule living thing trying to find out who I am, what surrounds me and my role in it. I can see only a tiny part of the whole flow. My mind can absorb only an infinitesimal bit of the gyan, knowledge that nature is made up of. The whole, an integration of innumerable interlinked elements, is flowing, progressing or evolving continuously. Scientists, ecologists, biologists, doctors, astrophysicists, experts in genetics and others are my new messiahs and gurus. With their help I'm beginning to see or understand my surroundings a little better. I've an objective image of the flowing whole, its force or vital energy and the information it contains. With this information or gyan, I begin to see the interrelationship and interaction between innumerable elements. This enables me to pull myself from the human flow and join the main Flow. Book-guru calls it Nam or Name."

I stopped, having delivered my exposé of religion.

"Where does it say this?" Bali's voice cut through the thick silence.

"Right at the beginning it says *jeta keeta teta Nam*, whatever has been created, that much is Nam, implying the Flow."

"If Nam is Flow, how does one meditate or practice Flow?" questioned Bali.

"Obtaining gyan and knowing the Flow is meditating on Nam.

It is something practical and tangible. It will enable me to be one with the Flow, the result of true meditation. For me, this is the Sikh way."

"What you are saying is that religious books deal only with the smoothing of inter-human relations. They do not guide us in safeguarding our environment. Ecology should become part of religious practice," Bali said.

"Absolutely. Sadly, this will not happen. The followers of Book-guru are more interested in safeguarding its word than doing anything practical. In the name of the Bible and Christ the Christian religious institutions set up many social welfare and educational services. The western governments inherited this formidable infrastructure. They not only took it over but developed it for the benefit of people as part of their programme. The followers of the Aga Khan, even without a country of their own, have set up an impressive community system functioning better than most governments. The Sikh people have not inherited any institutionalised legacy of welfare services, other than the very rudimentary langar, community kitchen, nor have they developed any new ones. It has the means and capability but not a cohesive socio-political community. On the contrary they are drifting towards division and dogma. Poor Book-guru has become a veritable glorified idol of worship."

"Why can't you stop being nasty again? You seem to hate Sikhs. There is no dogma in Book-guru." Dado was losing her cool now.

"You are right again. There is no dogma in Book-guru. It's the followers who are dogmatic. It results from the desperate marriage of hope in the Sikh way and ignorance compounded with apathy - a self-deception. They insist on enhancing symbols, rituals and ceremonies instead of liberating the word of Book-guru imprisoned in silks."

"You are insulting the word of God," Dado said angrily.

"Not really, all I want to say is that the Sikh practice does not conform to the tenets of Book-guru. For instance, the ritual of uninterrupted reading of the Book-guru doesn't do any harm to anybody, but it does take away the motivation or need to understand what the guru is saying. Divine-reading was not instituted by the Gurus. It is relatively recent. You know it well. The person who pledges divine-reading is usually not present to listen to it. He is sitting with us here and the reading is being done in the Golden Temple or in his home village depending on the strength of his faith and the bank balance. We believe that simply reading Book-guru anywhere by some person would resolve every problem. This soft dogma impedes us from learning anything from it."

"I agree with you there. Divine reading has become big business. Hundreds of uninterrupted readings are contracted out to Indian readers for special occasions," Bali added.

"Compared to the dogma in other religions, ours is minor." Satti was trying to defend the religion.

"The difference is that others can justify their wrong practice with quotations from their sacred writings, but we cannot. We hide our faults by criticizing others."

Bali raised her finger. "The Sikh ideal of service to human beings is limited to preparing and serving communal meals. In California, I call it Khalsa Dinners' Club. We offer groceries, we cook food, we serve it, we eat it, and we feed the well-to-do. There aren't many poor there."

Dado exclaimed in shock and many in the room appeared scandalised. To criticize the langar instituted by the revered Guru was blasphemous.

"We strongly believe that serving food to holy people and saints is a service and charity of high quality," I went on. "The Sikhs of Birmingham in England organized and transported truck loads of food to Barcelona and served free lunches, langar, to a horde of well-fed representatives of all religions attending the World Religion Parliament in 2004. It was a successful exercise in logistics. My argument about the langar or free kitchen is that it must be extended to the millions of poor and starving people in the world. Nanak after all fed starving, emaciated people. I doubt if they were fakirs and sadhus. But our preachers invariably recite this story and emphasize that Nanak had fed the holy men. Feeding holy men has become the supreme form of our charity. The preacher likewise expects to receive such charity."

Bali's soft voice caught our attention again, "To get out of self-deception we must know the Sikh way and comprehend the language of the Guru Granth. In California learning to read, write and speak Punjabi and Hindi might not be convenient but it is possible. The important thing is to know its ideas in any language. There is no interdiction to transmitting these ideas in other languages. Christians have done it in the remotest language on the earth. Nanak and Gobind Singh used various languages to expose their ideas, why not us?"

I gave Dado a sideways glance. She shook her head. "Look Dado, you have a brilliant guru in Bali. Why make me the target of your scorn? I'm ready to make Bali my guru."

"I know you like women," Dado laughed. "I wanted to prove that you are not as clever as you think."

"You are only confirming what I already know. I agree with Bali fully."

Bali, in her western attire added, "The Guru Granth does not prescribe turbans, salwars and head-scarves. Would wearing a particular type of dress lead me to nirvana?"

"I made a quick computer search and found that Book-guru refers to dress and symbols nearly one thousand times, usually to say that wearing them does not indicate saintliness."

"I'm concerned the most about our belief that just seeing Book-guru will solve all our problems," I interjected.

"You haven't heard about the risk our California Sikhs took to save the Guru Granth from hurricane Katrina. Our government declared an emergency and took measures to save and help millions of people affected. The entire nation was traumatized."

Someone shouted, "Bush did not do anything!"

"Yes everyone knows that, but this is different," said Bali.

"Did you mobilize Sikh teams to help stricken people?" I asked.

"No, Sikhs had a different priority, more serious and urgent than saving people. Their living Guru Granth was in dire danger of drowning."

"It is natural, we can sacrifice our life to save the Sri Guru Granth Sahib Ji," said Satti proudly.

"Wait a minute. Book-guru is all-powerful. He can take care of himself. Human weaklings need not worry," I countered. Satti looked pained at the rebuttal.

"This is not a joke," Bali continued. "It was in the newspapers, I have a cutting somewhere. A group of valiant Sikhs confronted a chaotic situation to save the Guru Granth from a gurdwara in New Orleans on Morris Road submerged in deep water. They used zodiac boats equipped with underwater cameras hired from a rescue services company."

"Who were these intrepid guys?" Satti asked in admiration. I wanted to laugh at the irony.

"A group called United Sikhs. It asked federal and state governments to rescue the Guru Granth. They sent a letter to President Bush seeking assistance to airlift it."

"Well, Americans do not know that for Sikhs the Book-guru is living," I said sarcastically. "It's more alive than the people who drowned."

"Stop taunting us!" Dado shouted. "Why can't you hold your tongue?"

Bali ignored her.

"The group got the help of a Kaur, a US Army National Guard, and hired a private helicopter from a special response company to launch the rescue operation. It took three days to obtain official clearance before the helicopter could enter the perilous area. Sikh volunteers and a priest teamed up with two rescue experts and advanced amidst curfew and random shooting. When the team entered the Gurdwara they witnessed a miracle. The Guru Granth was resting unperturbed on the wooden palanquin floating on five-foot deep water unscathed by the mighty hurricane. It's a miracle."

"You see," Dado affirmed, "Our Guru Granth is all-powerful. Don't you dare belittle him!"

"I submit," I bowed down with hands joined. "But don't take me wrong. You see, in the old days, Book-Guru was less robust and there were only a few handwritten copies. In those days it was necessary to protect it from the reader's humid breath, from his sweaty hands and from uncontrolled spittle spraying on the manuscript. Hence Book-guru's life was short. Now thousands of copies are printed using indelible ink and plasticised paper. Should it drown or become old, it can be replaced easily."

"The Guru Granth floated in New Orleans is a miracle, you have to accept," Dado insisted.

"No," I retorted. "The wooden palanquin is the miracle. It is the nature of most types of wood to float. The palanquin saved the Book-guru. Those guys simply collected it."

"So, you don't accept this as a miracle."

"Even cats and dogs sat on wooden planks and managed to survive without expensive rescue operations. No, I don't accept this as a miracle."

Dado glared at me again. I smiled back at her blind faith.

"Sorry Bali, What happened next?" I asked.

"Well, they all bowed down in front of the Guru Granth with their hands joined in deep reverence. The priest said a prayer and respectfully carried the Guru Granth on his head to the rescue boat. The operation lasted twenty-four hours. I heard that in honour of the saved Guru Granth the group opened a community kitchen, where they served hot meals to over a thousand evacuees. The article ends with a quotation from the Guru Granth: "The Wealth of the Fearless Lord is permanent, forever and ever, and true. This Wealth of the Lord cannot be destroyed by fire or water, neither thieves nor the Messenger of Death can take it away. BOLE SO NIHAL SAT SRI AKAL."

With this verse the Sikhs equated Book-guru with God. The irony of it was that God does not require human intervention. God can save himself or herself.

"I'm sure Book-guru would have been greatly pleased if the group had launched a mission to save the people first before coming for it," I mused.

"The operation was a true service to Waheguru," Dado exclaimed still blind to my argument.

"If a speedboat had passed near the gurdwara, surely Book-guru would have got uncomfortably wet or even drowned from the force of the waves it created," I could not resist saying.

"I bet the operation cost more than running the kitchen," Bali added, much to Dado's chagrin.

"Our faith is as twisted as the turban." I laughed. "Drowned in self-deception, Sikhs tear themselves down. They do not want to progress as Book-guru requires them to do."

Then I asked Bali if the California Sikhs have changed with the impact of the American way of life.

She laughed, "We are going to change the California way of life. We have revived traditions that died in the Punjab a long time ago. Our Nagar Keertan [holy procession] draws other Californians."

"I'm sure Book-guru must feel much more comfortable in the spacious American bus than riding the crude Punjabi truck."

"But we have one problem," said Bali. "Very few people can read the Guru Granth. However, with globalization that's not an issue. We import readers from India on short-term contracts. In dollars it does not cost much to bring them here. You know there are so many jobless there."

CHAPTER 20

THE THREE-QUARTER GURU UNSHACKLED

A few days before I flew to Delhi in November 2009, Simran asked me to participate in Nanak's birthday celebration. She is very devout and well respected in the city.

"We have put you down to sing two hymns and to give a short discourse on Nanak as you did last year," she said.

"Sorry, can't do. I won't be here," I informed her.

"Oh dear, I guess we will have to manage without you then. But would you mind if we borrowed your copy of the Sri Guru Granth Sahib Ji on that day and the portable palanquin?"

"Not a problem," I answered. "Arrange it with my daughter Atima. My two granddaughters love assembling and dismantling the palanquin."

Simran objects to my using the name Book-guru, though that is the exact translation of Guru Granth. It expresses the meaning well in two words. Out of respect, followers, like Simran, usually address it with a longer esteemed name. My copy of Book-guru is thirty-six by twenty-eight centimetres, which is about three-quarters of the full size, so I refer to it as my three-quarter Guru. However, it has served the community for more than three decades. It presides over the birthday anniversaries of its authors, Guru Nanak is the most popular. Atima walked around it four times to take her wedding vows. Hers was the first Sikh marriage in the city. Devotees, more Hindus than Sikhs, bow down in front of it lovingly and seek its blessing. For many years I performed the service of awakening Book-guru in the morning and putting it to sleep in the evening.

One day my nephew from Oxford gave me a Gurbani-CD. Gurbani means 'word of the gurus'. It contains the entire Book-guru in three scripts and a translation into English. Installed on the hard disk, a touch of a key makes the virtual Book-guru appear on my monitor. I found it pointless to disturb my three-quarter Guru every day.

"You don't service the Guru-Granth every day?" Simran asked curiously. She has the full size one at home, but does not offer it for religious functions. It's hers, very personal.

"No, I don't. But as prescribed in the Sikh code, I have draped it in its white underclothes and respectfully placed it with its silk scarves and the fly whisk on the cosy upper shelf of my wardrobe. Every time after performing a public ceremony it returns to the same abode," I explained.

"Pity you have stopped doing the daily darshan," she commented. Darshan means seeing.

"I can see it on my computer at any time."

"It's not the same thing, it has to be seen sitting on the throne."

"You mean I should place my monitor on a palanquin?" I joked. I found it funny trying to imagine myself sitting with folded hands in front of my monitor which would be draped in a silk scarf. I strike the ENTER key and with utmost respect lift the scarf to see the glorious first page of the Book-guru. What a magnificent sight! A close-up darshan! I bow down. I prompt GO TO and type a random page number. Lo, the page appears instantly. I read the command for the day. You see, it's so easy and clean: No problem of spitting and damaging the page corners with my sweaty hands. The beauty of it is that I can reach any hymn without turning and soiling the sacred pages.

After Nanak's anniversary celebration, Simran returned the Book-guru dressed in a new silk cloth. Atima, with utmost respect, placed it in the wardrobe.

"How can you leave the Book-guru like that?" asked Simran sounding annoyed.

Atima looked confused, wondering if she had done something wrong while returning it to its abode.

"It's snowing outside," said Simran, seeing Atima's expression. "It's so cold. Do you have a new woollen shawl to cover the Guru Granth?" Atima's expression changed from unease to sheer amusement. My daughter had the hardest time trying not to laugh at this absurd sentiment.

It was not the end of the parody. The following morning, Simran brought a thick blanket and lovingly wrapped the Book-guru in it. I wonder how it has survived thirty severe winters. I believe that the love for the physical Book-guru is more passionate than the Hindu love of idols of their many gods and goddesses and of the linga. Sikhs are an epitome of Granthophilia, blind love for the Book. I was born in January an Aquarian. It is said that it's the nature of Aquarians to rectify all faults of the world. My blood boils seeing rituals condemned by Book-guru, such as draping it in dozens of silk scarves offered by devotees. The following year a new group of Sikh devotees borrowed my Book-guru to bless their first general meeting. Out of the thirty devotees, only two wore turbans. The assembly decided to build a gurdwara. It was an emotional decision. Waheguru, the Almighty, would do the rest. No one recorded the minutes of the meeting.

The previous week, the Swiss had voted against the construction of a minaret for a proposed Muslim mosque. The group launched the campaign for the construction of a gurdwara by celebrating the birth anniversary of Gobind Singh, the tenth Sikh Guru. I offered my Book-guru to be placed in the new gurdwara, when built or when a new replacement of the Book-guru was found. Tradition requires that there be at least five full Sikhs when moving the Book-guru. It was a cold wet February morning. Two Sikh priests hired from Italy two half-Sikhs (one turbanless and one turbanned but with a trimmed and dyed beard) came to collect the Book-guru. I was the fifth in attendance. I handed it over wrapped in the warm blanket. The priests looking very unhappy at the blanket. They removed it and covered it in a white sheet.

I succumbed to my habit of sarcastic humour. "Be careful, the Book-guru might catch a cold. You know there is a dangerous virus around. The doctor will not know how to inject Timoflex into it."

An acerbic sneer stopped me from further comment. The Book-guru was placed on one turbanned head, the other started to sway the flywhisk over Book-guru.

"Do you have a spray-perfume?" asked one of the priests.

"Will this air-refresher spray serve the purpose?" I asked in return.

The priests ignored the remark, not amused by my sarcasm.

"Give me a bottle of water," said the priest. He wanted to purify Book-guru's passageway.

"But it's clean outside and there is no dust," I said. "Moreover the Guru's rain is falling. It's purer than tap water."

Anyway, I handed him the bottle of water and they walked in a line, barefoot on the wet cold concrete passage. The one leading the convoy sprinkled a few drops of water on the wet floor to purify the way. The second sprayed the air freshener. The one behind swayed the flywhisk furtively in the cold air. They entered a car parked five metres from the door. After the end of the anniversary prayers, my Book-guru was to be reverently returned home to its his abode.

"I'll go ahead to open the house," I said to the newly nominated president.

"No, it's being taken to Langenthal Gurdwara." Langenthal is a small Swiss village some two hundred kilometres away near Bern.

"Why?" I asked at this change of plan about my Book-Guru without my knowledge.

"Well, there it will be awakened every morning and put to sleep in the evening. He is our Guru, our Parmatma, God, it must receive our total respect, something you cannot do here."

"Oh? So are you liberating the poor Guru from my prison? What if someone needs him next week?" I asked.

"We promise that someone will bring it here if it is needed."

"Can you assure me that the daily ritual will be done in Langenthal? Or will they store it in a cupboard just as I did?"

"There it's in a respectable place. At home, we drink and eat meat. It is not correct," replied the president, who had earlier invited me to share whisky with him.

"Are you saying that during the past many decades, I have made the Book-guru perform arduous tasks under duress and kept it shackled in my prison? Though a slave, it was always available. Please return me my Book-guru. I'll store it in the same cupboard and I'll take the blame and punishment that Book-guru might inflict on me. You do not need to worry about it."

The car left before I could even think of saving it. Agitated, I walked back to the house. Thoughts wafted through my mind of the absurd manner in which the Book-guru is treated, reducing its enlightened writings to nothing. Some priests in England take the Book-guru for a walk in a car in order to exercise it in fresh air. An equally crazy thought went through my brain of my Book-guru being put out to sunbathe on Brighton beach.

My Book-guru was dethroned by a full-size Book-guru which travels two hundred kilometres to my city every time it is needed to perform a ceremony. Now the three-quarter Book-guru lives somewhere in Geneva. I have not felt the desire to locate it. I get much satisfaction every time I see it preside over religious congregations. Reverently I bow down and place my offering in front. Often sitting quietly in its presence, I reflect on the significance of the holy books. The Jews are not obliged to spread their Word locally or globally; they are supposed to know it. Christians and Muslims are required to take their Word to every human soul. While Book-guru's message is kept shackled, many copies of the Bible are sold or given away every second in more than two thousand and four hundred languages. The Koran and its language have come directly from God. That impedes its translation into other languages, but enormous wealth and human resources are being poured into putting millions of Korans in the hearts and hands of people. The Sikh Book-guru on the other hand has not progressed much in disseminating its message of universality and human brotherhood. Even though it invokes the scientific concept of the Big Bang, its followers have gone nutty protesting against mundane issues. A Delhi publisher was accused of stacking the printed copies like bricks on the ground, leaving them uncovered.

The internet has overtaken traditional printing. I can log on to God directly with my smart phone and download His message, display the words and listen to them. The Book-guru has still a long way to go if it is to catch up with the other two Books on the internet.

Does it matter if an average person's koranic or biblical or gurmukhi knowledge is negligible? Three-quarters of Muslims do not speak the archaic Arabic of the Koran, and even educated Arabs find it difficult to understand. Christians have overcome this hurdle; the Bible transmits its message in the local language of the people. The battle between the Bible and the Koran has persisted in various forms since the days of the Crusades. Muslim governments do not permit distribution of non-Islamic literature in their countries. The internet has overcome this problem. Only a small fraction of the

Islamic-Christian population which constitutes more than half the world's population has access to the internet. So publishing the Bible and the Koran is still big business, employing extraordinary marketing skills and tricks financed in a big way with Islamic petrodollars and Bibliophilic donations.

Book-guru copes rather badly in this battle of the books and in spreading its message to the larger global community. The main occupation, sadly for the Sikhs, has been to safeguard it in de luxe abodes. I just read on the internet a news release from the central authority in Amritsar announcing the unique journey of faith – four hundred and fifty copies of Guru Granth as passengers in a ship will reach Italy. Each copy will be kept separately on seats accompanied by Granthis (priests) to maintain the sanctity of the Granth. The copies were sent to Mumbai in a special bus. In 2004, a Canadian Sikh missionary society airlifted a planeload - one copy of the Guru Granth was placed on each aircraft seat, with a special canopy and mattress. What next? A seat in a spacecraft heading to another planet?

CHAPTER 21

WAITING WITH PATIENCE

❧

"Sardarji, I want some photocopies done." I approached the Sikh man with a long grey beard standing behind the counter of a small shop. Before he could reply, Bholla arrived and greeted the man with a loud "Sat Sri Akal".

"Meet Iqbal, he is one of ours – a nephew. This is his father Babu Singh," he said, pointing to an old man sitting at the entrance of the shop.

"It's easy to tell that you are from abroad", said Babu, shaking hands and displaying a very splendid long white beard. "When you came the other day to refill your SIM card, I was sure you were Inder, Mela's uncle."

"How do you know Mela?" I asked.

"Mela is my cousin," replied Babu.

In the Indian extended family system based on villages, we were hence related. Babu had a relaxed air. There was a power cut and he was not going to let it stress him. "This is India," he stated, very matter-of-fact. "Just wait, it'll be back soon."

The copying machine whirred – the power was back. "It's the first time we have met. Come, sit down. You cannot go without having tea."

"Thank you very much," I said. "Now that I know you, I'll come again. I must hurry because we have to catch the Patvari, the Jatpur village land registrar, to give him these documents. How much do I owe you?" I took out my wallet.

"Nothing from you", chimed father and son in unison.

"Let's not mix business with family, otherwise you will go bankrupt," I said. It was useless. The two men simply would not accept money from me.

Sitting on the back seat of Bholla's motor cycle, I mused, "I went into this shop as a stranger and now I have met some distant relatives."

"It might be strange in your country, you do not have many relatives there. It's not unusual here. But people's attitudes are changing here too. They do not want to know you. Life has become very fast, even in Raikot. People do not have time for each other. We are becoming like machines."

"Even relatives?" I asked.

"Yes. You'll discover soon. You think that the Patvari is waiting for us. I bet he won't be there."

"He said he would be there, didn't he?"

"Yes, but tomorrow is Diwali. Everyone will be shopping and then there will be four days of holiday. All the offices and schools will be closed until Monday."

"Diwali is for one day. Why do they close on Friday and Saturday?"

"These babus, civil servants, and teachers do not like to work. They demand holidays at every opportunity. This is the Indian way of providing services to her citizens".

"Will the shops close down as well?" I asked.

"No... the bazaar will be open till late at night, selling clothes, gifts and sweets. It's big business during Diwali because people want to buy more than they did last year and outdo their neighbours."

Memories flooded back. As a child in the village, I made little clay lamps and baked them in preparation for the Diwali evening. We – the village kids and I - would roll cotton wool wicks and fill the beautiful lamps with mustard oil. As the sun went down, we'd light them to welcome Ram, Sita and Luxman returning from fourteen years of banishment, symbolically inviting happiness into our homes and chasing away the devils of sadness and misfortune.

"I see houses lit up with garlands of electric lights in the forms of lotus flowers, arches and showers. Things have changed," I reflected. "Do women make baolis from clay to house lamps as my mother did in 1941? I think I told you that the baoli brought bad luck to her and us."

"Nobody makes them now. The tradition has disappeared, and with it the word in Punjabi. But the tradition of lighting at least one oil lamp in every house stays," commented Bholla.

"That's because the electric lights cannot frighten away the evil spirits," I joked.

"The sacred fire is still the only potent weapon. In the old days these lamps were the cause of many a house fire. Now people get electrocuted; safety rules are non-existent. Fireworks have become a bigger danger because everyone wants to have fun bursting crackers. But when the burning projectile lands on a stack of dry hay you can imagine the light it produces," said Bholla with sarcasm.

"That I suppose would chase the evil spirits forever!" I replied. "Tell me, do all the Sikh families celebrate Diwali?"

"Most families do, but we don't".

"Why?"

"Diwali is a Hindu mythological religious festival. It has nothing to do with Sikhs, but many outdo Hindus in celebrating it. They claim that on this day our sixth guru helped set some Hindu rajas free from the Mogul prison. How that guru's gesture can become religious is rather difficult to accept, but for us any excuse to celebrate is valid."

I did not want to say anything about many like me who in western countries light up our houses at Christmas and have turkey, and a select wine on the table for dinner. Bholla would have continued the discourse for longer.

Early on Monday morning Bholla took me to one of the five village chiefs, known as numberdars or lumberdars in Punjabi.

"Why do you have five numberdars?" I asked. "I remember there used be only one, Jaginder, whose house was near our workshop. Every time the policemen came, they went to his house."

In those days only a jat owning considerable land could become the village chief. The district administration designated him to ensure that the land rent was collected on time and help them with any investigations.

"Now the village has grown fivefold," explained Bholla. "There are more than two pattis, and each demands its own numberdar. The other castes also demand to be represented. We go to our patti numberdar Avtar Khangura. Of the five, Avtar is the only educated numberdar. We have always worked through him."

"Can't the village patvari do our land transfer?"

"All patvaris now sit in Raikot. I do not know how many there are. Each one is responsible for a certain number of villages. For Jatpur, it's Bant. He does not know everyone in the villages. So our numberdar must accompany us and personally certify every detail regarding your ancestry and the right to inherit land."

We reached Avtar's house. He was middle-aged with a long beard turning grey-white. He was dressed in a clean white Indian chemise and pyjamas, and on his head sat an orange turban, the small type. He led us to the sitting room, which was furnished with basic furniture. He had arrived from Canada a few days before. Addressing me, he said "Uncle, things are not the same here. You must find it odd returning after so many years."

I admitted that I did.

"It is worse in the towns and the cities. I have two sisters and a brother living in Surrey, Vancouver. My parents are with them. They look younger and they are more active than I am. Surrey is full of our people," said Avtar.

I agreed with him. In 2006 I was in Surrey and it looked as if the whole of Jatpur had migrated there.

"Guma of Kishangarh organized a get-together at your cousin Harban's house," I recalled.

"You mean Gurdial's brother?" asked Avtar.

"Yes, we were in the same class," I said remembering my young days.

"Anyway, I see people here are doing quite well," I commented. "With so many new multi-storey houses the village is no more a village. The rooftop water tanks shaped like pigeons and aeroplanes fascinate me."

"What you see is deceptive," said Avtar. "Less than ten percent of the landowners live reasonably well. The rest are poor peasants. The few who are rich are supported by their sons and daughters in Canada and California. Unlike in Canada, the villagers here have to face the corrupt administration. I should not be saying this, I'm at the lowest rung. Take your case: you want to transfer your land and all your papers are in order, but it cannot be done without paying. This system of payment operates from the lowest to the highest level proportionate to the rank. The villager pays the patvari who pays his superior, the Tehsildar, who pays the District Commissioner, each one to safeguard his job, and so on up to the minister."

"But the system existed even during the Mogul Empire and the British Raj," I remarked.

"But now it is different. You go there and you will be asked to sign again, otherwise the sahib will not approve it or you have signed at the wrong place. These are signals to which you must respond with bribery. No amount of anger, rhetoric or religiosity can help you," Avtar lamented.

"So, your endorsement is not enough. The machine has to be greased."

"We'll see. Keep two thousand rupees ready. I'll meet you at the Patvarkhana (patvaris' office] on Jagraon Road later."

It was a sunny morning. I rode on the back of Bholla's twenty-year-old scooter with dead shock absorbers. To protect my backbone, I kept my eyes on the potholes and bumps ahead and lifted myself on my hands, holding a steel bar behind me.

The patvari was not in his office. "He must be at the Tehsil Office in the town centre," said a clerk. Squeezing through cars, push carts, oxcarts, scooters and of course people, Bholla stopped the scooter in front of the Tehsil gate. A huge banner read: The Revenue Patvar Union. Behind it, I spotted six patvaris on strike sitting cross-legged on a mat.

"Is it to welcome me? How did they know I was coming?" I teased.

"They are very smart. To give us the maximum trouble, they chose to strike the day after the Diwali holidays."

The crowd flowed through the gate. I waited next to a young man seated on a crude wooden bench operating an old ribbon typewriter placed on a wobbly table. There were two rows of such machines, a few computers and photocopiers lined up in the passageway of the dusty courtyard to offer services such as typing legal documents - affidavits, wills, and contracts - in English, Gurmukhi or Hindi. All one needed was a lot of patience, because typing takes time.

Bholla, who had gone inside to find the Patvari announced, "Nobody knows where to find Bant. All the patvaris are on dharna, strike. I called Bant on his cellphone. His scooter has broken down and he has asked us to meet him near the strike banner."

We had wasted an entire morning without achieving anything. "What are the strikers demanding?" I asked.

"Better pay."

"They look well-fed, rather overfed. They do not need higher salaries," I remarked. "But they have a case. Their big bodies require more food."

Bholla laughed aloud, drawing the attention of people around. "They claim that they are overworked," he said. "Actually they are scared. The government has decided to computerise all the land records. Many of them do not know computers. They are afraid of losing their jobs."

Just then Bant arrived. "This is my uncle," began Bholla, pointing to me. "His younger brother died and left his land to his children. You know Avtar is our numberdar…"

Bant cut him short. "As you can see, I'm not allowed to work today, we are on strike. Call me on my cellphone to fix an appointment, possibly on Friday. By then the strike will be over. Bring all the documents, and Avtar has to be there to certify. He takes full responsibility."

Having said that, Bant took off his shoes and sat down with the strikers.

"Where I live, the transfer of land is done almost automatically. And here, we have not even started," I commented wearily.

"You know, in India we do not have to practise yoga and meditate for hours to learn to be patient. You have no option but to wait and be patient," said Bholla, tongue-in-cheek.

CHAPTER 22

LINGAS OF JATPUR

～

In March, the wheat fields surrounding the villages in Punjab are lush. The morning breeze sways the ripe crop like sea waves, so pleasing to the eye. As on other mornings, I was up before sunrise to jog. On this morning the fresh air was replaced by a pungent smell when I turned to Kishangarh. Someone must have emptied the dung pit, I thought. The smell became stronger, and when I reached the fields, I saw a cloud hanging over the crop. Two phantom figures appeared out of the cloud carrying cylinders on their backs. They had been spraying pesticides on the crop. The noxious air tightened my chest. Turning back served no purpose, the nauseating air was omnipresent.

When I passed the cloud, weird images made me shudder: disfigured faces, squint eyed, red pimples all over, snub noses, extra fingers, twisted toes, shrunken testes, shrivelled penis. For years the villagers have been inhaling bouts of this toxic air. An hour later when I returned to join the family for breakfast, my nephew's young wife handed me a stainless steel plate containing a bowl of yogurt and a hot stuffed paratha. When she turned I saw she was limping.

"Why are you limping?" I asked. "Did the buffalo step on your toes this morning?"

"It's not that," she laughed. "My toes are hurting. It's nothing to worry about."

When she placed the second paratha in my plate, I noticed her fingers. "You have swollen finger joints. Is it from milking the buffaloes"?

"I do not milk any more. My fingers are not strong enough."

"And your toes, you don't use them for milking, do you?"

"We have to clear the dung and make dung-cakes."

"Have you shown them to a doctor?"

"I'm taking some desi [local medicine]. Foreign medicines poison the body, they tell me." She would not name anyone.

I told, rather instructed, Bholla sitting near me, "Take her to a proper doctor today. If you don't, I'll take her. Is there a good doctor in Raikot?"

"No, a doctor in Jagraon treats such ailments. He is there only on Sundays. I'll take her to him."

An angelic Bhag walked in, having served Book-guru.

"I heard you singing this morning when I jogged by your gurdwara. Behind it on the edge of the pond I saw a newly-whitewashed domed mini temple about three feet high. Actually I have seen such mini temples on all the access roads to our village. The number seems to have increased. It looks like your gurdwaras aren't effective."

"It's a matti, the abode of Matarani, the mother-queen or smallpox-queen. In Punjabi, 'mata' means both mother and smallpox. You find them everywhere. People have more faith in them than in Book-guru."

"I have been telling white people that Sikhs do not believe in spirits and ghosts and have got rid of superstition and belief in spirits. Do people cast charms and spells?" I asked.

"Every village hangs on to primitive practices invoking spirits of the dead. Even the well-educated believe in them. Book-guru forbids such practices. Unfortunately, if you go to any village, you will find people worshipping the linga."

"I've seen in southern India lingas as high as a multi-storey building. But in your mattis, the lingas are very small. What happened to them?" I asked. That drew every one's attention.

"I guess spraying pesticide has shrunk them." Bholla's response provoked a loud burst of laughter.

"There may be some truth in what you say."

On the train from Delhi, I sat by a young lady. She was reading a medical journal. I asked if she was studying medicine. 'I'm a doctor' she replied.

"I beg your pardon, you look so young. That's why I thought you were a student. My name is Inder, and yours?"

"Gitanjali."

"Isn't that the name of Tagore's famous poem?"

"Yes, it is."

"Do you work in a hospital?"

"My husband and I run our own hospital in Ludhiana," she replied. "My husband is also a doctor and I'm a gynaecologist."

She didn't ask but I volunteered to tell her about me. "I live in Europe and this is my fourth trip in two years. I'm trying to get to know the people here. May I ask you about something?"

She nodded.

"Last October I participated in a medical camp organized annually near my village by a group of Californian doctors. At the end of the day they concluded that the rural people are becoming less healthy. In the last four years average blood pressure and blood sugar levels have risen. People have all sorts of problems, like knee joints and hips bones needing replacements. Do you think their finding is correct?"

"Yes," Gitanjali confirmed. "People overfeed themselves and they are not active. But there's worse. More pesticides are used to spray crops. More and more women have serious problems. Their menstrual cycle is disturbed and foetus malformation has become common. Nobody has shown any concern."

"Crop spraying swells the grains but shrinks lingas," remarked Bholla one day. "The house behind yours is called the Abode of Martyrs".

"Which martyrs?" I inquired.

"No one really knows," replied Bhag. "Some say a Sikh took shelter and died here a long time ago. He was a survivor of the Great Ghallughara, massacre or holocaust inflicted by Abdali of Afghanistan in 1762. This was his sixth attack on northern India, primarily to subdue the Sikhs and lay control over the Punjab. Originally there was a small stone monument that villagers associated with spirits of the dead and sought blessings."

"Who has built this hall?"

"The plot belonged to old Deyal. You know him well. He was your class fellow and you met him in Vancouver. He sold the plot to a group of ten Sikh farmer families of his Khangura clan. In four days, that's 10 March, the villagers will celebrate the martyr's day in this hall. That is the only function held in this hall. Sometimes it is used to say prayers after a cremation."

"What a waste of money" I remarked.

"Tomorrow morning I'll take you there. You will see Sikh women carrying buckets of milk mixed with water. Secretly each one washes the stone with milk-water and seeks blessings. Can you believe it?"

"Surely they ask for sons?"

"And cure for some illness."

"But I haven't seen any person performing a ceremony at the Mataranis."

"People do it secretly at night. They also place charms and cast spells. For the charm to work the queen must be fed. So some food is offered to the mini-linga. It's women who do it more than men."

"What do they seek?"

"The same thing: to get rid of a family calamity or a curse presumed to have been cast on them by another person, or to cast a spell to harm another person or family. The reason can be anything: jealousy and hatred, not uncommon traits of peasant behaviour."

"But why is it called the queen-smallpox?"

"In the past an epidemic of smallpox was so dreaded that people tried to appease the deity, the all-powerful Matarani who they believed caused it. The only cure they could think of was to appease her by paying her homage and ceremonially transferring the disease from the patient to the immunized smallpox-queen."

"How can you allow this when you piously sing hymns daily from Book-guru condemning such practices?"

"I've told you before, my singing has become a ritual. Who cares what Book-guru says?"

"Does Book-guru recommend the celebration of the puranmasi, the full moon day?"

"No."

"I visited the Golden Temple last year on a Sunday. It happened to be the full moon day and it was crowded. Now I realise why so many of our family wanted to get into the van that was already full. I thought the trip was planned because of me. When we entered the Golden Temple compound, I saw a long line, eight to nine people wide, of devotees trying to enter the sanctum. For an ordinary soul like me it would take two hours to enjoy the privilege of bowing down for less than a second in front of the superbly-dressed Book-guru. It seems that the timeless Book-guru has no time for ordinary souls."

"Not if you display a five hundred rupee note. Someone will gently usher you aside and a priest will honour you by placing round your neck Book-Guru's sacred kesari, a saffron-coloured, scarf, just like Dalai Lama's, though his scarf is white. Depending on the amount you offer you will be allowed to lie on your belly stretched full length like a stick in front of Book-guru, the literal meaning of 'dandaut bandna': supplication like a stick."

Everyone laughed.

"Are you implying that Book-guru takes bribes like the Punjab police?"

"How can Book-guru do that?" Bhag said. "Those who take care of it do what the Hindu priests practised for thousands of years: hoodwink the gullible masses. Rotten traditions must be maintained, it's the basis of our culture. Book-guru has not failed."

"Isn't the reading of Book-guru's word the Sikh practice of meditation?"

"Why do you ask me?" Bholla reacted. "You have done it. Yesterday you went to the historic gurdwara of Tahlisahib in Raikot to participate in the monthly full-moon day prayer. Our workshop is nearby, but I rarely go there.

"What did you see there?" Bholla asked.

"The first time I went there was three months ago. Six women and girls came with me in our little Maruti. I expected to hear the soothing music and merge in the spiritual bliss."

"You're old but you have no experience, you expect too much." They all laughed.

"The crowd was thicker than that in the Golden Temple. There was no place to park the car. Seeing the crowd pouring into the gurdwara I decided to stay in the car to watch people stream by on each side of the dusty road - mostly women - carrying something in shining stainless steel containers." Bholla laughed again. "There is nothing pious in that place. It's a meeting place for the young. Parents happily think their daughter has gone to pay respect to Book-guru while she is actually meeting her boyfriend. There is more sin than faith in these holy places."

"Yes, I did see many young people milling around. I'm sure some people go to pray."

"They are mentally disturbed people, especially women. I mean they have insecure lives. They neither have enough to eat nor basic necessities of life, often because their men are lazy or on drugs. They believe that offering parsad and contributing to the community kitchen will bring them material happiness or correct the husbands. In the shining steel containers you saw, they bring milk or butter that they cannot afford to eat at home, hoping that Book-guru will multiply it."

Bhag intervened, "For many it's a ritual. They go without any preconceived objective. For them it is a therapeutic outing, dukh bhanjan, riddance of pain."

Bholla chimed in, "This ritual among women has replaced the Hindu fasts observed to obtain a long and healthy life for their husbands or to conceive sons or grandsons, and fructify milk producing cows and buffaloes? I'm sure many go for that. Our society lives on hope and miraculous redemption from all types of woes."

Bhag said laughingly "Tahlisahib gurdwara is famous in the region for animal welfare. Did you notice vendors selling freshly cut pegs?"

"I did and I wanted to ask you why sell pegs, rather odd. In one vendor's basket each peg carried a ceremonial red string tied in the cleft cut at the top."

"People buy a peg and plant it near the buffalo or cow. They believe that this will make the animal produce milk if it has not done so, or not in the quantity expected after giving birth to the young. There are two legends regarding this. You know the word Tahli is the name for a rosewood tree, once very common here: they used to line all the main roads. You hardly see them now. Well the tenth Guru, Gobind Singh, camped at this spot for a few days in 1705. One morning after cleaning his teeth with a green rosewood twig he planted it and announced that it would grow into a big tree. No one must cut it. Whoever disobeyed risked his family perishing. In due course the twig became a big tree. A rich Muslim decided to cut it and use its wood in his new house. It is said that within a short time all his family died. That's why the Gurdwara is called Tahlisahib and those pegs are made from Tahli branches."

"I thought people used the twig of an acacia to clean their teeth. I do not believe the guru would inflict such curses at random, especially at that gruelling moment in his life. It is contrary to his gracious character. Anyway, what has that to do with the production of milk?" I asked.

"People are very smart here," Bholla continued. "They have linked this story to Gobind Singh's other miracle wherein he got milk from a young buffalo or a he-buffalo. So if you hammer the Tahli peg in the ground near the buffalo or cow, surely it will produce milk profusely. This is India. Sikhs have total faith in the efficacy of these miracles."

"Did you plant a peg when your buffalo gave birth when I came here four months ago?" I inquired.

"No."

"You see, the baby buffalo died because you did not plant the sacred peg. Be more careful next time."

"The milk you drink every day comes from the same buffalo."

We all laughed. Suddenly, we heard loud abusive voices coming from the back street.

"People are fighting," shouted Bhag's wife, who was feeding the buffaloes in the back yard. "Some jat boys are fighting, it's the same rival families: Surpanch's and Dyal's. These boys are on drugs. How many times I have told Manj not to associate with them!" Manj is her grandson.

The Dyal boy floored his rival and was sitting on him when his mother came and started beating the poor boy on his head with her shoe. The rival parents rushed out and were about to bash each other when the villagers intervened and separated them. The following morning they were out again: this time the Surpanch challenging the others to come out.

"One day someone will be killed," Bholla predicted. "Last month these boys had a fight in Raikot. You see, uncle, villagers have not changed. Old family vendettas persist, just as among the Afghans."

"A person is killed almost every month," said Bhag. "A week ago, a young man we know from Halwara came to the workshop. I asked him what happened in the fight the other day. Who killed the boy? The man proudly claimed that he hit him first with his sword. Why did you do it, I asked him? He said he didn't remember. He was high on drugs like all others. It is as simple as that, life has no meaning here, in our spiritual world. Such young people crowd gurdwaras: what do you then expect of the Sikh way? We have lost the Sikh way. We do not even know it."

"You were going to tell me about the full-moon festival," I reminded Bhag.

"I know, it's good to go to pray at least once a month. But we also celebrate the new-moon-day and the first of every month. Nothing in Book-guru says that we should do it blindly. Anyway, no one listens. One sheep follows another."

"Amazing, you have such views, and yet you sing ritually. Now I'll tell you about my full-moon day pilgrimage to Tahlisahib. We parked the car in your friend's car-repair garage near the gurdwara. I do not need to tell you about the hazards of walking one hundred metres through a narrow dusty side lane blocked by buses, cars, motorbikes, bikes and people, going in both directions. When I saw the devotees milling in the Gurdwara compound, I handed Preeti a ten-rupee note and told her to pray for me in front of Book-guru".

"Why didn't you go inside and offer your obeisance as well?" Bhag asked.

Bolla replied for me, "What for? People who go there are screwed up mentally. No one really prays. I never go to any gurdwaras just to seek favours that Book-guru cannot give and never gave in the past. You have to pray in your heart and work to get what you want. We are sick of these thousands of gurdwaras fleecing poor people of their money."

I continued, "We agreed to meet under the neem [margosa] tree. That gave me time to read what is written in big blue letters on the board in the compound temple."

"I have read it too, but I don't remember all." said Bhag.

"I have a photo of it. It lists the ideals of the Sikh way. Look at this picture," I displayed it on my digital camera. Bholla read the bullet points:

■ *A Sikh is a person who accepts and follows the teachings of Book-guru.*

■ *Does not worship deities, gods and goddesses.*

■ *Must not have faith in caste differences, untouchability, mantras, charms, magic formulas, lunar-phase and planetary influences, evil stars, feasting for the dead, ancestor worship, offering food and water to deceased relatives, funeral rites, sacrificial oblations, ritualistic sacrifice and feasts, death anniversary feasts, lighting lamps, dancing as for Krishna, austerities, head-shaving, new-moon and full-moon fasting, painting signs on foreheads, sacred thread, basil plants, rosary, tombs and monuments on graves, image and idol worship, delusion (pilgrimage only to Sikh places), mullahs, Brahmins, ancient books such as Vedas, Gita, Koran and the Bible.*

■ *Stays away from opium, alcohol and tobacco.*

■ *No ceremonial piercing of nose and ears.*

■ *Does not kill girls.*

■ *Considers the needs of the poor, helping them as offerings to the guru.*

Bholla commented, "We do not follow any of these. People are going in the opposite direction. We find comfort in the fact that we have such wonderful values on paper and billboards."

Bholla continued, "You will not see the rich villagers or the town merchants. The few who still believe in such fads perform their genuflexions early in the morning before the crowds form."

"I timed the rate of parsad serving at the counter. A server standing in front of each line prompted the devotee-buyer to move faster. On average ten devotees per minute were served in each line. I assumed that on average each devotee paid five rupees. Am I being impolite? Should I say donated for charity?"

"Five rupees is nothing these days, ten rupees is more correct. You don't know how desperate people are. They are prepared to pay big bribes to Book-guru, expecting a many-fold return from Baba Nanak. Why should you expect anything less? According to Janamsakhis, the tales of his travels, Nanak invariably made poor people rich and even kings. He made cool sweet water gush out in the most parched regions by just lifting a pebble. He gave sons but rarely daughters to childless parents, usually rich ones."

Everyone laughed. "I didn't look at it that way. But what you say fits the situation. OK, let's assume that each donation is ten rupees. Now tell me at what time does the big crowd start to form?"

"About eight, by then the villagers have finished their morning chores, they continue coming until four at least."

"That makes five hundred rupees per minute, that is two lakh and forty thousand rupees for getting the parsad, most of which is donated by devotees."

"Add at least the same amount that other devotees, like you, place directly in front of Book-guru," Bholla added. "That's a lot of money. No one knows what happens to it."

Young Manj took courage to say, "I've read that the daily collection in the Golden Temple, Amritsar is in many millions, second only to the Hindu temple of Tirupathi near Chennai".

A few days earlier when I returned from yatra to the Golden Temple I was taken aback. The moment I descended from the minibus Bhag and others bent down and touched my feet. I asked him why they did that. "Your feet have been to holy Amritsar," he said. "You are now sacred and we pay our respect, just like the Muslim who makes the Haj to Mecca gets respect and receives the honour of being called a Hajji."

CHAPTER 23

COITUS INTERRUPTUS

❧

Roshan placed the tea tray on top of the sawn-off tree trunk she uses as a table and poured us some tea. "Did you heat the milk?" Malika asked.

"Yes my queen, how can I forget?"

Malika smiled, picked up her cup and said, "It's chilly. I'm going inside."

"Ok – but don't fall asleep," I said, teasing her.

"I'm going to watch TV."

"I'll watch you."

Malika glared at me, then smiled and left Roshan and me to enjoy our tea.

"Roshan, thanks for the pictures you sent me of our trip to Spain."

"My pleasure," she acknowledged with a smile. "It was a great trip."

"You know, the one picture that really stands out is of the last day when we were heading for Barcelona," I reminisced.

It was late afternoon and the slanting rays of the sun shone on the bright yellow sunflower fields and the undulating hills studded with quaint old whitewashed villages. When our car dipped over the hill a loud "Wahoo!" escaped from my lips. My inside shuddered. My eyes could not accommodate the panoramic view of the vast bowl with a patchwork of rectangular and square fields in numerous shades. The landscape was surreal. It was like an impressionist painting by Monet or van Gogh.

"How can I forget that? In front, behind the far-away hill, appeared the tops of giant windmills gyrating," Roshan recalled.

Roshan had asked me to accompany her to Spain because she hated travelling alone, and I willingly agreed. She was an active fundraiser for the Aga Khan Foundation, which restored sites of Islamic culture that flourished at the turn of the first millennium found in the world today. From Barcelona airport we rented a red Renault diesel car and took off to see the remnants of the Arab rule between the eighth and twelfth centuries. For a week, she immersed herself in the Andalusian Arab culture of the Moors in the Iberian Peninsula. She was fascinated by the Alhambra because of its purity and the essence of Islamic culture. I was impressed by Cordoba, because of the immense size of the mosque in which Roman, Jewish, Islamic and Christian architecture merged into a confused monument built by its successive rulers. We walked across the old bridge to see the Roman tower.

"The haunting music in the tower mesmerised me," Roshan recollected. "I was awed by the life-size figurines of the four wise men. I did not know of them before. I love Ibn Arabi and his poem: My heart has become capable of every form... I often recite it to myself. It's beautiful – if only the world could follow it."

"It's amazing, that he wrote it a thousand years ago," I remarked.

"Do you remember the names of the other three?" asked Roshan.

"Maimonides was the Jew, Ibn Rushd was another Muslim and Alfons X, called the Wise, was a Christian," I answered. "These four wise men had foreseen the catastrophic inter-religion and intra-religion collision ten centuries ago and had warned followers of religions to avoid carnage and replace it with love. Not far from Cordoba, at a meeting of the world's religious leaders, a Swiss wise man, rejected and excommunicated by the Roman Church, declared there would not be peace between nations unless there was peace between religions. Religions continue to be the foremost cause of conflict between humans. The Parliament of Religions is a talk shop that does not want to follow the advice of the four wise men."

"It's so easy and simple and yet so difficult. What's wrong with us humans?" Roshan asked.

"To answer you," I said, "We have to backtrack to Maimonides. The problem is that we do things the wrong way round or upside down. We start building spirituality from the top, without first laying a foundation of knowledge and education on the ground. You see, Maimonides' approach corroborates the idea of the Flow in my Big Bang Yoga."

Roshan squinted. "Yes but how does one incorporate Maimonides' principles for the everyday person?"

"I'll answer that in a moment, but first, do you know what Mohammed has said on this subject as reported in the Hadis?"

"I've no idea."

"He has said two things, both as important as the five pillars of Islam. First: From the cradle to the tomb dedicate yourself to learning, because he who seeks knowledge loves God. Second: The study of science has the value of a fast, and teachings of a prayer."

"That's a revelation. If we had stuck to that, we would be far ahead."

"That's true and that's why I want to see how religious concepts or beliefs perform in the face of the knowledge that human beings have accumulated in the last few centuries especially since they landed on the Big Bang idea. Yoga is the union, a perfect marriage of knowledge and spirituality. But unfortunately, every attempt to consummate this marriage has ended in coitus interruptus, no fertilization, which I translate into no peace. We need a potent Viagra to dispel fear and hatred and bring in peace and love."

Roshan burst out laughing.

"Won't Kama Sutra help?" It was Malika walking in. Thankfully, she hadn't lost her vintage one-liners.

This time, I joined Roshan in an explosive laugh.

"I think we should visit the famous Hindu-temple sculptures in India depicting the attainment of spiritual bliss through the art of kama, sex," I suggested. "The clever ancient Hindus tried to marry dharma, karma and kama without much success."

"A good idea, let's visit India," said Roshan excitedly.

"I'll have to get some Viagra before we visit the temples. Can I get it without a doctor's prescription here?" I asked jokingly.

"I didn't mean that," said Roshan, hitting me on the shoulder. "You're incorrigible. All you'll get is another cup of tea."

Roshan went inside to fetch more tea. Malika became quiet.

Roshan returned with the pot and continued. "Overall, I found your Big Bang article well researched, even if some aspects are debatable."

"Such as?" I asked.

"What you have not fully explained is the dynamics of why and how. Your answer is anecdotal. I don't think that any philosophy has the explanation. Not yet anyway."

"You do not need to be a philosopher to answer that. The Flow of Big Bang explains it all. Francis Collins was the head of the Human Genome Project on DNA, the code of life. In his book, The Language of God, he accepts the Big Bang and the theory of evolution. Yet he concludes that the existence of a supernatural God explains why all this happened. Roshan, your religion does not allow you to abandon God. Many do not accept the Big Bang idea. However, the Big Bang facilitates my answering the question why with a simple logic: The Big Bang happened because things, matter and non-matter, got concentrated, they got concentrated because they were scattered, they got scattered because there was a Big Bang, there was a Big Bang because they got concentrated. And so on from infinity to infinity. No more why! Would you accept that?"

Roshan looked perplexed, uncertain whether a response was needed immediately.

"This morning when we were talking, the sun disappeared, followed by a hailstorm, after which it snowed. The weather-woman announced that it was temporary. Just like the Big Bang, spring will restart in the morning." I heaved my shoulders and sighed: "*Quod erat demonstrandum* - that had to be demonstrated."

Roshan did not want to give up. "My faith does not accommodate your Big Bang theory, it's all wrong. I will not get into that even if science is moving in this direction, including the concepts of multi-universes and parallel dimensions. The word you refer to repeatedly, anthropocentric, is more central to the issue we are discussing".

"The problem is not God or the Big Bang," I stated in defence. "The problem is the selfish nature of human beings. God is their scapegoat, someone to blame for our ills, defects and errors. When I pronounce that it's God's will, I acquit myself of errors and politely tell Him: You, are the culprit. Poor God." I sighed again.

"I look at it from another angle." Roshan's reasoning sharpened. "Your flow idea has many dimensions plus time entrapping everything. We humans are as yet unable to think in multi-dimensional terms. It is a serious limitation. Philosophy and religions enable us to transcend this state and visualize the universe conceptually."

There was a heavy silence for a few minutes as we tried to digest Roshan's contention. I started, my words coming out slowly so they made some sense.

"Gods and religions exist as they do, perhaps as a consequence of historical issues and events. Their relevance has been reduced by the fact that present flow-related concepts apply literally, but not as proclaimed by the interpretation of scriptural material. What religions talk about is not the same as the all-powerful relatively eternal Flow composed of Information, Interaction Interdependence and Vital Energy. With these elements we derive universal laws, principles and truths. What I mean is that scriptural depictions may actually be accurate, but they may not refer to God or gods as proclaimed by religious entities."

"You have put a lot of effort into your Big Bang ideas, but you are not going to shake any belief systems too easily," said Roshan.

"I don't expect to. These structures, belief systems, and issues of identity resulting in wars frighten me. They are egocentric, directed at human needs and values, very strong and bad restraint for the evolution of the human species."

"Can you imagine Maimonides and his illustrious colleagues like Al-Farabi, Avicenna, and Ibn Bajja having access to the vast store of present-day scientific knowledge and other information at that time? I'm sure we would have been spared the horrors of the clashes of civilizations. The marriage would have been consumed, coitus interruptus avoided and the human race would have treaded more cautiously," reflected Roshan

"Yes, the consummation of the marriage of science and thought, God and systems of science: what a blissful honeymoon," I said in support.

"Kama Sutra, in practice," Malika chipped in. "Off with petty traditions."

"Don't you realise that God will become jobless?" I pointed out.

"We'll see Him lining up for unemployment benefit," Malika laughed.

"You know, poor God gets worn out solving the problems of the Jews by Friday evening. He is forced to rest on Saturday (Shabbat),

Christians exhaust their god by Saturday evening, he is obliged to recuperate on Sunday, and God gets tired with Muslim complaints by Thursday evening and He must rest on Friday. Obviously the economics of division of labour require that their gods be different. Imagine if there were only one working god and problems arrived together, for three days God would not be available to run the world," I laughed.

"What would happen if He were unwell or decided to go on strike"? Malika wondered aloud.

"Well, I suppose that is a good reason to get in the Flow and go wherever it takes us," Roshan concluded.

CHAPTER 24

WHITE CROWS

∽

Meeting Malika completed the cycle. It was an anticlimax. There was no reunion of hearts, there was no return to romance and love, no hugs and not much holding of hands. I had expected more. But having met her, my past memories will not trouble me any more. Nevertheless, I wanted to talk to her and fill the memory gap. And I wanted to know her feelings. She had travelled to New Mexico to meet me and was curious to see me. But why? Did she want to confirm whether she had made a youthful blunder falling in love with me? Every time I touched on our romantic memories she diverted the conversation to some other issue as if I had touched a live nerve. Yet she said a few times, "Why do you think I have come here? I've spent my life… just like that". She did not dare say, thinking of you. "My brain does not want to recall my return to India. For that, I hate my father. Two days after we reached our village, I conspired with my twelve-year-old brother to escape to Mumbai where I was supposed to meet you. Our Gujarati head master offered to help us. What was his name?"

"Desai."

"Yes, he had arranged with his family in Mumbai to shelter us. No one could have found us."

"A day before you left Eldore, your father promised me that he would write to me when it would be convenient for me to join you."

"He didn't tell me, that was a lie. To hide my trail we took the train from Ludhiana northwards to Amritsar. When we reached Amritsar my brother was ill. We had no choice but to return. I'm blank after that."

"Did you visit Amritsar this time?" Malika asked, a little more cheerful.

"Yes, three days before I flew from Delhi"

"I've been there many times. The Golden Temple captivates me."

"This was my second visit. The first one was forty years earlier. The gold-plated domes and walls glitter as always. I didn't notice any change, nor did it evoke in me any special feeling of reverence different from that for temples in Tirupathi, Jaganath or Varanasi. You know the same Maharaja Ranjit Singh who got this temple gilded gave gold for gilding the famous Vishnu temple in Varanasi. Was he a Hindu, or was it a political ploy to please Hindus? Between my two visits the Golden Temple complex was attacked, damaged and repaired."

"Sikhs and non-Sikhs revere the place, why are you indifferent?" Malika asked.

"My daughter was not yet three when I went there the first time. Since childhood I have heard about the healing potency of the sacred pool and that of the dukh bhanjan beri , the berry tree that cures all afflictions. You know the legend was turned into a film. The girl was carrying her crippled husband in a basket that she put under this tree at the edge of the pool and went away to look for food. He saw crows dip in the pool and fly out as white swans. He managed to crawl into the pool. Lo - a miracle! The cripple was completely cured. My heart throbbed with much expectation and reverence. Nervously I made my daughter sit on the first step and dip her feet in the sacred pool. Promptly, two tall Sikhs wearing white togas and blue turbans appeared behind us. They struck their spear shafts on the marble and menaced me: You dip the child in fully or take her out. Don't you

know this? Frightened I pleaded, Please forgive us. We have come
from abroad, we do not know the custom. We are leaving and will
not visit your temple. We started walking towards the exit gate. The
guardians of spirituality cooled down, Don't go away, do the darshan
[seeing] of Darbar Sahib. There is also the library, foreigners like to
visit it. That is how I paid my first respects to our holy gurdwara, the
like of which is found nowhere else. For me, it's not the place but
people that invoke peace. That minor incident left a lasting impression.
A pilgrimage to holy places has no place on my road to spirituality."

"Did you go alone this time?"

"No, I was with a family of eight, all packed at the back of a Tata
diesel pick-up driven at its maximum speed wherever the road and
traffic permitted. We stopped for a Punjabi breakfast at the Haveli
restaurant. I ordered tandoori parathas for everybody. It was a big
mistake: they were too rubbery to chew. But the others relished
everything. It was their first time in such a restaurant."

"It's fun to go out with the family," smiled Malika.

"Yes and no. Our driver could not count how many times he
had been to the Golden Temple. Yet it took him an hour to find it
and not without asking passers-by. The roads around the temple
complex are congested with every kind of moving device one can
think of, besides throngs of people. Later I realized why there were
so many people: It was pooranmashi, the full-moon day, and a Sunday
– holiness combined with convenience."

"One should avoid going out on such days."

"The Sikhs have embraced this Hindu ritual although it is
condemned by Book-guru. I follow the verse: uttering the word
'Waheguru' once equals bathing in sixty-eight of the most sacred
places of pilgrimage of India. First we visited Jallianwal Bagh the site
of the massacre by the British in 1919, then through the milling
crowded street to the Golden Temple hidden behind crummy
buildings. From the main entrance gate I saw the glittering temple

in the middle of the srovar, sacred water tank. I performed the clockwise circumambulation of the tank and joined the eight-abreast line to enter the sanctum. I was not prepared for that and the first shove threw me against a woman. I apologized to her, saying it was not my fault. She gave me a no-harm-done look. Squashed from all sides and expecting a two-hour wait in heat, sweat and smell, I stepped out of the line and walked along it to find out why the line was moving in surges."

At the first arched entrance the line is split into two and fenced on both sides with steel pipes. Two wooden poles are put across as flow locks. Two hefty men pull the pole out to let about twenty persons flow through and thrust the pole back to stop the flow. A few moments later men on the other side do the same, causing a twisted surge behind. I saw people swooning in the hot crush. Men on both sides holding water buckets passed glasses of water to the suffering devotees.

"You didn't go inside. You are a coward. Wasn't your family displeased with your irreverent behaviour?"

"I do not know. They just watched me with eyes wide open. I told them that I would see them at the outlet of the human flow in two hours. I recalled the story our driver told me just before entering the city. It was about the Chief Minister of Punjab's visit to the Golden Temple. One of the guards announced loudly, "Step aside! Make way for the Chief Minister of Punjab". The devotees squeezed themselves to each side to clear the passage. The Chief Minister was also the head of the Gurdwara Management which runs the Golden Temple complex and controls hundreds of other gurdwaras. A woman held his arm and said respectfully: Brother, wait for a moment. She stood in front of him, took out a hundred rupee note, kneeled down in front him and placed the note at his feet. Sister, said the Chief Minister, This is not the place for your offering. Pointing to the sanctum, he said: You should offer it to the Guru Granth inside.

She humbly replied, In the end my offering there is going to reach your pocket, why go to all that trouble when I can give it to you directly?"

"Aren't you ashamed of telling such jokes? Malika laughed. "You are ill-fated for not genuflecting in the sanctum in front of the exalted Guru Granth."

"Maybe. Surely people know about the twisted practices. What happens to the enormous amount of money collected every day is not transparent. I expected the Sikh government to be more correct than others. No. Nearly seventy percent of the revenue budgeted for the development programme is not spent on the projects. Book-guru is powerless."

"What did you do for two hours?" Malika asked.

"I observed people, their devotion and their dipping in the sacred tank. The water is quite clean. The tank water is expected to wash away your sins and cure ailments, just like the waters of the Ganges in Varanasi and Hardwar. The German-made water purifying plant has difficulty filtering all the sins left by bathers. I saw green algae accumulated in the corners. I visited the four gates and looked at the community kitchen. My two hours passed reverently and positively."

"Did you see the new machines for making chapattis?"

"No, I didn't go inside. I only saw steel dishes being distributed at the entrance."

"The first machine was also a German make, now they are made locally."

"I saw my people emerge from the human outlet. I expected to see their faces radiating with Book-guru's glory but instead they all looked tired and miserable. We sat down to rest at the end of a corridor away from the crowd. I had hardly stretched my legs when a short woman accompanied by three young boys, without turbans, appeared. She did not look Sikh, but there is no way to identify a woman. They placed a cardboard box and two metal buckets near the end wall and asked us to make room for them. In the twinkling of an eye, one of the boys started distributing bowls moulded out of leaves among the people and the others followed him serving small fried chapattis, curried vegetables, halva (parsad), and purified butter dripping to the marble floor. A crowd swarmed with arms outstretched asking for food. These were not poor people. Two well-dressed fat women were the keenest of them all. Soon the white marble floor lost its lustre."

"People are supposed to eat in the world-famous sacred community kitchen," Malika commented.

"Pilgrims struggled to get food and snatched chapattis – just short of turning into a brawl."

"Weren't there any Temple guardians?" Malika asked.

"Two of them appeared just when nearly all the food had been distributed. They asked the woman to stop. She resisted: This is the Great guru's house, I can do all the charitable work I want. I approached her and said, 'I see your devotion to serve pilgrims nearly turned into a scuffle. How do you feel about it?' She retorted: 'There are no pilgrims here, many are temple servers. I've distributed food here many times before but nothing happens. My conscience is clear. My true guru, my master, has entrusted to me this duty and I'm doing it in this holy place. I'm fulfilling my mission'. Evidently she was sent by some holy man.

"I asked her: 'Doesn't your heart pain when you see your charity provoking unholy behaviour among pilgrims? She tersely repeated: 'This is my mission given by my living guru. My feelings and heart do not matter.' I continued: 'If it's seva [service], wouldn't it be better to feed the numerous poor and the beggars I see outside the Temple?' The three boys nodded their heads, concurring with me. She retorted: 'It's not for me to decide. My master decides. I do what he instructs me to do'. She looked brainwashed, benign, and harmless.

"The Temple guards turned up again and asked the lady to take away her material because the cleaners were coming. As I stood, cold water splashed at my feet. A team of cleaners lined up across the tank periphery passed buckets full of water from the tank and emptied them onto the marble floor. Water flows back to the holy tank, dragging with it all the dust and debris and the spilt food. The water that has been used to wash the feet of visiting devotees becomes even more sacred, pure and miraculous – charan pahol. I saw a woman walking behind the line of the men washing the floor. Every time a bucket was emptied near her, she collected a small quantity of water with her hand from the flow and licked it. I noticed that she just wetted her lips, did not swallow."

Malika did not comment and walked away to her room to rest.

I brooded over what we had been saying. Malika represents the Sikh mindset, determined yet unsure and reactionary in some ways. She had mentioned that the Sikhs are not like the Moslems who have a Koranic mission to convert the whole of humanity to Islam by any means and at any cost. She has a point.

I looked deeper and felt that the Sikhs' intent is similar, although there is no binding injunction. Our religion is universal, implying all human beings should follow the Sikh way - no coercion. One is born Hindu, one cannot become a Hindu. Proselytizing is not possible. Anybody of any faith can become a Sikh, like the community of white American Sikhs. Do we accept all religions? We tolerate them. Gobind Singh, the tenth Sikh Guru, instituted the Khalsa military brotherhood. He recognized the role of Hindu and Muslim religions in politics and the welfare of people. Hindus did not have any significant religious institutions that would safeguard the people from misrule and tyranny. The caste-based Hindu system exploits its own people. The state used Islam as a political and economic tool, especially during the second half of the Mogul rule. People were forced or obliged to convert. Gobind Singh drew a clear line between the Sikh panth (way) and the state. Perceptively he assigned the role of the Sikh way to Book-guru and gave political power to the Khasla. In order to perform socio-political responsibilities in the right manner members of Khalsa must behave in the Sikh way detailed in Book-guru. The individual interacts with the Sat Sangat (saint congregation), to acquire the art of living and enhance personal qualities. He uses these qualities for the benefit of society through socio-political institutions.

Some Sikh factions do not recognize the two complementary but distinct aspects of the Sikh way of life. Often there is a tendency to copy the integrated Muslim model, in which religion and politics are inseparable. A few among such groups succumb to extremist ways. Nevertheless Sikhs have inherited some Muslim manners. We are supposed to say five daily prayers. The pilgrimage to the Golden Temple is similar to Haj to Mecca. Building new gurdwaras is not unlike the Muslim practice. California probably has more gurdwaras per capita than places of worship of other faiths. Then prayer is the core of the Sikh way of opening mind and spirit to a divine presence. Hence the need for so many places of worship.

Why do we need to pray so much? Are we more sinful, or is our prayer faulty? For many every song of Book-guru is a prayer. But this is not so. I recalled one hymn:

They have their head hair plucked, and drink filthy water:
They beg daily and eat the remnants which others have thrown away.
They spread their own excrement inhaling its foul smell though the mouth,
Clean water frightens them.
Like sheep, they have head-hair plucked out with hands smeared with ashes.
They have abandoned the lifestyle of their mothers and fathers,
Their families cry out in distress...
They remain filthy day and night;

They do not paint the sacred mark on their foreheads.

They sit grouped together heads bent as if in mourning;

They do not go to the Lord's Court.

With their begging bowls hanging from their loins, and their fly-brushes in their hands,

They walk in single file.

They are neither Yogis, nor disciples of Shiva, nor Qazis nor Mullahs.

Estranged from the Lord, they wander around in disgrace,

In fact their group is contaminated...

They go without giving charity or bathing;

Their shaven heads become covered with dust...

The Guru is the ocean, and all His Teachings are the river. Bathing within it, glorious greatness is obtained. O Nanak, if the shaven-headed ones do not bathe, then seven handfuls of ashes are upon their heads.

Imagine singing it lovingly as if it were a prayer when in fact it's a criticism of some bad practices. Few realize that a large part of Book-guru consists of descriptions, critiques, instructions and guidance. It clearly says that simply reciting them is a waste of time. We are not only keeping Book-guru out of reach of the rest of the world, which does not understand its language, but also from our own people by worshipping it like an idol.

The famous 20th century philosopher Bertrand Russell said that Sikhs are committing an unpardonable sin. Of course it's not all negative. The overall impact of the Sikh way makes our people relatively generous, broad-minded, adaptable and less prone to superstition and taboos. Being extroverts, we enjoy life. Often these are individual traits. As a group, community or nation the thinking is not broadening further. Take for example, Book-guru's emphasis on human brotherhood and service to humanity. The group's scope of service is limited to cooking and serving communal meals, langar, washing dishes, arranging and cleaning shoes of devotees, a centuries-old practice which has outlived its purpose of bringing social equality and helping the poor and the hungry.

The main purpose of the langar today serves as a social get-together. Transforming such traditions to community action by helping the poor of the world, setting up social and sports services, family counselling and similar welfare activities is still beyond the pale of Sikh thinking. Watching Book-guru online and on TV being loaded with hundreds of silk scarves and adorned with glitter and being carried ceremonially with pomp and reverence to its sleeping room. Let them build temples, for the followers believe that to be the best form of charity.

These thoughts depress me. Are we such an unfortunate group of people? Maybe. Sikhs do not know they have a miracle in their hands. They see the magnificent glowing light at the end of the tunnel, but are unable to take a step towards it to put into practice Book-guru's teachings and thus fulfil their claim of being universal.

Then my mind turned to Malika. If truly one Sikh nation or community were to exist, I would not be here in Santa Fe to meet Malika hiding from our own families and people - we would have married and had our own children and a different life.

Malika interrupted my dreaming.

"What happened? You are back so soon," I asked.

"I felt guilty leaving you alone."

"I was thinking of you. I missed you. I want to be near you, give all the support you need. Come, sit down."

"I have brewed tea for us. I'll bring it here."

Malika returned with two mugs and sat down near me.

"What have you been dreaming?" she asked.

"About us, married. How would we have ended up? Would we have had children? Where would we be, in Kenya, India or England? Would I have gone to the university?"

"I call it destiny. Let's leave it there," she said with a sigh.

"Tell me, if you were to marry me now would your father have objected?"

"Times have changed. He would not have stooped so low. Nevertheless, here in California and British Columbia clannishness is taking a new shape. Even now it's not uncommon for the girl's parents to resist," Malika said. "Change towards the right track is slow. Our religious and social institutions do not have the courage to promote inter-caste marriages. Gobind Singh's objective to create a casteless society has still to see the light. Inter-caste marriages happen from non-Sikh impetus through individual choice in universities and the multicultural work milieu. The gurdwara managers and preachers cannot take any credit yet. To say that Sikhs do not practice caste discrimination is a lie. It seems even the educated have started to look inwards, marrying within the caste and clan. This behaviour seems to arise from the western ideal of freedom of association."

CHAPTER 25

BEDTIME LURE – A DIALOGUE

﹌

- Our Adi Granth, the First Book, what I call Book-guru because it is a person, is an anthology compiled in 1604 under the supervision of Arjun Dev, the fifth guru of the Sikhs. He edited it with the help of other learned men. Gobind Singh, our tenth guru, expanded it in 1706. It contains more than 6,600 poems and couplets, forming a formidable tome of 1,430 pages. Two years later, in 1708, he designated it as his successor.

- Why a book as a successor?

- You can say it was God's wish. It happened that a few months earlier two of his sons were killed in a battle against the Mogul army supported by Hindu rajas. The local Muslim governor then captured the remaining two younger sons, aged seven and nine, and after torturing them, beheaded them. There was no one to continue the line.

- Didn't he have a daughter?

- No. Anyway, a woman has never become a guru.

- Why?

- Tradition. Do you know a woman in India or anywhere else in the world who has risen to that eminence?

- I can think of Mary, mother of Jesus and Meerabai.

- Not in her lifetime. The latter was relegated to a minor saint. A proposal to include her hymns in Book-guru was turned down. The authors of all religious literature are men. Book-guru is no exception.

- Why didn't Gobind Singh follow Nanak, the first guru, who had designated his ablest disciple as his successor?

- I believe Gobind Singh was hard-pressed from every side. He was left with a handful of companions chased by Mogul forces. Not only was it difficult to choose someone, he must have realized that in a family succession he could not create the just society he wanted. So designating the Adi Granth as Book-guru was a logical decision.

- Did people accept it?

- For some sixty years it remained the Adi Granth. Then the followers began to address it as Guru and added words of respect: Sri, Sahib and Ji. So, I'm not wrong in calling it by the name of a person: Book-guru.

- But, unlike the Bible, the Koran, and the Gita, it's our eternal living embodiment of a guru – our burning light.

- I realize that. That's why we address it as Maharaj and Patshah, true emperor. We seek blessings directly from it. That's why we drape it in the most expensive clothes, wake it up in the morning, place it on a raised decorated dais, put it to bed in the evening and symbolically feed it, just as the Hindu sects indulge their statues of gods and goddesses.

- Be careful, the Sikhs don't like to hear that.

- You think they'll brand me with a fatwa? They can't do that. I have read such views expressed in the Punjabi newspapers. Many universities, researchers and knowledgeable people condemn the absurd rituals and beliefs that Book-guru wants us to do away with.

- Few people know what Book-guru says because they do not understand its language.

- I'm sure the illiterate public of the fifteenth and sixteenth century understood the language of Book-guru's songs. Otherwise why did they write? I think it is easier to understand it today. I have seen high-school children in the village with their Punjabi textbooks which contain many of the Book-guru's songs. Its language is no more difficult than the language of Shakespeare and other English authors that children learn in school.

- All our children want to learn English. They are reluctant to use Punjabi and Hindi because they want to pass the exams which are set in English. I understand what you are saying. We are knowingly losing our way. Yet Book-guru's poetry is easy to understand once you begin to study it. It's rhymed, musical and metrical, arranged in musical scales to be sung in any place at any time. These songs connote a relationship with the divine that has no limit. It is love for its own sake, typical, sane, reasoned, rational and level-headed.

- That tells a lot about your Book-guru. Its songs assert that the guru in the book is neither the book, nor the words, nor the songs, but the ideas they express. If you do not know these ideas, you cannot learn from the guru. Book-guru says: The Word is the Guru and the Guru is the Word. Often we interpret the Word in a narrow way to mean the writings in Book-guru. They forget that Word is a universal all-encompassing idea of Nam, Name, which expresses the essence of God, the Flow, its vital energy, information, knowledge, interactions and interdependences. The Flow itself is the true Guru. The most striking thing is that it does not contain any fixed doctrine or dogma other than the idea of a supreme power.

- Nor does it frighten us with hellfire. It does not claim that it is the only source of ethical intuition.

- I agree with you. Book-guru's ideas are rational and applicable even today, except for some aspects which reflect the social customs of old times. By contrast, the Hindus and Muslims have an unsolvable problem with their scriptural ideas resulting in irrational practices such as caste discrimination and according women a lower status.

The Sikhs do not have such problems. Their problem is that they are unable to put them into practice. As a consequence, their social behaviour is irrational because they continue to follow some of the despicable Hindu and Muslim ways.

- Certain practices have become part of us. They cannot be wrong.

- Like what?

- The fuss we make over Book-guru. I went to the gurdwara for the evening prayer. At the end, the priest recited a short prayer in an incomprehensible mumble. Why was he in such a hurry? I assumed that Book-guru must be tired, having endured three days of uninterrupted reading. With utmost respect the priest wrapped Book-guru in white underclothes and covered it with a silk cloth. The Guru Maharaj was ready to retire to his sleeping quarters. A hefty male devotee aided by two assistants reverently placed the Book-guru on the priest's turbanned head. He walked carefully to the bedroom while we respectfully chanted Waheguru, Waheguru... You can see this ceremony on the Punjabi TV channels.

- Why does it trouble you? It's so calming.

- I do not deny that. But I'm curious about the role of women in Sikhism. I haven't seen them perform this ceremony. Does Book-guru forbid them?

- There isn't anything like that.

- Then is it dangerous if women put Book-guru to bed and one of them quietly stays behind? You know what women are like.

- What are you implying?

- You see, people believe that Book-guru is living. Don't you see? The presence of a woman alone triggers a delicate situation.

- Book-guru is above all that.

- Then why isn't a woman allowed to carry Book-guru on her head?

- You're asking for trouble.

- You do not want to admit that it's sex discrimination or fear of temptation.

- How can Maharaj be tempted?

- I remember the story of the famous Hindu Rishi, holy man. Deep in the Himalayan forest, he sat in meditation under a banyan tree. He remained in a profound transcendental trance for many years. He survived on air. All the celestial gods became alarmed that if the Rishi acquired too much power, they would be obliged to submit to him. After much pondering, they worked out a plan to break his trance before he reached the divine state of a god. They sent down a ravishing damsel who was an exquisite dancer. The seductress was instructed to perform in front of the Rishi. I have seen Bollywood films emulating this scene innumerable times, with a busty, hip-swinging dazzling girl in glittering outfits hiding very little of her body. This heavenly damsel appears in front of the meditating Rishi, and the forest awakens to the sound and beat of heavenly music. The damsel begins her slow and erotic dance. The rhythm quickens to an orgasmic pitch. The Rishi does not budge. The dance reaches its peak, emanating electric-laser shafts of light penetrating the Rishi's head. He opens his eyes, shooting back flames of anger. The seductress is unperturbed and stares back. The man is so mesmerized by her beauty that he gets up and starts to dance with her, and they slip out of sight into the forest.

- You mean Book-guru might wake up!

- Do you know that women are not allowed to sing Book-guru's songs in the Golden Temple?

- That's correct, I never thought of it that way.

- That reminds me of the Greek hero Odysseus. He was forewarned of the beautiful sirens living on an island. With the sweetness of their songs and charm they would lure him and his sailors, use them and then destroy them. Their ship approached the island. The sea was calm, the perfumed air conveyed celestial music to their ears. Odysseus quickly plugged the ears of his seamen with wax. He instructed his crew to bind him to the mast and whatever he might say or do, not to untie him until the island was out of sight. Hearing the ravishing song, Odysseus was hypnotized and struggled frantically to free himself. He screamed, he cried and made signs to his men to untie him. Instead, they bound him tighter and the ship stayed on course. The music grew fainter until it could not be heard. Odysseus calmed down and stopped struggling. All were saved and the ship reached home safely. So you see why it's dangerous to listen to women singing.

– To conclude, what you are saying is that in male-dominated Sikh society, Book-guru can do nothing, the principle of equality between the sexes is still to see full implementation.

CHAPTER 26

SAINT-THIEVES

"This sant is blessed by God," said Zora, my fifty-year-old nephew. "Without him I would be lost. He is my saviour. With his miraculous powers he helps everyone. One day I'll take you to him. I'm sure he will convert you."

People use the word 'sant' loosely for a saint, a yogi or a monk. The words sant and sadh occur frequently in Book-guru. They invariably mean a good man or woman who follows the will of the Guru in God, one who is self-controlled and peace-loving. That person can be any one of us, a normal person, living honestly and joyfully within his milieu and respecting it. Book-guru's sant lives happily like a raja or a queen with little money, and fame means little.

My curiosity aroused, I wanted to see Zora's sant. In the often-recited and much loved ode of Sukhmani, which translates to 'mind's bliss', there are seven stanzas which describe the benefits of being in the company of such sants (sadhs). Another seven stanzas describe the ill-effects of causing pain to a sant or sadh.

One morning Zora turned up in Jatpur unannounced.

"Uncle, are you still interested in meeting Santji?"

"Yes." I replied, curious to see the occult powers of Zora's sant. In a Maruti driven by a young Sikh, we headed for the dera (monastery) of Lopo, about thirty kilometres from Jatpur. Zora continued singing the praises of the current sant, fourth in succession. I expected to see a humble mud house like the dera in front of my old house in Jatpur where as a child I used to beat the cymbals with a wooden mallet during evening worship. The car came to a halt in front of a huge concrete building, still incomplete, looking bizarre amidst wheat fields. The building would have to be worth millions. The monastery-temple had two mausoleums containing the ashes of the first two sants – the great-grandfather and the grandfather.

"The palanquin with the Book-guru presiding over the first mausoleum is gilded with a ton of pure gold," Zora said, proudly adopting the role of a guide. "All these buildings were constructed in three decades. Isn't that amazing?"

If Zora was expecting to see me impressed about this, he was disappointed. I made no comment. Following others, I made an offering at the monument dedicated to the first sant with a ten-rupee note. Near it, under the same roof, is a simpler monument for the second sant. I reduced my offering to a five-rupee bill. We then walked into an open space covered by a six-metre-high concrete roof some fifty metres long and twenty metres wide, supported by two rows of massive round concrete pillars. At the end is the third incomplete mausoleum of the father. An urn containing his ashes has been placed on a decorated pedestal next to Book-guru to attract offerings. Sensing something seriously amiss, I did not offer any money here. The sant has hijacked the word of Book-guru to exploit the poor, innocent, gullible and superstitious people.

"This, last Santji has clearly instructed that a mausoleum must not be built for him. But we are collecting donations to build one!" Zora declared fervently.

"Why are you disobeying your santji? Are you not insulting him?" I hid my anger.

"All great souls must be remembered. We must keep his memory alive. People want it. Funds are pouring in. I can tell you, even this big building is not large enough to accommodate the devotees who gather here four times a year," Zora asserted.

"What happens during the rest of the year?" I queried.

"He has built over forty schools and a college which is the best in the Punjab," Zora continued.

"Who runs it? Is the college free?"

Zora was quiet - probably he did not know. Later I found out that the sant's family runs the college, an expensive one to study in.

"Now I'll take you to the shed where the sacred cows are. It shelters over five thousand cows. They are fed well and never milked, their calves suckle it all. Can you imagine the sacred work of the holy santji?"

Standing on the flat roof of the cowshed I saw that the enclosure was too small to house that many beasts. Five hundred would be a more realistic number. In any case, the cows looked weak. "There is never any shortage of food for them," continued Zora, blind to the state of the poor cows.

I could not take it any more.

"In Western countries it is not uncommon for one man to own more than five thousand cows" I replied. "He looks after them well. They have enormous udders and produce more than twenty-five kilos of milk per day. That is many times more than even your buffalo."

"I think those are all lies" retorted Zora. "I have heard other people also talk about it."

The current santji was nowhere to be seen. Zora was on a mission today. Torn between his ailing father and his wife, who wanted the father out, Zora had come to his sant for some solution. Bhag's elder brother, Zora's father Amar, was eighty years old. He had managed my land and house for many years in Jatpur. Two acute strokes had left him walking with the support of a frame. Amar had sacrificed everything for his younger son, an alcoholic and drug-addict, hoping that one day he would change. Zora, on the other hand, who had not continued beyond primary school, was an engineering genius. He designed and made prototype automatic machine tools for manufacturing nuts and bolts of all types and shapes.

For many years, Zora had not spoken to his father because he felt that he did not care about him but favoured his younger brother. The sant of Lopo had replaced his father. Yet Zora, feeling guilty for not looking after his invalid father, had expressed to me his desire to serve him in his last days.

Amar, having sorted out his affairs and settled his younger son in a new house, decided to quit Jatpur and accepted Zora's offer. He boarded the bus to Ludhiana with the help of some villagers and arrived at Zora's house trudging with his heavy steel frame and a small bag containing his few clothes and toiletries, showing his astute sense of self-reliance. However, another stroke a month later left him bedridden. Zora could not cope with the situation with his wife nagging him to send Amar back to Jatpur. On the point of breakdown, Zora had come to his sant, his protector. In the car, I reminded Zora of his desire to take care of his father.

While waiting for the sant to show up, Zora took me to the enormous kitchen. Five gigantic steel cauldrons were crudely fixed in the brick floor, perched on the low embankment of a flood channel, dotted with smelly puddles polluted with plastic bags and the discharge from the holy kitchen. The sant was in the dera. We climbed the steps to the first floor and entered the big hall and walked in a line towards the sant, sitting cross-legged on a metre-high pedestal at the far end of the hall with light from the rear window giving the illusion of a halo around him. Everyone placed money as an offering in front of him. I put down a fifty-rupee note. The sant's eyes widened at the large amount I had placed at his feet, interrupting his discourse momentarily.

I sat down at the back with a view of the whole assembly. The sant picked up a ten-rupee note and rolled it round his finger as if trying to hide his nervousness. I looked out of place in the company of about twenty of his followers and sycophants. My presence distracted him, and he kept looking at me shiftily. He leaned towards Zora and asked him in a low voice who he had brought with him. Satisfied, he addressed a young couple standing in front of him with joined hands. He assured them that their wish would be fulfilled and they would have a child. An elderly lady stood up and handed him a bundle of notes, some three thousand, and begged his holiness to do a reading of Book-guru for her. Seeing the bundle, he called one of his assistants to handle the request. Then he turned to Zora and asked if I needed something. I saw Zora's finger pointing towards himself. The sant's advice to Zora regarding his father was the same as mine. But the words from the sant's mouth were better than those of my simple self.

Zora stood up and I followed him to the exit where a police Jeep was parked, flanked by two stocky turbanned policemen. Police in a holy place!

I needed to go to the toilet. It was not easy to find a urinal in the huge dera complex and in fact there wasn't one. Someone pointed to a small brick outhouse across the dusty road. It was a storehouse, its wall serving as an open-air urinal, foul and messy. The holy sant, with all his amassed wealth, could not sacrifice a tiny fraction of it to provide clean toilets for his followers. I wondered how the thousands who assembled here managed.

When I turned around after relieving myself, I was greeted by a bizarre sight - the sant was running back into the building after talking to the police.

Zora was unperturbed by the incident. Instead, to my amazement, he continued to sing the praises of the man. "The Santji did not go to school, yet he knows everything, he is a treasure of knowledge" he said. "He can perform miracles."

"But that's against the teachings of Book-guru," I interrupted.

"All the gurus have performed miracles to save the world. There's nothing wrong with that. I have seen it with my own eyes. A poor family invited Santji to bless their new house. The Santji took many attendants with him and on the way he met a few others he knew and asked them to join in. When the owner saw the horde, he panicked. He could not see how he was going to offer jalebis (sweet syrup-soaked rings) to so many people. The Santji said, "Don't worry, there are enough for everybody". The jalebis were distributed to all from a basket covered with a cloth. At the end there were still some left. I saw this with my own eyes."

An elderly man accompanying us in the taxi recounted a similar story of the sixth Sikh Guru in the seventeenth century, without realizing that he was equating the sant with the great guru. In Sikh mythology nearly all miraculous stories are related to food, wealth and sons. The poor live on hope, the sant sells that hope.

"Why then does the sant need to collect money when with a flick of his fingers he can make stacks of it and feed the starving millions and eradicate poverty?" I asked.

Zora ignored my question. Nearing Jatpur, he drew my attention to a white building, thirteen storeys high, in the middle of lush wheat fields. "That's the Sikh temple of Jhoreran" he said.

From a distance it looked like the towers of Gomorrah and Sodom depicted in a Hollywood film. A rival sant had set up another redoubtable money-making-machine-temple paid for by the poor.

Back in Jatpur, Bhag asked me, "How was the Lopowala Sant?"

I shrugged my shoulders, angry at the farce played out by these so-called holy men. Bhag saw that I was not impressed.

"We call them saint-thieves. We are totally against them. These sant-families own vast tracts of land, buildings, colleges and schools."

Zora glared at his uncle and took leave, but Bhag continued, "Once a week, a Jeep with loudspeakers passes through our village urging people to give charity to the sant of Lopo and his sacred cows." I shook my head.

"Not long ago the current Lopo sant was punished by the Sikh central authority for malpractices. His face was blackened and he was made to sit on a donkey and paraded through the town of Jagraon. But the shameless man is back. Nothing can stop them. They are extremely cunning and smart. They are in cahoots with the local police and authorities. It's child's play for them to free a criminal from the toughest prison. You know, the Sant's wife operates another similar temple. They have built colleges with money collected from their worshippers and run them as private family businesses. The Sikh central authority in Amritsar has no control over them, and often they support each other."

As far as I can see, the Sikhs are committing the gravest sin by going against the teachings of their own Book-guru. They allow such saint-thieves to trick people and fleece them of their hard-earned money. There are thousands lining up to follow this easy profession and aspiring to become rich.

"I also see that any reason is valid for building a new gurdwara," I said.

"Yes, like the Tahli Sahib commemorating Gobind Singh's short respite in Raikot when he was being chased by the Mogul forces," remarked Bholla.

This magnificent gurdwara is famous more for the legends of Gobind Singh's fairytale miracles and less for the enormity of his mental and physical suffering, resulting from the lost battle and the news of the execution of his two young sons. From here, Gobind Singh trekked southwards, probably to meet the great Mogul, Aurangzeb. The area then was forested, and now there is not a tree in sight. We know very little about his journey, but much about the miracles he performed at each stop, now marked by temples.

"How they could locate the exact spots is a mystery," remarked Bholla.

The following Sunday I visited another gurdwara a few

kilometres from Jatpur. It was impressive, with a dozen two-metre-high pedestals bearing sculptured scenes depicting the brutality inflicted on Sikhs by the Mogul authorities. The temple stands on the edge of a pond where Gobind Singh is said to have bathed. Gobind Singh took several months to reach Nander on the Godavari River in South India, two thousand kilometres away. How many stops and how many miracles occurred is anyone's guess, but I won't be surprised if one day the route is chain-linked with as many temple-milestones.

I have pondered over why the sants have acquired such a powerful religious position. Book-guru is unable to talk to devotees and solve their spiritual and psychological problems or bless them. It demands effort and time to study. Hence, it's easier to go through a mediator who can obtain the blessings from the living Book-guru and provide takeaway solutions. The Saint-thieves have assumed a role that Brahmin priests have been practising for centuries. It goes against their interests to promote the physical and intellectual activity that Book-guru advocates - a healthy mind and body does not require sants.

Bholla, who was now taking charge of my estate in India, had organized a ceremony for the laying of the foundation stone of my new house.

"Whenever we undertake a major project or function, our family tradition is to make an offering of parsad and pray at the gurdwara in Kishangarh," he informed me. "Tomorrow is Sunday. We will go there at six to join the singing of Asa di Var, the ode of the morning."

"We have three gurdwaras in Jatpur, why can't we do it here?" I asked curiously.

"Our family had a special relationship with Sant Kirpal Singh of Kishangarh. Like Sant Isher Singh of Rarewal and Sant Attar Singh, he was a soldier in the British Indian Army. After the war he chose the spiritual path and became a sant. He was one of the few educated persons and spoke English. He was father's close friend. Both learnt and played music together."

I interrupted. "I remember him coming to our house once. I also remember the black car parked in the gurdwara. That was the first time I'd seen one. Its back was covered with a white cloth."

"Yes, how can you remember all those things?" Bhag wondered. "He had a car, I think a Humber. Well, he died of a tumour in his back at the very young age of forty-two. He asked to be operated on without anaesthesia. Before he died, father asked him why. Santji replied: "I'm carrying a heavy debt of living on the charity of people". Bhag shook his head sadly. "Father saw him often surrounded by women to whom he gave a piece of paper with some sort of a mantra written on it. Once father reprimanded him. "Why are you doing that?" he said. "Giving mantras is against your teachings." Kirpal Singh replied "Listen my brother, women are like flies. Give them a bit of sugar and they stay away for a month. The mantra I give them is simply 'satnam waheguru' (Wonderful Guru is truth). They go away satisfied."

I laughed, though I was curious at the good sant's reasoning. One also encounters sants who genuinely serve people by providing help.

It was getting dark. I was hungry. Bhola reminded me, "Uncle, aren't you going to jog this evening"?

"We'll jog together early in the morning. Will you come?" I asked. Everyone laughed. No one has seen Bhola run.

CHAPTER 27

STILL YOUNG

⌒

Shera, Malika's father, was a train guard. During his days off, he would start with a walk to the Railway Asian Club, where he read the week-old English and Indian newspapers, after which he continued to Eldore's European bazaar and then down Grigg Street to the Indian-owned shops catering to white customers. The parallel street with white-owned shops had recently opened doors to all races. In the middle was the common post office.

Shera caught up with local gossip over a cup of tea with the shop owners. On the way back his last stop was at the flour mill, to chat with my father. The mill was near the railway residential quarters where he lived. Standing at the entrance, listening to the deafening noise of pulleys, belts, grinders and rollers, he'd wait for my father to dust off the flour from his turban, beard and clothes. Once he had adjusted the machines to produce a certain type of flour, the black African workers emptied the sacks of grain into the huge, hungry funnels feeding the grinders. Only then would father leave his machines to spare a few minutes with Shera.

A pressing issue was the building of a separate gurdwara open to all. Both were for one united front and lobbied that the existing gurdwara run by the artisan, tarkhan, clan should be open for membership to all castes, especially the farmer-jat clan. The two men were also concerned about our future, as we were finishing high school. There were many proposals coming Malika's way from good families, but for Shera none of the boys were suitable for his daughter. My father was hoping for a suitable girl for me too – one who could keep house, cook and start a normal family. The question about a tarkhan boy marrying a jat girl or vice-versa was a no-go zone. To some extent people still frown on inter-caste marriages, especially when one caste is seen as inferior in the traditional Indian hierarchy.

Shera was instrumental in making me change my mind from joining the Indian Defence Academy in Pune, where I wanted to train as an engineer. "You should do the two-year teachers' training in Nairobi" he said. "There's a shortage of teachers, so getting a job will be easy and you will earn a good government salary. After that you marry and support your father who has burnt his fingers cooking for you all his life." He was expressing the notion of sacrifice in the Punjabi way. I was determined to become an engineer. A number of my classmates, who had performed not as well as I in the Cambridge examination, were getting ready to travel to the UK to train as doctors, which was a more prestigious profession. In order to stop me from joining the Indian army, the elders arranged a number of weekend meetings. One Sunday afternoon I gave in, vacillating between frustration and duty to my father. Then, even before I could enrol at the teacher training college, the elders persuaded me to get engaged to Santi.

Two years later I returned to Eldore with a very good teacher's diploma. Now more confident, I took the bold step to break off my engagement with Santi. It shocked the tightly-knit community, but gave it a lot to gossip about.

Then I met Malika in the penthouse where we declared our love and vowed to get married to each other. But would Shera transgress the jat tradition and give his daughter to a tarkhan?

"My father loves me. He will allow us to marry" stated Malika. I didn't feel so confident.

"Do you know that your father asked me to meet him outside your house last night so that no one could see us? He tried to convince me that what we are doing is not correct. He said he will lose face and no one will want to marry your sisters and brothers because of us."

"I did not know you were out there yesterday," replied Malika, taken aback.

On Monday, she reported sick. Two days later she reported back to school. My heart missed a beat when I saw her, but it instantly turned to shock.

"What happened?" I asked when we were alone in the staffroom. "Your left jaw is blue and swollen."

"I slipped and fell from the steps. Father took me to Dr Price. I've a fractured jaw. So I cannot open my mouth much."

I wanted to hug her, comfort her, because I did not believe her story. "You shouldn't be at school," I said.

Malika's eyes brimmed with tears.

"Tell me the truth."

"I did not fall from the steps, Father hit me."

I was red with rage. How could a man beat a woman? We were talking in hurried tones, afraid that someone might hear. All the teachers had lessons at this time except for us, which gave us half an hour to talk. I gave her a quick hug.

"I have money to buy air tickets to England. I think we should elope soon," I said.

"Father knew we would do something like that. He has taken my passport and withdrawn all the money in my account. I had more than sixteen hundred shillings."

In those days, that was a lot of money – more than we needed to buy two flight tickets to London with change left over.

The next morning Malika passed a note placed in a schoolbook to me. It read: "Come to our house at midday". I biked to the house and ran up the four steps from which Malika was supposed to have fallen. In the room, I was shocked to see my father and Shera. Before I had a chance to greet them, my father lifted his turban from his head and placed it on my feet, pleading with me to give up the idea of marrying Malika. Instinctively I picked it up and placed it back on his head. "What are you doing?" I asked, stunned. The turban represents the honour of a person. There is nothing above that.

"Tell Malika that you don't want to marry her. She will do as you say. You must not go against the tradition. You know very well that you cannot marry her," my father pleaded.

But I knew that Malika was more determined and stronger than I was. She would not give up her sacred vow taken in front of Book-guru.

"Father, Uncle – you have taught us that we are one people. We have worked hard together to get rid of the caste system. We used this argument as a basis for opening up the gurdwara to all castes. For that reason we did not hide anything from you," I pleaded. Silence. We could have heard a pin drop. Shera glared at me.

"We could have eloped. We didn't because we believed in you. We seek your permission and will not do anything unless you approve. Our mission is to set an example and unite the community."

"You are an intelligent young man," smirked Shera. "You have to understand that we cannot mix religion and social customs. Even our gurus and their children did not marry outside their caste. So who are we to go against them? Your father agrees with me. If you really respect us, you will put an end to this relationship."

I found Shera's argument about the gurus foolish because the Sikh way calls for a casteless society. I looked around for Malika. The corrugated-iron sheet, two-room house was built on wooden stilts with floor boards, a veranda in front. Across the small concrete compound were the kitchen, bathroom, store, and a bucket toilet.

The slightest movement in the house was audible. The door of the second room was shut. Was Malika listening in there?

A year earlier, my younger brother married Arti. It was an arranged marriage. Arti's family lived in the neighbourhood. In Punjab, it is unthinkable to marry within the same village. What counted in Eldore, thousands of miles away, was that the parents' villages of origin must be some fifteen kilometres apart, like Arti's family village and ours.

Arti came from a big well-to-do extended family and knew how to run a house well. Knowing that I would soon start earning a handsome salary, my father purchased land, where we built a decent house. Arti made it a real home and for the first time we ate delicious food and didn't have to cook any more. Our lifestyle changed and the year passed in bliss – except for the issue regarding Malika and me.

It was May. Like any other day I came home for lunch. My father arrived at the same time. A man of few words, he hissed, "She has taken some poison to kill herself. What are you going to do now?"

If Malika was going to kill herself over me, so should I. Without thinking or reasoning anything, I ran out of the house, hopped on to my bike and returned to school. I entered the chemistry laboratory and took the glass bottle labelled 'copper sulphate'. I knew it was used to poison dogs and mice. My hand did not flinch as I poured the shining green crystals on to a piece of paper and folding it, placed it in my pocket. After school I returned home, left my bike outside and walked across the dirt road through the African shambas (small cultivated fields) to Stony River some three hundred metres away.

I put half the green crystals in my mouth and drank the water from the river with cupped hands. I hiccoughed a few times before I could swallow. It was more difficult to gulp down the rest, but I managed. I lay down on my back and waited to join my Malika. The wait was short. A violent urge to throw up failed. I had not eaten anything that day. My stomach convulsed violently. I turned on my side, curled up and tucked my head between my knees to calm down. I had assumed that the end would come fast and painlessly. It did not. Instead I had convulsions, but nothing happened. I knew I had failed.

I got up and limped home through the tall savannah grass. An African man ploughing his shamba saw me stumble. Surprised to see an Indian in a smart suit so late in the evening, he asked in Kiswahili, "What's the matter? Are you OK?"

Seeing me fall to the ground, he ran to help me. "Please go to that house across the street and tell the servant that I'm dying," I whispered. I vaguely remember my limp body on the servant's shoulder. Next I heard my father say, "Take him to the hospital and inform the police, I do not want trouble." There was no emotion from him. At the hospital, I threw up into a big metal bowl.

"Committing suicide is a crime," the big Sikh superintendent's steely voice pierced through my ears in the morning. "I'll shut you up in prison. That will teach you to play Romeo. What did you swallow?"

"I took some chooran [powder against indigestion]," I lied.

"Where did you get it?"

"It was in on my windowsill, wrapped in paper."

"Who put it there?"

"We always keep it in the house."

"You wait, I'll have your vomit analysed," said the inspector, not convinced. A few minutes later an orderly entered the room, picked up the bowl and tossed the contents outside the window in the dust. A friend, a local businessman, had bribed the policeman, I learnt later.

Many men from the anti-jat camp came to sympathise with me.

"Inder, we'll help you. You are one of us. The jats will not accept you. Even your family has abandoned you."

A few months earlier these very people - hypocrites - had signed a petition to the Minister of Education requesting the cancellation of the scholarship awarded to me to study in a university. The petition read, "A teacher of bad character, like Inder, must not be allowed to teach our children." Knowing that their petition had been successful, they were thirsting for more drama, pretending to be my friends.

I was furious. "In other communities scholarships are awarded to their young!" I raged. "But you snatched away something that was not even yours. All the children in the class I teach passed their final exam with high grades. It was a first in school history, and you say I'm a bad teacher? Get out or I'll call the police!"

When I returned to school, a colleague took me aside. "Inder, you're intelligent. Our society is treacherous. You dared to confront its loathsome customs and castes. We need more people like you to amend its wrongs."

"So what do you want me to do?"

"You can't fight the system. But at least you tried. Start a new life."

I glared at him for being so audacious.

"You will do brilliantly in life. Our community has helped nobody: it's full of hypocrites. Don't waste your time and energy on rectifying social ills. The time will come for that."

"Malika and I have vowed to marry each other."

"Look, trouble is brewing. I hear the Sikhs – the jats and tarkhans – are ready to kill each other on the issues of the gurdwara and you marrying Malika."

"For me the Sikh community does not exist," I stated bitterly after a moment.

A few days later, Malika and her family left for India. Bitterness, anger and frustration tormented me. By some twist of fate, I was offered a job as an assistant instructor at the Outward Bound Mountaineering Training Camp on the foothills of Mount Kilimanjaro. The army-style training in a remote forest full of wild animals required me to push my limits, both physical and mental, to survive. I could not have found a better treatment for coping with my broken heart. For the first time in the camp's history the entire group of fifty young men reached the summit of Uhuru Peak, the highest point in Africa.

I continued my treatment a few months later by joining a less strenuous expedition to Mount Kenya. On New Year's Day - Malika's birthday - I stood on Point Lenana, five thousand metres above sea level and sent her, telepathically, my good wishes.

My luck took a turn for the better. The Ministry of Education decided to ignore the malicious petition by the Sikh community against me and reinstated my scholarship to study science. A few weeks later, a letter from Cambridge informed me that I had passed the examination in economics, geography and history required for university entrance. After a long time, I found something to be happy about in life.

Professor Loadman, who had been my professor in the teachers' college, was now the chief inspector of schools. He drove four hundred kilometres from Nairobi to Eldore to ensure that I was admitted to Trinity College, University of Dublin. He became my guardian angel.

In August 1959, I took a Britannia turbo-prop to London, from where I boarded a train to Holyhead and then a ferry to Ireland. But Malika's memory travelled with me and remained a powerful motivation.

Now chatting with Malika in California half a century later puts me back on the train I missed. But I am no longer stranded in some barren country; I am a passenger. I have traversed seven decades of life full of excitement, turmoil and happiness. My teenage grandson is my loyal fan. "I have often heard him tell his friends, "My grandpa is the best. He's always doing something and that's why I call him Dada - for dynamic, atomic and grand. He's my biggest inspiration, a superhero, running and cycling at seventy. Five years ago he climbed Kilimanjaro, again."

Richard, my best friend, uses his Germanic logic. "Inder has two ingredients: a healthy mind and a healthy body. He is the living proof of the Roman saying 'mens sana in corpore sano' - a sound mind in a healthy body. That's why he'll keep running marathons, giving us philosophical talks and recounting travellers' tales."

Atima's husband, Yaniss, is a mountain climber and has scaled the Alps countless times. One day he asked me: "You have climbed Kilimanjaro three times. Would you do it again?"

"Why not?" I replied. "It would be fun."

Like a typical Swiss, he took me seriously, and a month later he booked us a flight to Tanzania. I was approaching sixty-six and not quite sure of my capabilities. We climbed from the Moshi side in Tanzania with a young guide and two porters. It was a relief to have the porters because on previous trips, all from the Kenyan side, we had carried everything, spending two nights in rock caves and the last one in the little wooden Kibo Hut.

The Tanzanians had set up three campsites with good wooden huts and common cooking facilities. Some fifteen thousand climbers start every year, but only half reach the top. Meeting others of my age gave me confidence. It's not the climbing that breaks people down but the fast rate of ascent to a high altitude. Many wrongly assume that it's just a tough walk on a well-trodden track.

We opted for the normal programme, with two night stops, reaching Kibo Hut at an altitude of 4730 metres on the third day at about three in the afternoon.

The multi-dormitory hut sits in the saddle between Mawenzi and Kibo, both volcanic peaks. On my previous trips reaching this height, I suffered mountain sickness. The slightest movement triggered a hammer in the brain and I threw up. This time I was fine, but Yaniss was throwing up. While he tried to sleep I walked over the ridge to see the old Kibo hut.

We were sharing the dormitory with a Spanish couple. The husband was a professional cyclist and his wife a marathon runner and both looked extremely fit. There were also two young and very sporty Swiss girls from Grisons.

At six in the evening, the porters served hot soup and everybody sat at the table except Yaniss. He was miserable and sick and said that he would not go any further. The last assault starts at midnight so that climbers reach Gilman's Point, about two hundred metres lower than the summit, to watch the sun rise behind Mawenzi. The extraordinary panoramic view makes one forget the agony of the climb. Those who still have some breath left continue along the rim of the crater to Uhuru Peak. I did not want Yaniss to stay back. This was his first time in Africa and he must not return disappointed. With our guide's help I managed to persuade Yaniss to get out of bed. Head wrapped in his blanket, he said, "Touch my forehead, it's hot. I have a fever."

At that moment, without thinking, I assumed the role of a mountain school instructor, a job I did many years ago. I touched his forehead and said, "Give me your arm. It's cool, you do not have fever. Drink some soup. You'll be all right soon."

The young Spanish woman, when she heard that this was my fourth climb up Kilimanjaro, asked, "Why do you want to climb again? Are you crazy?"

I replied, "I want to know if I'm still young."

She retorted, "There are other ways of finding that out." Everyone laughed.

We took off just before midnight. We had hardly climbed for half an hour when the Spanish cyclist, who had earlier claimed that he never suffered mountain sickness, fainted, and his guide had to carry him down. Yaniss had recovered and took the lead. At five-forty-five in the morning he welcomed me at Gilman's point. Just then my hands froze and I became short of breath. I realized that my anorak was not protecting me from the cold, and my breathing did not improve. I should have worn the heavier ski jacket. After a short walk on the crater rim I decided to give up and was content to come down from the second highest point of Africa.

Yaniss reached the top. When he returned to Kibo Hut his first words were, "Never again." I replied, "You will change your mind when we get home." I had said that on my first climb, but I returned.

CHAPTER 28

MALIKA'S TRAIN

❦

Malika has never spoken to anyone about being taken to India. It took some effort for her to tell me her ordeal for the first time. She said that she had been drugged. She never saw me standing on the railway platform wanting to bid her farewell. She only remembers being woken up in her village in Punjab; so she claims.

Sitting in Roshan's garden in Santa Fe, I asked her, "What happened after you returned from Amritsar with your sick brother? Your father?"

"I told him we went to Ludhiana to see the city."

"And then?"

"I have told you before, my memory is blank and I have no desire to recall anything."

"My boss in the Kenya Water Department was from your village in India" I told Malika. "He knew your father well. He told me about your wedding because he was on leave at that time." Shera had invited the entire village to Malika's wedding. The groom was from a well-to-do farmer family. It was a grand wedding, never seen in the village before.

"Were you happy?" I ask.

Malika goes back in time before her marriage. "The first year, I refused to marry. Then one day, Babuji Uncle from Eldore turned

253

up. I know he was closer to you than to his son. He told me that you were married."

"That was a lie" I said.

Babuji Uncle was a widower like my father, bringing up Nimu his son and his younger sister, who were our contemporaries. Babuji owned land in the European bazaar. They lived in a temporary wooden house little better than a shack propped against the high stone wall of a workshop. He invited my father to build our room and my father added two walls to make a small room next to Babuji's and roofed it with flattened petrol drums.

Babuji was a kind man. He invited many other families who were pressed for money to live in the same compound. Always dressed in a navy blue coat and pants with a silver pocket watch chain looped between his breast pocket and the coat's buttonhole, he treated me like a son. He told me that he was in favour of our marriage, but at the same time he tried to persuade me to give up the idea because he said ours was a passing youthful crush.

"I'm not surprised he lied to you" I said. "Your father must have manipulated him to say so. There was no way for you to verify this. By then I was in Ireland thinking of you. I sent you letters, knowing that they would be intercepted."

"I was mad when I heard that you had got married. My resistance snapped" said Malika. "That's when I accepted the arranged marriage. It was also a question of father's job. He had used his home leave for my sake. Then there was the question of my younger brothers and sisters who had to return to school."

"What a lucky guy, to get a beautiful cultured wife."

"He looked after me well. But he had barely scraped through high school, so we did not have much in common. Anyway, he took me to Assam, near Darjeeling, where he was a foreman on a tea estate. The green countryside and the cool air reminded me of Eldore. The manicured tea plantations looked like the tea estates of Kericho in

Kenya. Often he used to take me on a tractor to see the forest. I was so homesick and still reeling from shock that you had got married." I shook my head.

"However, I held on to my British passport. After a few years we moved to England. Being a qualified teacher I landed a teaching job in a good school in north London. But my husband did not know any trade and could not find a job." Her marriage had been no fairytale.

"With two children, cooking and running the house was very hard on me. Then came the third child. My husband longed to return to India. There he could live without doing anything. So he left me alone. At the point of breakdown, I joined him in the village. It was a big mistake. There was nothing in the village for us to do and the children kept falling sick. In those days there were no clinics in the small villages. I decided to return to England. I lived alone with the children."

"Was your father near you?"

"Yes, they had also migrated to England. He was supportive but there was nothing much he could do to help me. I blamed him for ruining my life at every opportunity. He died of lung cancer. I loved him but never forgave him. Anyway, my grandchildren are a wonderful gift and their love is all I need."

During the two weeks we were together Malika did not ask me about my children or my late wife. Preoccupied with her sickness and the fear of separation from her dear ones, she abruptly changed the subject.

"Every Wednesday, our local gurdwara holds a meditation session. I used to feel so much at peace there, but I have lost interest now. I know in times of adversity people find hope and solace in prayers and gurdwaras, but strangely enough I have not. Maybe it's because once upon a time I had prayed so hard for something that I felt I could not live without it, only to come to realize that not all prayers are answered."

Malika looked at me with tenderness, but none of the affection I was looking for. Women fascinate me. In order to seek their attention I did things out of the ordinary, undertook adventurous trips, and learnt new skills. Above all I travelled to Santa Fe, wanting to hear from Malika's mouth that she still loved me and had prayed to be with me all her life. But she refused to utter the words. I told her my story, even though she did not ask.

"After finishing university I returned to Kenya. Dado told me that you were married and had children, living in England. It was painful listening to her. She never gave me your whereabouts because she was afraid that I might contact you. Thinking of you motivated me to study hard. I wanted to prove my worth to your father and to the narrow-minded Eldore community. My obsession narrowed my vision and deformed my judgement. I knew that after Kenya's independence a lot of the good jobs would be in Nairobi. But I rushed to Eldore. Stupidly I declined the offer to be a college lecturer in Nairobi. Instead I opted to be a teacher at our high school. The Ministry was happy because few wanted to teach in a rural town."

As luck would have it, on the first Sunday I went to the new gurdwara that Malika and I had been against, and saw Malika's father chatting with my father. He looked uncomfortable seeing me well-dressed and earning good money, someone who had wanted to be his son-in-law.

"It's strange" I said. "Every time I go to London I encounter someone who knew us from the Eldore days. They always ask me about you. Nobody believes that we never reconnected."

I told Malika about meeting Lallu, a common friend from our childhood days in Eldore. He and his wife had been friends with Malika and her husband in London.

"Lallu told me about an outing to Blackpool" I said. "He said you never spoke to your husband once. He said, 'You know Inder, if you had appeared at that moment, she would have walked away with you'. That rekindled my desire to meet you. You avoided me for too many decades. Yet you set the wheel of fortune in motion towards our meeting in an enchanting country."

"How?" she asked.

"Two weeks after we chatted over the phone in January, I landed at a training centre in Trieste, Italy. I gave two lectures on telecommunications and disaster preparedness. There I remembered the book EAT-PRAY-LOVE. I read it on the aeroplane. The author, Elizabeth Gilbert, describes her visits to three 'I's': Italy-India-Indonesia. Carrying a heavy bag of personal emotional problems and seeking solutions, she spent four months in each of the three 'I' countries. Her newspaper paid all her expenses. Without realising it, I followed in her footsteps. Like her, I ate a lot of pasta and seafood washed down with champagne and wine. Every morning I tried to burn calories by jogging along the sea shore and skipping breakfast. Eating became my pastime. I was paid to sit in discussions and listen to other lectures most of the time. I thought of you and wished you were with me."

"Now that you have seen me looking like a whale, you would have regretted it if I had turned up," Malika laughed.

I continued, ignoring her jibe at herself.

"Like Elizabeth, I flew to the second 'I', India, in March. She spent four months confined in an undisclosed ashram, barred from the world outside, observing total silence, cleaning floors, chanting Sanskrit verses, meditating and praying, but I just observed how people prayed."

"Elizabeth claims to have attained some sort of spiritual illumination. I didn't have any intention of meditating or fasting. But it happened that I went to temples more often than during my earlier trips. I prayed little but played the dholk [Indian drum] often to accompany the hymn singers in the village gurdwara. I also visited many deras, as well as the Golden Temple in Amritsar and Hindu temples and ashrams. I ate simple vegetarian village food and slimmed down again. Then Elizabeth took off for Indonesia, the third 'I', where she experienced a balanced life of love, sex and bliss. Fastened to her wheel of destiny, I thought about going to Bali to find love. But my wheel of destiny brought me to an 'A' – America. And now here I am with my love trying to shape my destiny." I looked tenderly into her eyes.

"I'm glad you came," she smiled.

Not a word more, she had shut her heart again.

"Life will go on" she said. "I would like to live longer. It's the family that matters, all else is secondary. Temples, meditation, yoga, are our crutches. I use them sometimes. Once upon a time I boarded the train with you and started on a journey of love," she said softly as if in a trance.

"Are you still on it?" I asked.

"My train stops to collect more people. Through the window I see another train going in the opposite direction. It screeches to a stop. I see you in the window of the other train. I stretch my arm towards you and you lean out to hold mine. But then my train rolls away, never to meet you again in this world."

Suddenly she got up and went inside. When she returned a few minutes later, her eyes were red.

Love is timeless and mysterious. In a restricted society, it succumbs to taboos and interdictions. Yet we are powerless under its spell. Romance, on the other hand, is the story of a brief period of happiness. It is usually coupled with death. True love is eternal, beyond human understanding. If love is not the lasting type, is it worth the pain?

CHAPTER 29

MASTER OF NONE

❧

I spent four years in Dublin's Trinity College, probably the happiest in my life. *Trinity News*, the in-house newspaper, featured me. The shortened story read:

> When Inder goes into the remote parts of Ireland he is sometimes besieged by the locals clamouring for autographs, seeing him as a prince or maharaja because of his turban. Being the only student at Trinity wearing a turban makes him the most recognized face around. Although he seems the embodiment of everyone's romantic concept of an Indian, his home is in fact in Eldore, Kenya. Before coming to Trinity he qualified as a teacher and had three years' practical experience. A keen sportsman, he is a qualified mountaineer and has scaled Mt. Kenya and Kilimanjaro. In addition, he is a fine hockey player and athlete. Inder's hobbies include Indian music: he plays several Indian musical instruments and sings.
>
> On a broader scale, Inder is keen on science and technology as well as world affairs and politics. He can also discuss religion without getting worked up, believing that each has something to offer, and has a good knowledge of many religions of the world.
>
> In addition to his degree course he is studying for a post graduate Diploma in Geography and Public Administration. As well as being chairman of the International Affairs Association he works for similar organizations in Dublin, such as the Irish U.N. Students' Association. He

was awarded the Omolulu Trophy for the promotion of understanding between students of all nationalities.

Inder has represented the societies at international student conferences in The Hague and Stockholm, although the badge Irish Delegate pinned to his chest must have come as a surprise to those who were expecting something savouring more of a bog and a brogue, he was nevertheless a great success. In Sweden he was seen on television, and appeared in papers under the heading Exotica. He was invited to be a family father at an International Children's Camp held last summer near Klosters, Switzerland. He feels slightly reserved when meeting people socially for the first time, but anyone who knows him at all well finds him delightful intelligent company. He is not a man to parade across Front Square with a girl on each arm, anything smacking of exhibitionism is totally alien to his nature. However, we believe girls do find him extremely attractive, and when they do the chasing, he is content to let them.

It is largely his exceptional capacity for organization that makes him such an outstanding chairman of The International Affairs Association. In the autumn he will return to Kenya to teach. Concerned about underprivileged people, he is committed to improving their living conditions.

Looking back, I realize that being at university showed me how to embrace life positively. Dublin was a student city. The country was too poor to attract foreign workers. Most of the Asian students, including five turbanned ones, were studying medicine in the Royal College. The Dubliners assumed that every foreigner was a medical student. My friends called me Trinity Singh. For a number of seasons I played field hockey in the Royal College team and no one noticed that I was studying at Trinity. On weekends, we usually met at the pubs off Grafton Street, drinking being the main pastime.

Onewintry Sunday, Pami, a close friend, phoned, "We'll be at O'Brien's at six, are you coming with someone?"

"Only sva lakh is coming," I replied. Metaphorically one full Sikh is equated to one hundred and twenty-five thousand persons, which is sva lakh.

I entered the pub as the five medic friends lifted their whisky glasses and shouted: "Cheers to One two five K", and put them back on the table without taking a sip. Their empty pockets made them stretch drinks for the longest time possible.

"Sit down," Pami said, pulling me down to the thinly-cushioned bench. He caught the attention of a blonde waitress and ordered Irish whisky.

"What's niggling you?" Pami asked.

"Nothing. Why? Do I look different?"

"Yes."

"With my turban I feel I'm from another planet, always unsure what others think of me."

"With your handsome youthful looks, you are a hit with the girls, that's what counts. The other day I saw you with three girls at the front gate. Don't keep them for yourself, introduce me to one of them. There aren't many in our college."

"That's the problem. Some white students are jealous and accuse me of using my turban to attract girls. That is not my fault. I'm split between the real me and the image I project."

"Here is your whisky. Cheers, and stop philosophizing," said Pami.

Pami was also from Kenya, the youngest son of Nairobi's superintendent of police. He had finished school at sixteen. When his parents heard I was going to Dublin, they asked me to take care of their son. Very bright, Pami was the youngest pre-med in the Royal College. I shared a room with him in the Harcourt Street student hostel. He missed his mother very much and was homesick.

The few girls studying medicine were too sophisticated and serious to befriend us. One place where we could meet girls was the

Swiss Chalet dancing hall. However, only those who knew how to dance were allowed to enter. So Pami and I enrolled in Wheelen's dancing school, next to the famous Gaiety Theatre on King's Street where I once watched Orson Welles play Shakespeare's Falstaff.

For our first lesson, we arrived feeling very nervous. Mr Wheelen, the owner and teacher of Wheelen's Dance School, was a short man wearing a moustache and was smartly dressed. He wore a bow tie and pointed black shoes to emphasize the importance of etiquette in dancing. I concentrated on learning to dance while Pami concentrated on the girls, who were attracted to his young face.

After the third lesson, Pami befriended Betty, a very pretty and innocent-looking girl, and soon she was in love with him. Swiss Chalet was one of the few dancing places where turbanned students were allowed. Soon I mastered dancing from slow foxtrot to cha-cha-cha and tango. Rock and jiving were catching on.

Crystal Palace Dancing, off Grafton Street, was more formal. Every time I tried to enter it, no matter how well dressed I was and how white my turban, a hefty guard barred my entry. How a Malaysian turbanned Sikh, a second-year medical student, managed to patronize it was a mystery to me.

Betty started to visit Pami at weekends. The hostel permitted daytime visits on the condition that doors must not be locked. Often Mr Pedesta, the warden, would walk in unannounced. One afternoon he entered my room and saw me with a white band of cloth round my chin knotted on top of my head. It was to keep the beard neat.

Mr Pedesta exclaimed, "I'm sorry, you're not well. I hope your tooth is not too painful. Should I call a dentist?"

"No. Please don't worry. My toothache will be all right," I stuttered. The warden quickly closed the door.

Pami would ask me to stay away when Betty visited him. Once they lost track of time and I walked in. They disengaged hurriedly, their faces red, and Pami placed a hand on his wet pants. Betty wanted to marry Pami, yet he had not even started his medical studies proper. I managed to persuade him to get out of that relationship.

As for me, the memory of Malika shielded me from any long-term relationship. I concentrated on studies. My first-term geography essay on 'Climate and man' drew the attention of Professor Houghton, head of the department.

"I expect such work from a final-year honours student" he said. "Where did you get all these references?" he was looking very impressed at my paper.

"I'm a certified teacher and I'm here on a teachers' scholarship," I explained to him. "I've covered most of these topics in the teachers' college and I know where to look for the information."

"I see. Recently we started an honours programme in geography. Wouldn't you like to change to honours?"

"My government wants me to do a general degree so that I can teach more than one subject. There is an acute shortage of teachers in Kenya."

"I understand. We have a postgraduate two-year diploma course for Irish geography teachers who have obtained only a general degree. I would be glad to admit you to the course. Look at this course programme, see if it interests you. Three teachers have enrolled. The third and fourth-year honours lectures cover most of this course. You will have to attend them besides your normal degree course. Think about it and let me know," he said encouragingly.

The next day I enrolled. Before the end of second year, I had attended all the geography lectures. I sacrificed my summer holidays to prepare for the six exam papers, studying in the college library most of the time.

In the middle of a lecture Prof. Houghton entered the hall, excused himself for interrupting and handed me a large envelope. My girlfriend, Hilary, was sitting next to me. Placing the envelope across our laps, we quietly pulled out the big Postgraduate Diploma in Geography. I had not seen anything like this before. Hilary pinched me. I was elated. My confidence shot up. From then on, I wanted to exploit my potential fully. I dreamed of projects to correct the wrongs of the world.

I did not let my emotional lacuna, rooted in my insecure childhood, motherless and almost fatherless, become an excuse for not doing anything. I moved to a comfortable room on the campus facing the much-photographed Trinity bell tower. I learned to comply with centuries-old campus traditions, including wearing black gowns to attend lectures and entering the Commons for meals. I made many friends. I bought a used Fiat 600 that took me across Europe to Greece that summer. In addition to the BA and Postgraduate Diploma in Geography, I obtained a Diploma in Public Administration. My supervisor-tutor found me a most intelligent and hardworking student. In addition to studying, I took an active part in sports and debates. I was popular among my fellow students and well liked by lecturers, who remember me as an outstanding undergraduate who made his mark in many fields.

But in my old age, I regret that I have been a jack of all trades and master of none. Why didn't I specialise in some branch of medicine or engineering or genetics and researched into the very roots of nature? I would have loved to be a university professor or a specialist in something. I feel that I lived for the instant. I did not navigate my life skilfully. I let it drift in the sea of circumstances and social trivialities. Often remorse and a sense of worthlessness set in. Yet success and happiness have always awaited me.

CHAPTER 30

GOD'S COMPETENCE

∽

I was surrounded by eight women singing devotional songs with me on a Sunday afternoon in November. Their pious enthusiasm was reviving the practice of celebrating Guru Nanak's birthday after a break of almost two decades. Sitting like Lord Krishna among his milkmaids I played the tabla and the harmonium, but unlike Krishna there was no dancing, no bathing naked in the pond and no running away with the maidens' clothes.

Simran, the lead lady, announced the programme. "Inder, you sing two songs. You do not need to practise because you already know them."

"No, I much prefer to present a short talk in the form of a dialogue about Nanak."

Simran remarked, "Everyone knows about Nanak, let's stick to singing."

"A day before the function Simran phoned to tell me that I should present the dialogue. The text was ready, but nobody had practised it with me. An hour before the start of the function, I managed to persuade my daughter Atima to play the role of an inquisitive young person. She was playing the harmonium as well during the function. I knew she would do a good job. She has played many roles in a number of plays. She agreed reluctantly."

We launched the dialogue after the hymn singing. It went like this.

Me: This morning we have reverently recited and listened to Nanak's Japu. It is the first poem in Book-guru. I have often asked myself why I recite it. Is it a prayer? On closer examination, I found that there is no prayer in any of Japu's thirty-eight songs. What is it then? I'll tell you. Japu, is Meditation. It contains Nanak's thinking and ideas. So Nanak's Japu does not mean meditating with closed eyes or repetitious recitations, at least in this case. Nanak wrote his many thoughts in beautiful songs in simple language that illiterate people could learn by singing. For example, in Arbad narbad dhundhukara, Atima will recite two couplets from page 1035 of Adi Granth in English.

Atima:

Through uncountable ages,
Complete darkness pervaded over utter emptiness,
There were no worlds, no skies.
The infinite Will alone reigned.
There was neither day nor night, nor sun nor moon,
But only a multidimensional Force,
Forming a perpetual, unfathomable flow in unstoppable trance.

Me: In this song Nanak describes how the universe and our Earth in it came into being. This idea is similar to the Big Bang that CERN in Geneva is working on. Note the words 'unstoppable' and 'flow'. Nanak often sings this idea even more simply: *tu daryao sabh tujh he mahen.*

Atima: You are the River and everything is in you. Why does he say 'tu', 'you', all the time and not God?

Me: Because he has defined the nature of that River in the introduction to Japu: Ek onkar, sat nam... that everyone knows.

In this basic definition, Nanak has not used names like Brahma, Bhagwan, Ishvar, Krishna or Ram. Why? The reason is: names do not convey the image of the dynamic, unstoppable flow of the River. Nanak wrote the whole Japu to answer one question: *kiv sachyara hoeyai*? How can one become a knower of the truth and how can one break and pass through the wall of maya? He starts his answer in the next line: *Hukam rzai chalna Nanak likhya nal*.

Atima: Abide by His order, all information (that is in the Flow) is also in you.(Pause). Doesn't it mean: know the River and its Flow?

Me:Yes it does, Nanak expresses the flow of the River as a Force and often as Guru. As you know, Guru means: anyone or anything that gives light and removes darkness. The following six songs describe the nature and dynamics of the Force or Guru and the information it carries. Nanak calls it Nam, literally 'Name'. '*Jeta keeta teta nao, bin navai nahin ko thao.*'

Atima: As much as He has created that much is Nam, there is no place without Nam.

Me: Here comes my second question: In that case what is Nam japna, meditating on Nam? *Thapya na jae kita na hoe…*

Atima: It cannot be installed like an idol, nor can man shape its likeness.

Me: *Gurmukh nadn …*

Atima: Following the Guru is inner music, following the Guru is the highest all-pervading knowledge. The Guru is Siva, Vishnu, Brahma and the mother goddess.

Me: Nanak places all these gods inside the Force, the flow of the River, the Guru. (Pause)

The following four songs give us practical advice. By listening to and understanding Nam the disciple becomes the master, gets access to the vast store of knowledge, yoga, all the secrets of the body and mind, divine wisdom and bliss. Bathing in the joy of Nam is to bathe in holy places. Having understood Nam, we have to accept and believe in Nam. The next five songs describe what happens if we do so. The next eighteen songs define qualities of the Force or Guru and of Nam and also futile rituals and traditions. *Asankh jap asankh bhau* …

Atima: There are countless prayers and worships.

Me: *Munda santokh saram pat jhol dhayn ki kere bhibhut.*

Atima: O yogi, make contentment your earrings, modesty your begging bag, meditation your ashes.

Me: *Asan loe loe bhandar…*

Atima: The Force or Guru is everywhere and his treasure houses are in all places. Obviously Nanak is referring to Nature that surrounds us, without which we cannot survive.

Me: *Karmi karm hoe vichar…*

Atima: We are judged by our deeds and actions.

Me: Having described our moral duties or dharma, in the next three songs Nanak describes the importance of knowledge, gyan. Gyan khand mai gyan parchand, *tithai naad binod kod anand.*

Atima: Gyan allows us to hear heavenly music leading to enormous joy and beauty.

Me: *Tithai gharria surt mat man budh.*

Atima: When we reach this stage, we acquire understanding, discernment, and the deepest wisdom.

Me: *Karam khand ki bani jor.*

Atima: At the stage of Grace, we attain supreme spiritual power.

Me: *Tithai sito sita mehma mahe…*

Atima: At this stage we are completely stitched/sewn into His admiration, that is, we merge in the Force, the flow of the River, the Guru.

Me: In the last thirty-eighth song, Nanak summarizes his advice in a beautiful analogy. Some of you might appreciate the pure Punjabi words. Jat pahara…

Atima:

In the furnace of countenance,
Let patience be the goldsmith,

On the anvil of understanding
Strike with the hammer of knowledge,
The fear (of the Force) is the bellows,
Austerities are the fire,
Love is the crucible,
In it melt the nectar of life,
Thus in the mint of truth,
Make the coin of the Word.

Me: This brings me back to my question: Why do I recite Japu? Is it a prayer? Why should I recite Japu? Is it not like reciting daily a book on medicine to become a doctor? I carry Nanak's ideas with me and not his image. I feel that Nanak is not my Guru, but the knowledge he has left behind is my Guru. So, by the same logic Book-guru, the book, is not my guru. My Guru is the knowledge that it contains. Singing Nanak's songs gives me anand - bliss and harmony.

It was a big hit. The Ambassador of India, a Sikh, asked for a copy of the dialogue. "I want to send it to my son in India, he is interested in that sort of approach to Book-guru" he said. "I'll also read the Japu again in that light."

People like Simran have absolute faith in singing and reciting from the Book-guru, but what it says matters little to them. I was happy with Atima. She had made me so proud that evening.

"You played the harmonium very well," Simran complimented her. "I did not know you were also interested in the Almighty. The young nowadays don't care for such things."

I wanted to rattle Simran because she had not been impressed with the dialogue bit.

"Simran, is God really almighty? What if I said God is a weakling, incapable of thinking logically since he created the Universe? Did He really create all that?"

"Be careful what you say. You might lose your tongue and receive a fatwa for blasphemy. You will be hanged from a tree in some Arabian desert."

"There aren't any trees there," I laughed.

"Where there is Allah there has to be a tree."

"Irrigated with petrol."

"You have more than a cracked mind, you're going crazy."

"You know, once I encountered God and asked him: Why did you take billions of years to set up a metabolism in living things so that they could live, love, and proliferate to suffocate themselves with poisonous gases? First He failed to understand me, maybe I did not speak his language as you do. Then I guessed that the world has become too complicated for Him."

"Who are you to judge God's competence?"

"It would have been so easy for Him to make more blue algae to reduce the carbon dioxide and enrich the air with oxygen and block the ozone hole as well."

"You are advising God, do you mean that humans are cleverer than Him?"

"No doubt there, many times. Now listen, it took humans less than three hundred years to accumulate poisonous gases and upset the climate cycle. Humans have pillaged gas and oil reserves that God took millions of years to manufacture. He could not correctly estimate the requirements of His creatures. He has been governing with a debit budget. He does not even remember when he last had a balanced budget," I chuckled.

"I see, you badly need help. If you truly pray from the bottom of your heart God will surely help you," Simran advised.

"You have told me that before. You know, I have asked Him to send me a magic prayer or mantra that would enable us to narrow the widening rift of incompatibility between human beings and Nature. I'm still waiting for His reply."

"Be patient, He will surely send."

"It's already too late."

"Why?"

"I see a catastrophe brewing. The Apocalypse is near. By the time His agents supply Him with intelligence reports His actions will be too weak to be effective."

"I've full faith in Him, He will save us, we deserve to be saved."

"Do we deserve that honour? A big NO, our species is the most destructive. Its removal will be a good riddance and universally beneficial."

"If the worst comes, I'm sure God will organize our migration to another planet."

He has no clue of the intricacies of life on Earth, and you expect God to organize our move to another planet. Forget it."

CHAPTER 31

NO GIRL FOR YOU

I was not even five years old when my mother chose a bride for me. In India, child-marriages have existed for centuries. This outdated custom persists in modern-day India and many a marriage ends in disaster. I was told that when my mother saw a pretty, fair-skinned girl in the village of Rakba, she was smitten by her beauty. I have been told that Mother insisted. "I want to make this girl my daughter-in-law. It does not matter if she is older than my Inder" she is supposed to have said.

Mother fixed a date for betrothing her to me without seeking the advice of the astrologer-cum-pundit. All I can recall is that some men came to our house in Jatpur. One of them placed a silver rupee on my palm. Someone put a cotton scarf on my right shoulder and made me hold the lower end with my left hand to form a pouch. In it someone poured sukkar, raw brown sugar. I shakily balanced the weighty pouch. The men, chuckling at my childish innocence, asked me to distribute the sweet stuff with my right hand. I had no idea what the occasion was. My mother died a few months later.

When I was in high school in Eldore my father mentioned a few times that I was engaged to a girl in India. It implied that after school I would marry her. I ignored him. I did not even know the girl's name.

As a normal young man I was attracted to girls in my class, to some more than others. I did not dare talk to any of them because parents forbade communication between girls and boys. One day my father handed me a letter. "Read it. I think it's from Colonel Vakil." A short text said that the girl I was supposed to marry had done well in school. It was a signal for marriage. I handed the letter back to my father as if it did not concern me.

It was the beginning of 1954 when my father brought another letter from Vakil Uncle. It announced, army style, that the girl had fallen sick and died, giving no further details. Neither I nor my father bothered about this news. We were too far away and had never met her, so there were no broken hearts.

Many years later Vakil Uncle related to me what had happened. One hot summer morning, the girl's mother had asked her to fetch dry dung cakes for the hearth fire. The girl walked to the back yard, where the dung cakes were stacked. The cool of the stacks attract cobras seeking shelter from the scorching summer heat. The girl slid her hand in the stack for the dung cakes, and the cobra struck. Deaths from snakebite are common in villages. No one stocks anti-venom serum. By the time the girl reached the hospital in the nearby town, it was too late.

A motherless childhood did not teach me to be sentimental. Often I felt I was nobody and I did not exist. I craved to prove that I also had feelings, but did not know how. My father was thirty-eight when he lost his wife. I lost the girl I was to marry without seeing her. I wondered if we were cursed.

Vakil Uncle was the only family member who kept some contact with us. When I was about to finish high school he suggested that I should join the National Defence Academy in Pune so that like him, I could acquire a degree in engineering. My father could not afford to send me to a university in England or anywhere else. Kenya did not have a university in those days.

A few days later, I received application forms which I completed on the same day, indicating naval engineering as my field of interest. I knew nothing about oceans other than those in the school atlas and swimming in the shallow sea water at Bamburi Public Beach in Mombasa. I chose to be different, and the idea of going to sea fascinated me. This news spread like wildfire in Eldore.

Every Sunday afternoon four or five of our fathers met at Babuji's house to play cards, drink tea and gossip, sharing news from their villages in the Punjab. The most talkative and amusing was Shera, Malika's father. Often I filled in for a missing adult card player. During weekdays, Babuji lived a hermit's life in the forest forty miles away. He supplied cedar fencing posts hewn from the remains of felled trees to white farmers. He lived in a big cedarwood house. A few years earlier it had belonged to the manager of a big sawmill guilty of sawing up the virgin cedar forest. He moved the sawmill to another cedar forest to continue the crime. The original forest has been replaced with plantations of quick-growing pine tree. Now it is difficult to find cedar in Kenya.

At the end of the war Babuji lost his army job as a clerk in charge of transport. He did not have any other skill. He owned a Bedford truck which he used to transport fencing posts and drive to Eldore on weekends. He spoke English with a colonial army accent. Reading and writing letters for the town's illiterate earned him the title of Babuji. He was everybody's Babuji, much respected and liked. He was the lead reader of Book-guru. He used his organizing skills acquired in the army to assemble young boys on Saturday evenings and lead them to sing hymns in the temple. Under his tutelage, I learnt to play the drums and the harmonium.

One Saturday evening after the hymns at the temple, Babuji asked me to his house. When I entered, I saw a group of seven elders sitting in a circle - the pack of cards on the small tea-table in the middle was absent. I thought I had been invited to play cards.

"Sit down," said Babuji pointing to a stool.

"Well done," Shera congratulated me. "It is important to get good marks in Senior Cambridge. Malika also has good grades."

After a brief silence Shera addressed me again. "What do you want to do now?"

"I am going to India to join the National Defence Academy in Pune to study engineering. I have filled in the application form and will post it tomorrow," I announced proudly assuming that the elders would be equally proud to see me doing what Sikhs are good at, soldiering.

"You know your father does not earn much. He can't pay your expenses" Shera pointed out.

"My uncle has confirmed that all expenses will be covered. I won't have any problem."

"In the army a degree can take many years," Babuji intervened. "It's not like in universities."

"Uncle says that if I study hard I can graduate in three years."

"After that?" Shera quizzed.

"I will become an officer with good prospects of rising to a higher position."

"That means you will stay in India for good," Shera continued. "Have you thought of your father?"

A pause. I did not know what to say.

"You know why your father did not remarry when your mother died?"

"Yes, he told us once. It was proposed that he should marry my mother's younger sister, Bibo. I used to play with her. She is a little older than I am. He declined because he did not want to ruin our lives. He said a stepmother despises other children when she has her own."

My father said nothing.

"You do not want me to study. Is that what you are saying?" I asked him, angry at bringing this on me.

"You have enough education now. Very few have reached that far in this town," Shera replied instead of my father.

"But I want to go to university. I'll study day and night."

Seeing me annoyed, Shera smiled. He placed his hand on my shoulder and said, "We don't have to decide just now. Think about it during the week. Talk to your friends and we can discuss it again next Sunday. We have two weeks before sending your application to Nairobi. Malika has already applied. She wants to be a teacher."

It was he who had decided for her, girls have little say in these matters. Young Dado walked in with a wooden tray loaded with the unbreakable glasses faded with daily cleaning with ash. We did not use washing-up liquid in those days.

Nimu's younger sister placed a plate of savoury titbits and Baring biscuits on the wobbly table in the middle. The subject was closed.

Confused between duty to my father and the desire to study, I was torn – and there was nobody I could turn to for advice. The following Sunday afternoon, I simply announced, "I want to go to India". There was a steely silence.

"There is a need of a woman in the house," Babuji finally spoke. "Anything can happen to your father. He has sacrificed his life for you. Now he needs to rest."

"Yes, you're right," everyone chorused.

I stood up to leave, but Babuji asked me to sit down again. In those days, the elders' authority was absolute. He cleared his throat and continued, "Santi was in your class. You know the family well. Her father likes you. It's an excellent match. She has not passed the exam but she will repeat the year while you are in Nairobi. Your father agrees."

I could not hold back my anger. "I am not going to Nairobi!" I burst out. "I'll stay here and find a job and get married so that you have a woman to run the house. Happy? Is that what you want? For me not to study further?" I was shaking.

My father had not uttered a word.

"Inder, you must become a teacher," said Shera. I glared at him. "It's a noble profession."

"The boy has agreed to marriage," said Babuji. "Let's make a simple ceremony of placing a rupee on your hand. It's not a full betrothal but just to say that you are spoken for."

I felt powerless. Words failed me. I gave in with silence. Babuji immediately sent Nimu to tell the go-between in this match-making affair to alert the girl's family. "Tell them we will be there at four", he said. According to tradition the correct procedure is that the girl's father goes to the boy's residence to place a silver rupee in the boy's hand. The opposite happened here. Anyway the ceremony could not have been accommodated in our small rented room in a corrugated-iron building. There was just space to fit three beds and a table.

I do not recall how everyone travelled the two miles to reach Santi's house. Shera did not come. In less than half an hour I was betrothed to Santi.

I completed the two-year teachers' training with outstanding grades. During that period I did not communicate with Santi. I returned to Eldore and began teaching at the Eldore Asian primary school. Everyone was waiting to celebrate my marriage. Six months later I finally broke the engagement, upsetting the community. A year later the dormant seed of love with Malika flowered. We wanted to marry, but Shera put her on the train to India.

Five years passed. I returned to Eldore after graduating in Ireland. I lived with my younger brother Mohi, his wife Arti and their two young sons. The pressure returned for me to marry. I was hesitant to marry a girl from a family I did not know. I finally accepted the proposal to marry Arti's cousin Jito, eight years younger than me. During the school days I used to spend part of my holidays at their sawmill, where I learned to repair cars and trucks. They were the first

Sikh family in Eldore which had done really well in business and were millionaires. The men drove big American and German cars, wore expensive clothes and owned well-furnished modern houses, one at the sawmill and the other in Eldore. They were the first family in town to own a television, a video camera and a videotape player when others had not even heard of such devices. Their material comfort led me to misjudge. I did not see that their traditional values contradicted the modern lifestyle.

Every Saturday they descended to Eldore from the sawmill. The men attended the Lion's Club dinner and then joined friends at a bar for a couple of whiskies, driving home drunk. On Sundays, everyone went to watch the latest Indian film. Like most families, they were caught up in a culture clash, leaving a schizophrenic impact on all. It takes a few generations to digest and consolidate material and cultural transformation. The 1930s values of a Punjabi village on one side and the attractive westernised life style on the other were confusing for the younger generation. In any case, I was drawn to the family, its friendliness and gentle loving manners, something I had not experienced before.

Malika's memory lingered in my mind. How could I abandon her? The girl I was going to marry had once been my student at primary school. Jito adored sewing, knitting, cooking and sports at the expense of study. Everyone loved her cakes, so artfully decorated. The children called her Cake Aunty. What triggered me to choose her? One morning I looked out of my little office in the high school and saw the profile of a smartly-dressed girl walking on the footpath. It was her. The light fell on her. She was athletic with a firm bosom. That fleeting vision overruled my heart. To the great joy of all, I agreed to marry her.

Twenty-seven happy years of marriage ended on Christmas Eve 1991. The drunk driver of a minivan drove head-on into my car. Jito died on impact; the family curse had repeated itself. My father did not remarry. I did not remarry either. Was it to evade the curse? I did not think of it then.

CHAPTER 32

THE PATH OF
CELESTIAL VISION

⁓

Kashi is Arti's niece. She's forty-six years old. She visited me in Geneva one summer.

"Why did you write that you are in awe of me? Do you see the devil in me?" I asked her, strolling along a trail in the Swiss Alps.

On a June morning I parked the car downstream of the bridge on the Rhône River at Branson just in time to catch the waiting ubiquitous yellow post bus. It slalomed along the riverbank through green vineyards punctuated by sunlit villages and lush forests for half an hour. The road ended in a little village at the foot of a rocky cliff where coffee and croissants primed us for a dizzy climb in a small, shaky cable car. It ferried us up a few hundred metres to the steep rocky ledge overlooking the Rhône, where it makes a sharp bend. Coming from the flats of Winnipeg, Kashi was speechless.

We took the trail into the nature reserve of Les Follatères, signposted with the image of a gentle, wise-looking donkey and marked 'Voie de la vision celeste' (Path of celestial vision).

Kashi got her tongue back. "Now that I have met you I feel ashamed of harbouring a groundless fear" she said. "When I was growing up I was always in awe of you - I had heard so many good things that in my mind I was not only fearful of my own inability to live up to you if I ever met you but what you would think of an awkward shy girl."

"Have you noticed that even at this height it's not cold?" I asked her to draw her attention to nature. This sheltered corner remains relatively warm. As a result one sees hundreds of species of Mediterranean-type plants and flowers, rare insects, birds and reptiles. Flowers bloom in February and climax at the end of spring to the song of nightingales and other birds. A bright sun in a blue sky and a light morning breeze cooled and honed our spirits. Walking downhill, most of the time under the shade of deep green mainly conifer woods, saved my cranky knees and ankles.

"This flower is magnificent. What is it? Kashi asked.

"It's Jupiter, not the celestial body. You see, the sky and the earth merge here," I laughed.

I showed her the viper's bugloss, white cephalanther, wild lettuce and many others that now escape my memory. At every break in the woody cover she rushed to the right to look at a new, stunningly picturesque view of the Rhône valley below, with the bridled river flowing amidst green fields, orchards and vineyards, overlooked opposite by high snow-clad peaks sculpted by deeply-cut hanging valleys, some spouting out glittering waterfalls.

At midday we perched on the promontory and ate our picnic lunch while joyously admiring the view of the Rhône stretching for kilometres in both directions, ignoring the industrial sector of Martigny, rather a blemish on the paradisiacal image.

The last donkey sign guided us out of the woods into open vineyards. The sun which had seemed so soothing a moment earlier now began to scorch us. The trail changed to a grassy path and then a steep dusty track descending to the village of Fully and refreshing drinks. Another country bus took us back to the car.

"What an enchanting walk, like a dream" Kashi recalled. "Those flowers in their innumerable shades of colours varying from van Goghian deep to soothing pastel in all those shapes: stars, bells, loops and strings."

"I hope the angelic walk has cleared your hangup and I'm no more your devil," I laughed.

"It's the way I have grown up. It stems from my mother's insecurity. I guess I'm always envious of others."

"But you have a good life too, travelling around the world, going to conferences, meeting all types of people, three lovely grown-up kids. You can't ask for more." I shook my head. "You're past all that."

"I know, but mother always lives in the past. She's forever telling me how happy she was with my father and how loving and handsome he was."

"I remember that," I confirmed. "People looked at them with envy. They were so happy. Your father's death shocked everyone. There was no one who did not shed a tear. You were born a few weeks later."

"Growing up was not easy" continued Kashi. "I lived with a stepfather who did not care for me and a mother who was always too busy. We lived in semi–poverty in Bradford with little money and the usual problems a dysfunctional family brings. Please don't get me wrong - this is not a sob story, I am well past that. But my mother cannot put aside those two years in Eldore when she was married to my father and she cries often. She talks of the big house, the cars and the beautiful clothes she wore – it was a life of comfort. She made me feel that some day I would be called home, where there was love and security."

"And?" I asked raising an eyebrow.

"But there is another side to it. Growing up was not easy."

"How does Eldore come into it?"

"It's my image of the glamour of the Eldore family - the wealth and brief attention showered by them a few times when some of them came to see me in Bradford."

Kashi became quiet, trying to find words to continue. The silence lingered uncomfortably, until I finally took over.

"Your father and grandparents spent their lives on a farm surrounded by forest, away from Eldore and its social life. I used to go there to learn how to repair car engines."

Silence again. Kashi was lost staring out of the window. I let the silence linger. She finally spoke.

"My father's younger brother visited us in Bradford a number of times when he was at Sussex University. I was ten or eleven years old. Every time he visited, Mum cried a lot. She never told me why."

"My wife, your aunt, was also very keen to meet you and your mother. When we were in London, your uncle took us to Bradford in his car."

"Yes, he owned a car. That impressed me a lot. I began to feel very secure with him. I vaguely remember your visit."

"What I remember most is that I have never felt as cold at night as I did in your house. It was like a fridge," I laughed. "Your mum cried a lot, happy to meet us but also remembering the past."

"Well, like I said, every time Uncle came, Mum cried. But what my uncle did five years later..." Silence again. "Do you remember Uncle and I visited you for a couple of days when I was sixteen?"

I nodded.

"He said he was deeply concerned about me." She took a deep breath.

"Uncle wanted me to meet my grandparents and aunts in Kenya. So he arranged this trip. After staying with you, we flew to Nairobi."

"I remember you were very close to your uncle." The words came out of my mouth before I could stop them.

"I saw that I shared many of my genetic traits with them. I so much wanted to belong to that family. I had the chance of moving to Kenya but I didn't. I feel I missed out on something."

"Look at it this way. If you had stayed in Eldore, you probably would not be the cultured career woman you are today, managing a big educational institution for children. You would have been married off and probably become just a housewife. If you had been a boy things probably would have been different."

"Why do you say that?"

"Don't you know what happened to the dream family?" I asked. "It was a house of cards that crumbled with a puff of wind. Your grandparents died. Your aunts and uncles don't talk to each other. They fight over the inheritance, which is not much. I wouldn't like to see you among them."

"I still can't get over the glamorous image I have of the family - even after..." She did not dare not say what I had already heard. I let Kashi continue.

"I went through a harrowing experience, you cannot imagine. What Uncle did was very wrong. The shame and disgust that followed confused me even further. After a few years, I met my husband-to-be. While we dated it was great, but once we were married it was a lonely experience. He is very quiet and I am a talker."

"In the photos he looks very handsome, a party animal," I said. "I'm sure you have many other friends to talk to. A perfect couple is rare. There has to be some give and take. I believe that a true marriage is of differences and not of similarities. If the couple can accommodate their differences a marriage can be heavenly."

Kashi was with me because her daughter had finished university and was travelling through Europe. She was arriving from Spain. The following day, I took them to see the vineyards of Lavaux and Château de Chillon. In Chamonix I put them in the cable car to Aiguille du Midi to have a close view of Mont Blanc. I loitered in town, recalling Arti's letter full of angst. I did not tell Kashi about it.

"I've never seen anything like this before. It is wonderful up there. You should have come with us," Kashi said in one breath. In the car she continued, "I'm sorry Uncle, for burdening you with my pent-up emotions."

"You have done no sin" I said. "You should not feel ashamed. In spite of all that, you studied and went to university. You have a profession and a talented family. Enjoy them. For your own sake shed the memory and forget that teenage incident, it was not your fault."

"But uncle, that family. I feel I have missed something important in life. I feel dissected."

"A large part is your imagination. I have told you what has happened to the family. The beautiful home you saw no longer exists."

"I feel very lonely," sighed Kashi.

"I want to help you. But I do not know how. I hardly know you."

"Uncle, you have already helped me by listening to me. Just talking to you has calmed me down and I can think logically now."

"Let's toast that," I said, pouring us each a glass of wine at the roadside restaurant.

"Ironically, I feel that my childhood helped strengthen me in many ways. I just needed a shoulder to cry on. I couldn't turn to mother or anyone else. It came down to you. Thank you."

CHAPTER 33

RIVERSIDE WALK

～

Malika, Roshan and I were driving from Santa Fe to Dallas. The landscape was beautiful. "I always thought Texas was dry and barren," I remarked, surprised.

"You've watched too many John Wayne cowboy movies," Malika teased me.

"Texas is much greener than what you see in the cowboy movies," Roshan added.

"Didn't you watch *Dallas* on TV?"

"I did. My eyes were glued to the beautiful women and their deeds and misdeeds."

We were driving through lush green forests interspersed with luxuriant patches of grass, and there was a long way to go. I continued, "It's amazing how a handful of Europeans eliminated the indigenous people and took over this vast land."

"Yes, it's a land of plenty," answered Malika in the back seat.

"No wonder Texans are so spoiled and they have oil," I remarked. "With the skills they brought from the old continent and freedom to operate and exploit these natural resources it was easy for them to industrialise on such a large scale and dominate the world."

"You know that Texas has the highest population of followers of Aga Khan?" Roshan interrupted. "Houston is our capital. My husband has many relatives there. It's very hot and humid and I didn't want to settle there."

My habit of expounding on things took over. "Your people, Ismailies, originated from the Gulf of Kutch in western India where it is hot, arid and humid. You are genetically attracted to settle in similar lands. You will not find many Sikhs in this climate. For them California is more like the Punjab."

"Really?" quipped Malika from the back.

"Yes, really. Look, it took you fourteen years to leave the comfort of California to meet Roshan and three decades to see me," I laughed.

"It's not that," Malika defended herself. "You men never understand. I was busy raising a family."

"That's an excuse. Lots of women raise kids, work and travel," I countered.

"Well, in our society, things are different." Malika was on the defensive. "Nothing has changed, even though the Sikhs have been in America for decades. We continue to live like the villagers in Punjab and remain stuck in tradition. Women have to worry about the house, the children and everything else. Nothing has changed. In many ways our values have become narrower. Pride in the clan overrides everything, an ancient trait reinforced by the right we have acquired in America to exert freedom of association."

One good way to shorten a journey is to start an argument. I turned around to Malika.

"Our Book-guru gives us this right also, but we do not know it," I stated playfully. "You can find all the answers in it on how to lead your life. Sikhs are fortunate to have such a wonderful Book-guru that is not too difficult to understand."

"I wish it was that easy," retorted Malika.

"It is. We have forgotten that its objective is to show us the Sikh way, not to make it an object of worship."

Roshan intervened, "When we lived in Eldore, I thought the Sikhs were the most dynamic people. Although you were a small community, you went to the same gurdwara, organized annual sports day for all Asians and regularly played field hockey and tennis. You built a big sports club while we stuck to business, shopkeeping and making money. What you are talking about?"

"Yes, while your community was making money and had a good leader, each one of us is a sardar. You cannot blame us, because sardar means chief and so we do not accept leaders."

Malika and Roshan burst out laughing. I continued, "Under the leadership of your Imam you built a hospital in Nairobi in the fifties, the biggest in Africa. It is still the best in the region. You started *The Nation,* the most popular newspaper in the region, unbiased and promoting democracy. You still own it. Many governments listen to your Imam. We have left no such legacy other than constructing more gurdwaras. Book-guru is our leader."

"How can Book-guru become a leader?" Malika asked.

"I don't know. One thing is clear; we continue to defy our gurus and Book-guru by turning them into idols."

Malika and Roshan sighed. I wasn't sure whether they wanted me to stop or go on. I took the silence as a sign to continue.

"We should be the spiritual leaders of the world. Instead we carry on with absurd rituals. We are ready to sacrifice our lives to protect religious symbols and forms and have little time for humanity. We do not listen to Book-guru, yet we want the whole world to follow it. Can there be a bigger insult to Book-guru?"

"Hey, we're quite near San Antonio," Roshan interrupted, cutting off my ramble. "Inder, take the map and guide me to our hotel."

Unusually for America, the car was not equipped with a GPS. Holiday Inn is near the city centre. I rolled Malika's suitcase to their room. My door was opposite. I handed my duplicate chip-card to

Roshan. She passed it to Malika and quipped, "This opportunity will not arise again."

I hoped that Malika would cross the corridor to spend the night with me - just to be with me, nothing more. But fear travelled with her. She was afraid that her family and children would come to know of it. She didn't even want them to know that she knew someone by the name of Inder. Roshan could not understand Malika. I think now that Malika has seen me, her fifty-year-old romantic image of me as a handsome young man has faded.

We came out an hour later. The evening sun's reflection was mirrored in the glass panes of the city's skyscrapers. We strolled along the San Antonio River, which flows through the city a few metres below the bustling street level. It attracts thousands of visitors.

Spontaneously, we decided to have a sunset cruise on the river. It's an amazing feeling to sail through a city, passing through locks and watching beautiful pathways on both banks, gurgling waterfalls, and silvery pools where people relaxed. The sun hid behind the tall buildings and the city lights went on. The river looked different with the river walk lamps reflected in it. Soft lighting illuminated every plant, monument and bridge. I felt as if I was in an enchanted fairyland. The picture would have been complete if I could have put my arm around the woman I loved and enjoyed this moment in perfect bliss.

We lingered in the city, enjoying its tranquil atmosphere, and sat at an outdoor café on the river's bank to enjoy a bottle of red wine and a delicious meal. Roshan hugged me, recalling our youthful days in Eldore and our travel in Andalusia. Malika did not show an ounce of jealousy. I held her hand; it was limp. Where had that beautiful woman I fell in love with gone?

Early the next morning I jogged through the sleeping city and saw the sun reflected from the other side of the towering buildings.

After breakfast Malika accompanied me to the pulsating urban village market and enjoyed choosing two embroidered linen dresses that I bought for my granddaughters.

CHAPTER 34

BLUE HORSE

~

Driving back from San Antonio, Roshan stopped at a quaint tea house by a small lake for a cup of tea. It was a warm Sunday afternoon. The waitress brought a trolley of cakes around.

"What's your choice?" Roshan asked.

"Everything looks delicious," I answered.

"Let's order three different things and we'll share," Roshan suggested. "I'll have a chocolate cake."

"And you, Malika?"

"Apple tart with cream."

I went for a plum tart. Roshan excused herself to go to the restroom.

"Now, what were we talking about in the car?" Malika asked.

"You were going to tell me about the procession to celebrate the three hundredth anniversary of the creation of Khalsa."

"Oh yes" she said. "In 1999 thousands of people turned out to watch the Khalsa procession in London. It was fantastic." I was quite surprised to see Malika talk about it with so much enthusiasm.

"The Sikhs were dressed in bright blue and yellow outfits – to portray the Khalsa colours. Some even wore the entire uniform complete with swords and spears in eighteenth century style."

"It must have been something," I remarked.

"Yes, it was unreal," she said.

"You know, a few weeks ago when I was in India, I followed a nagar keertan, a religious procession, in Jatpur. It reminded me of the Hindu Rath Yatra that I saw a few years ago," I told Malika. "A big-eyed deity of the god Jagannath of Puri was loaded on a heavy carved wooden cart which was drawn by many dhoti-clad devotees. In Jatpur, Book-guru was enthroned in a plush well-lit cabin of a luxury Tata coach, richly decorated."

"I have not heard of a nagar keertan procession before," Malika remarked.

"The practice is relatively recent," I replied. "It's an attempt to set up a cultural identity separate from the Hindus. Each gurdwara, usually associated with a particular Sikh clan or caste, organizes its own nagar keertan. I see it primarily as a way to collect money from gullible people."

"You're still at it!" Roshan laughed, back from the restroom. "Don't you have anything better to talk about?"

Malika took a sip of tea and delicately placed the cup in the saucer. I ordered a second round of tea. Malika was quite animated about the Khalsa procession and started to talk once we were back in the car again.

"In England, the processions serve a useful purpose: they build self-confidence in our boys who wear turbans" she said. "You see, they are often bullied and taunted for wearing turbans."

"In that sense, the comical Bollywood movie *Singh is King* has instilled more self-assurance in the Sikh youth than all processions put together," I remarked.

Malika and Roshan let out hearty laughs. "Yes, I agree," replied Malika.

"You know what?" Roshan cut in. "You discussing the procession reminds me of the processions in ancient Egypt headed by the pharaohs representing Ra, the Sun God. I remember a Hollywood movie of Cleopatra where the people fell on their knees with their eyes lowered to offer total submission to the queen."

"Oh, I remember that one," Malika recalled. I continued. "The Sikh tradition comes from the Hindu Rath Yatra. Book-guru disapproves of exhibitionism, because it promotes worshipping the book. Nevertheless, it boosts the Khalsa way. As you know, establishing the Khalsa was the first attempt in modern India to reform the broken-down social and political structure, instil confidence in demoralized people and create an egalitarian society.

"Gobind Singh unfortunately did not live long enough to consolidate what he had started. His revolution attracted the lower sector of the society, mainly peasants, who quickly organized themselves into small armies to fight the tyrannical regional government and defend the people against the invaders from the north. Maharaja Ranjit Singh, the nineteenth century Sikh, was the first and the last great Sikh ruler. Rising from the position of a village chief to the ruler of an empire, he still captures the imagination of many a Sikh. What he gained was lost in less than thirty years. The Khalsa lost its momentum. However its values were used by the smart British. All we are left with are these processions that fulfil the dream of the Sikhs when singing at the end of every prayer: Khalsa will rule."

"You mean these processions express the political aspirations of Sikhs," asked Malika.

"Exactly. They want to be recognized as a separate nation with distinct customs and traditions. To realize that dream, the Sikhs need to replace antiquated traditions with a modern organisation encompassing all types of Sikhs, like Roshan's Ismaili community under the leadership of the Aga Khan. We camouflage our political aspirations with the garb of Sikh spirituality that is in contrast to the teachings of Book-guru, which says:

I have made a pact with the Supreme Lord
All other pacts are for worldly power.

For worldly gains the fools dispute and struggle.
In this Dark Age, five dominant passions cause factions:
Lust, anger, greed, attachment, and self-will.
I am in the Lord's faction,
Who has destroyed all other factions!
False is all love besides that of God
That divides men into warring groups.
The many factions decry and malign each other
And vanity consumes them.
As a man sows, so must he reap!
Nanak has signed a pact with Righteousness
That can conquer the whole world."

"That is beautiful," Roshan gushed.

"I recited this during an inter-religion prayer for peace in the Geneva cathedral."

"Now I understand why Gobind Singh handed the spiritual guruship to Book-guru," said Malika.

"Good!" I exclaimed. "Establishing the Khalsa brotherhood three centuries ago was a social and political necessity. Baptism raised the common person's self esteem. It gave the person the morale and courage to face tyrannical rulers, oppressive domination of the upper castes and the marauding Muslim invaders who descended in hordes from central Asia to loot, plunder and enslave women and children. Those who chose baptism donned the Khalsa uniform and became soldiers. The most important and revolutionary significance of the creation of the Khalsa brotherhood was to change the structure of the caste-ridden society, and distil in people a sentiment of fraternity and social welfare."

"Hmm," murmured Roshan. Malika listened with concentration.

"Gobind tried to consolidate the tithe, a system of taxation levied on Sikhs, to finance the Khalsa army which, guided by the Sikh way of Book-guru, would have evolved into an efficient, transparent administration and regional government."

"I have read that Gobind Singh was so committed to establishing a disciplined government that he had his corrupt representatives arrested and burnt alive because they kept the tithe for personal use despite being warned against it many times. Khalsa's role was to protect the poor and the weak in the community and not to be exploited. This was the time when the rich Hindus and Muslims collaborated with the invaders and the Mogul emperor to overthrow the Sikhs."

"Despite all that," Malika said with pride, "the Sikhs have retained dignity and many moral values. You will not see a Sikh beggar anywhere in the world."

The State of Punjab, from which most Sikhs originate, is one of the richest but also the most corrupt in the country. Up to seventy percent of the state revenue is not spent on the budgeted projects. What we practice is Sikhism, the religion, and not the Sikh way.

"Has the Khalsa force any role in these times?" asked Roshan.

"It has no role and does not exist. Actually, the Khalsa army forms the Sikh regiments of the Indian forces."

"You remind me of an anecdote," Malika laughed. "It spread when we celebrated the Khalsa tercentenary in London. Somebody started a rumour that Gobind Singh was coming to participate in the procession. The old Sikh men of Slough whiling away time on a park bench claimed that they saw the Guru's hawk. It flew ten times around the gurdwara. Then someone claimed he saw the Guru riding his blue horse in the blue sky with the hawk flapping its wings on the finger of his outstretched arm. Another spread the news that the Guru would land in front of the gurdwara at ten in the morning."

Malika took a deep breath and continued.

"A parking space was reserved for the Guru riding the blue horse at the gurdwara. Everyone who heard the news put on his Khalsa uniform and rushed to Slough in cars, trains and hired buses. Some even decided to walk, thinking that the great guru would recognize their devotion to him. They stood dutifully with hands folded while others held their swords upright. Their eyes scanned the sky when a falcon flew across. A shiver of excitement traversed the crowd. At that moment, a thunderous noise which made many hearts shudder. A squeal of screeching tyres pierced the ears. All eyes turned in that direction. Like lightning, a flashy galactic-blue Porsche GT Carrera swung around and came to a perfect halt in the reserved parking place. With arms raised and swords lifted, the menacing crowd howled at the car owner "Remove the car, can't you see this place is reserved? Our great guru's blue horse is expected to land at any moment".

The gull-wing door opened and out stepped a tall and extremely handsome man. He was dressed in a metallic bright blue skin-tight suit and a superb plume adorning a sleek golden turban. He had piercing blue eyes - a superman from outer space. Some people in the crowd saw a bright halo around his head and a celestial blue aura radiating from his body. The beau looked over the gathered and said in a robust electric voice, "I am Gobind Singh". The crowd fell on its knees. Someone tried to shout "Bole so nihal", but his voice failed.

"The great Guru said, 'I am not surprised that you did not recognize me. I know that I have changed. And you guys, I made you like this three hundred years ago and you are still the same, stuck in the past, while the world has gone so far ahead'". Roshan and I had a hearty laugh.

"The Sikh panth (way) has become a rigid religion, authoritarian and idolatrous. Though we have acquired an unprecedented amount of information and knowledge in every field, zealous fanatics do not want to use it to reinterpret the scriptures and make them useful to people in present times. Book-guru is very flexible. It can easily accommodate new knowledge. Yet our preachers continue to believe in the golden age, the Ramraj of the Hindus. The Christians and Muslims are waiting for the day of judgement and resurrection. Each has its own image of the golden age and the chronology of its arrival. How many such forecasts have passed?"

"In a way we have gone backwards," said Malika. "Why don't we do what Book-guru tells us?"

"Your question is not new," I said.

I narrated the story of Moses Maimonides, who lived more than a thousand years ago. He wrote a book called *The Guide of the Perplexed*. He lived in Andalucía in Spain, then ruled by Arabs. In those times Islam was very tolerant and open. He was a Jew but wrote in Arabic. He was a great thinker and master of many sciences. He was the personal physician of the great Sultan of Istanbul, who ruled over most of the Mediterranean countries. In Chapter 1.34 of this book he states: "It is certainly necessary for whoever wishes to achieve human perfection to train himself first in the art of logic, then in the mathematical sciences according to the proper order, then in the natural sciences, and after that in the divine science". A little earlier in the book he wrote: "He who knows how to swim brings up pearls from the bottom of the sea, whereas he who does not know, drowns". He goes on to say, "Not completing such preliminary studies... would lead to all people dying without having known whether there is a deity for the world, or whether there is not". He also says it is difficult for one person to pursue these lengthy studies, or even one branch, and acquire all knowledge before being cut off by death.

"This explains Nanak's point that birla koi janiyai - rare ones will know - and few will reach the goal. Effort is required, few are prepared to put in the effort.

"Maimonides has clearly stated that His favour and wrath, His nearness and remoteness, correspond to the extent of man's knowledge or ignorance. You know how much Book-guru emphasizes the need for acquiring knowledge. Without knowledge the mind remains blocked, says Nanak."

"Where did Nanak get his knowledge? He didn't go to a university."

"There are many individuals who are genetically gifted in one or more aspects of knowledge: mathematics, astronomy, psychology, philosophy, art, logic and the universe in general. They study, observe, reflect, test, discuss, meet people and get deep into nature itself. In fact they become one with nature. Their experience and findings leave an invaluable legacy for the world. Nanak was one such person who studied available ancient writings, travelled over half the world and acquired a tremendous amount of knowledge.

"The world as an element of nature was his guru. Knowledge is all there around us. To access it we normally need a teacher, a professor, a human guru, books, and the internet. Nanak's genius allowed him to learn directly from his surroundings. We have more accurate and more readily-available knowledge and better means of acquiring it than ever before. Yet few are able to understand in the modern context the ideas so simply portrayed in Book-guru.

"I'll illustrate his point with a few examples. Offerings do not bring happiness, says Book-guru. Not even once does the Book-guru seek wealth and material offerings. The gurus had introduced a system of taxation. It was abandoned because the collectors became corrupt. Now the Sikh gurdwaras and preachers have adopted the old Brahman swindle: to become happy and rich you must make offerings.

"Mind, body and wealth are all God's gifts, so Book-guru questions what anyone can offer Him in worship. If we return His gift to Him, how can it be an offering? Sikh preachers have cleverly instilled a fear in the Sikh psyche that bad luck will occur in their present life and the next one if they don't make a donation. The Roman Catholic Church has perfected this scam. With the power of fraudulently-acquired wealth it ruled over the whole of Europe. Tell me, what can I offer to Him? Everything belongs to Him. I should surrender, offer and dedicate all my body and mind to Him, Book-guru guides. The third guru refused Emperor Akbar's donation of several villages. Nanak helped the poor with a part of his earnings. Book-guru collects millions now. What happens to that vast wealth is not transparent. We address Book-guru as maharaja and emperor. Imagine the Raja asking for donations! Why do we give to him? The human mind feels contented when thinking of giving, but the giver asks a thousandfold more in return and expects the world to honour him. According to Book-guru a donation is charity given to a beggar or for helping the hungry, the poor, the needy and the handicapped.

All are thugs: seeking money for religious purposes is tantamount to plundering, taking away what the poor merit."

Roshan said, "I thought it was only the Muslims who have problems because the Holy Koran is subject to various interpretations."

"It's neither the holy books nor God if such a being or thing exists," I replied.

"I guess it's in our genes. All the prophets and gurus have failed to put us on the correct path knowing very well that we are incorrigible," replied Roshan as we drove into Santa Fe.

CHAPTER 35

USE IT OR LOSE IT

～

At sixty-seven I was fitter than ever. I ran my first half marathon – twenty-one kilometres - and was looking forward to many more. That year I did not see a doctor or make any medical claims. I was at the top of the world, ready to run my first full marathon. Then disaster struck.

If you've retired and you're over sixty-five, don't play football with children. They love to be goalkeepers and make you kick penalty shots. I played for an hour, kicking the ball and feeling super good and oh so young. But the exhilarating feeling only lasted till the morning after. When I woke, I was a sight to see. My knees were swollen like melons. Twice during the week the left knee gave away, and each time I collapsed with excruciating pain. It was devastating to think that this could be the end of my new-found running career. You can imagine my chagrin. No more meeting running mates in weekly competitions. No more silent nods and handshakes with all those I recognize at the starting line. No marathons.

"There is nothing I can do to repair the used kneecap cartilage and the damaged inflamed cross ligaments holding it," said the sports doctor, who was also a knee-specialist. "I see a touch of arthritis here and there."

I felt my world almost crumbling around me.

"You have to do something, doctor," I pleaded.

"Look, people run even with such a condition," consoled the doctor. "Keep to even surfaces. Avoid running downhill, cross-country or on packed snow tracks as you did in March. But do not stop moving!"

I was elated when he said that – do not stop moving. If you don't use it, you may lose it. I recalled the seminar I attended on health and retirement. I learned that it's a common belief that the reason for memory loss in old age is the inability of the brain to replace the dying neurons. Dead neurons are replaced only when they are going to be used. In many cases, after retirement the use of the brain is abruptly reduced to such a degree that a few neurons are adequate to meet the reduced need, hence a reduced memory.

Similarly, reduced physical activity means a reduced need for food intake, leading to the shrinking of the stomach, the digestive system and metabolism in general.

In 2005 the first marathon was run in the city streets of Geneva. I enrolled for the event. The first Sunday in May was a beautiful, cool morning. At eight, thousands of runners lurched across the electronically-monitored starting line in front of the United Nations building. The route was lined with cheering spectators. We ran past the railway station, criss-crossed the Rhône River, passed through the city and its suburbs, ran along the lake and through the lakeside parks to the finishing line. I finished 580th. Nobody was really impressed with the result. So this time around, I announced the result a little differently. Clocking in two hours and seven minutes without suffering from cramps, I said that I ranked first among ninety-six. I did not mention the nine hundred and seventy in front. After crossing the finish line I said, never again - but everybody says that and then they are back to the starting line.

Looking at the results on the Internet I noted that the gold medallist in my group was born six years before me. He had finished twenty-five minutes ahead of me and was probably taking his shower at home when I crossed the finishing line. A seventy-six year old was ninth. Four others before me were four to five years older than me.

I still have many years to improve. Why stop now, I said to myself.

I ran my first 7.25 kilometre Escalade race in 1995 when I was fifty-eight. It took me 42.5 minutes at a speed of 10.26 kilometers per hour to complete the distance. I reduced the time to 36.75 minutes in 2003. At that rate of improvement I would have topped the all-time record in 2011 if I had not played football in 2004. Blast!

The Geneva Escalade is not a competition. Everyone runs against himself. There are no referees or umpires. It is so heartwarming to see the crowd on each side of the route clapping and encouraging the runners in the freezing air - below 4°C. In 2003, my family and my Swiss friends were there to encourage me. I heard them shouting "Allez Inder! Allez Inder!"

I saw my friend Allen standing at the Cathedral bend to inform me of the time I had taken so far, which prompted me to run faster. At the end of the race my daughter Atima, who was also running her first ever Escalade with her friends, rushed to hug me and announced that I had beaten my own record by more than a minute. I forgot about the self-imposed torture of running up and down the narrow cobbled streets of the old city three times and was overtaken by sheer joy. My knees improved without medication and continued carrying my weight in two or three half marathons a year and many shorter races.

Many of my colleagues who have returned to their mother countries after retirement pass through Geneva in summer. In 2008 Rudi and Shashi came to see me. Rudi retired as a deputy director in 1992 and lives happily in a vineyard on the shores of Lake Balaton in Hungary. Making wine does not require as many neurons as managing a scientific and technical institute employing a few hundred persons. He asked me, "Do you remember when and where we met the first time?"

"How can I forget that?" I replied. "It was in November 1967 in Kisumu, Kenya, where I was in charge of the regional office of the Lake Victoria Project. You drove in a Ford Zenith from Entebbe with Mr Krishnamoorthy, our dynamic project manager."

"Yes," Rudi said. "It was my third week and I was totally inexperienced in the art of working in Africa. Mr Krishnamoorthy decided to throw me in at the deep end and sent me on a safari to Kenya to survey Kenya's Masaai Mara area and find suitable sites to install meteorological stations."

"A Sudanese assistant accompanied you and the Land Rover driver was Kironga," I added.

"We did not know a word of Swahili and the driver did not speak English."

"You returned two days later with your left hand bandaged. I think you cut it with a panga."

"Yes. That happened in Maasai Mara National Reserve."

Maasai Mara National Reserve is the most famous of the Kenyan wildlife reserves. It's known for the annual migration of wildebeests from the neighbouring Serengeti in Tanzania and its big cats. The short November rains turn it into an enormous mudbath. The vehicle Rudi was in got stuck deep in the black soil. Against the instructions the warden had given at the reserve gate, they came out of the car and were digging under the wheels. Then they heard the lions roar. Apparently they had invaded their watering place.

"We left the car doors open so that we could jump inside if necessary," Rudi continued. "Night comes rather fast there. There was a thunderstorm. We heard a lion roar quite close. We got into the car, hungry and tired. Looking back, our fear was more psychological than about lions. We did not see a single lion, only heard them roar. We chatted about lions before I fell asleep. Nightmares woke me up many times. I asked myself why I had left the safety of Budapest to come to perish miserably in the bush. I was cramped and miserable in the car with the lions roaring around us. I had come to Africa to do scientific work, not for adventure. I had no business with lions, but they might chase me if I stepped out of the car and finish me off. It was really most unfair."

Shashi, always quick of wit, responded, "You were never in danger of being eaten by a lion because animals do not enjoy human flesh - too many toxins. Animals, unlike humans, do not pursue the uneatable."

"I felt that I was being chased when I ran the marathon," I blurted out. The men looked at me with a confused expression.

"It must have been a two-legged one chasing you," Shashi teased.

"At the fourteen kilometre mark I was struggling through the Jardin Anglais when a young woman started to pace with me. We did some yo-yoing for a kilometre but she fell back," I explained. "To save my knees, I looked for flat surfaces, often shifting from the middle of road to the footpath. Wherever I ran I felt someone chasing me – silent soft padding. I did not dare look back in case I got distracted, just like an escaping prey animal. The crowd kept cheering the same name: Muriel. I realised that it was the woman who had been running alongside me. She was the lioness who had been chasing me for an hour, holding back for the kill just before the finishing line. In order to save myself I accelerated to the finishing line and she finished a few steps behind me. I turned round to face her. "Thank you for chasing me, my guardian angel", I said to her. "You made me run faster." Still out of breath, she said, "I thought you might be upset that I was sticking to you. I was worried that you might stop at the last climb near the bridge and that would have killed me." The chaser and the chased - I let you picture it: we made the hottest hug imaginable, two unknowns."

"Here it is not the Masai Mara," Shashi remarked. "Putting me in your shoes and being chased by a lioness in this city is quite amazing. I might have reached that mark too if I were chased by soft padded feet like you. I allow you poetic licence here. But this was not a lioness in Masai Mara. That would have been a multi-pronged strategic hunt with not one but many lionesses, all plotting your demise. The final chase would have been very short, and you would not be talking here. For that, I am glad. Otherwise who else would be describing a marathon run in these terms for us and the rest of the world who have forgotten how to run at all? The chaser and the chased. Fascinating. Hottest hug. Two unknowns? I dare not ask any questions about this. I give you a word of wise advice: do not try this in Africa. If you hear soft padded feet behind you, climb a tree as fast as you can. Running will not save you. But there are no trees in the wild game reserve. Moreover, you are trained for running, not climbing trees. But, lacking trees, what would your next strategy have been? I'm most curious."

In my eighteen years of running in hundreds of races, the official race photographer has never failed to send me my photograph in action. For the photographer, depicting my torture is good business. That torture is nevertheless easier to bear when running in agreeable company. The last time I was photographed running with a girl, we were both wearing red T-shirts and blue shorts as if we belonged to the same team. To show that I was enjoying the summer I sent the photograph to many friends with my best wishes. A girl running by my side gave rise to a lot of comment. Joe wrote from his deckchair on a Caribbean beach, "I envy your physical status. Many thanks for the picture of your beautiful running mate. I wish you both happiness."

Shashi was quick to take the opportunity to laugh at Joe. "Are we to conclude that Inder sent the picture to impress us lesser mortals with his running skills and endurance, or was it to impress even lesser mortals with his running mate? I believe that you, Joe, have been lured into the trap, so to speak. Of course, we need to be, and justifiably are, highly impressed by Inder's marathon efforts. When I attempt accelerating on a treadmill at the gym, I believe that I actually move backwards, such are my stupendous running skills."

Shashi then shot his sting. "Nice picture, and I saw only one. We missed perchance the picture where both Inder and running partner end up in the lake in an embrace!"

Marie, a woman friend from Brittany, emailed, "Now that I know your track companion, I understand why you always run so well and so often."

I tried to cool down the remarks. "My running mate exists only in the picture, which was shot a little more than one kilometre from the finish. I do not know her. It just happened that we were wearing similar colours. I think I managed to overtake her, and after that I never saw her again. But I greedily keep your good wishes."

Shashi emailed back. "Well we are disappointed. On the other hand, we should also be suitably impressed that you overtook the running mate, who looked fit enough to run a hundred miles without tiring. Indeed, we see you are straining a bit for the pass. Are you sure that spurt was not just for the camera, with a coffee soon to follow? We have suspicious minds!"

"Well, I am not disappointed," Joe argued. "I hold on to the original announcement and do not believe in any change of story that Inder is now trying to show. I also agree, Shashi, he does not look like an overtaker at that point in the race. So full marks Inder, go to the top of the class and carry on with otherwise or picture mating!"

Shashi wrote, "I think I managed to overtake her, and... I never saw her again. Note that this was the last kilometre or so of the race, at which stage brain function and cognitive capacity could be subject to question."

Roshan's daughter from Texas wrote – and she's a regular jogger and marathon runner: "The picture appears to show the woman walking while you were gently running. You were making an effort to overtake her and she was slowing down". Then she continued, "I think you run because you like the company of women."

My son, either sitting in front of a slot machine in Las Vegas or lying on his belly at the edge of the Grand Canyon wondering at the river down below snaking between the cliffs, sent just two words, "Nice picture". Surely he meant the girl and not my contorted face. His wife views it differently. "Love it, how come you are always running after women? Or is it the other way round?"

I replied, "Normal men run after women, it is fun! I am one of them. As to the second part of the question, I don't know. If women are attracted to me, I want nothing better."

Another former colleague, a non-runner, overawed by the lady's powerful physique, wondered if her posterior gyrating before my eyes, kilometre after kilometre, had perturbed my concentration or rather encouraged me to run faster.

A runner is a lonely creature among thousands of participants, unless he or she is a member of a team. The only object is the finishing line. A cousin from the Punjab emailed, "Your marathon photo is beautiful. It appears you had a pleasant run in the company of the lady."

The sexual overtones regarding my running mate made me look up the race website. I discovered that the girl is Annick. I beat her by 1:03 minutes, so I did overtake her. Joe and Shashi must forgive me for savouring my satisfaction. I had correctly recalled the event and so still had some strength in reserve, and my cognitive capacity was intact. Without the girl in the picture running beside me, no one would have shown much interest. Sex remains the primary human obsession.

One thing I often miss is that in all these years of running in the city I have not seen any Indian cheering me on or telling me later that he or she had seen me running. My desire to seek the attention of people has not diminished. Running does not appear prominent in the Indian culture. I have failed to impress them. Nevertheless, I regularly meet two Indian women, Anne and Judith, who have been running marathons longer than I have. Obviously by their names they are not Hindu or Sikh. I get much satisfaction discussing our experiences with them. I recall our last encounter on a beautiful September morning. Anne and I lined up with hundreds of others to enrol in the thirty-first fifteen-kilometre cross-country in a village on the city outskirts. Nervously I looked forward to do the annual run through the challenging hills of the Mandement region, the heart of local vintage wines.

Anne, born in Kerala, is thirty-six, looks like a teenager and is always smiling. We conversed in French because she was with Swiss friends.

"Are you going for thirty kilometres?" I asked.

"No, I'm just back from holidays. I'll stick to fifteen. Last month I ran the Sierre-Zinal. I'm still recovering," she replied.

"You look really fit. I should have brought a cord to tie one end around your waist so that you could pull me today" I laughed. "Have you seen Judith?"

"Yes, she is around," replied Anne.

"We are still the only three Indian runners here. I wonder why the others are not interested in running," I remarked. "Do you keep a record of your races?"

"Yes, in my computer."

"Can you email it to me? I'm tempted to do a write-up on our exploits for the benefit of our compatriots. They do not know your achievements or Judith's. I'll circulate it to the Indian Association members."

In 2006, Anne ran the world-famous Sierre-Zinal mountain race. It is one of the foremost challenges a long-distance mountain runner can face. She took off with over seven hundred starters from Sierre at five hundred metres above sea level. She ran up two thousand metres and then down nine hundred metres to the final destination, Zinal, at sixteen hundred metres, thirty-one kilometres away. Anne is one among the eighty thousand runners who have pitted themselves against the mountains since the first race was held over this extraordinary course back in 1974. She completed the run in five hours and seven minutes, and was ranked seventy-sixth out of ninety-two women. She did not expect to see any of her compatriots drive from the cities to cheer her on because they do not even know about the race.

Sierre-Zinal is also called The Race of Five 4000s because the runners can see five mountain peaks culminating higher than 4000 metres.

Standing in front of Anne in the long line I daydreamed: The residents of the Dev-bhumi, the Land of Gods, in the Himalayas have migrated to the Alps. Five celestial mountain devas and devis, gods and goddesses, tired of crowds, pollution, climate warming moved to the Alps, but at a price. They willingly agreed to lower their lofty status by some 2000 metres. They naturalized and assumed new names in the Horn family. Nanda Devi now rises as Weisshorn, the unmarried virgin Kangchenjunga has become Zinalrothorn, Sri Kailash is now Obergabelhorn, and Amarnath proudly stands out as Matterhorn. The fifth, a Chinese called Cho-Oyu, the Turquoise Goddess, got the name of Dent Blanche. Here they felt free from hordes of pilgrims seeking miraculous cures and the cacophony of temple bells and smelly litter. Instead of pilgrims, they encounter healthy walkers of all ages seeking nothing other than to look at and appreciate their beauty. They all cheered Anne whenever she was in view. Then in my reverie I saw the little boy in Orissa running sixty-five kilometres as fast as or faster than the top marathon runners, and my Indian compatriots sweating as they watched him on television.

Suddenly he disappeared. What happened to this supernatural runner? I looked towards the sky. There he was descending to earth as God's latest avatar. I saw hordes waiting for his darshana (sighting) to receive his benediction so that they would be cured of minor and incurable physical and mental ailments.

Anne shook me out of my reverie when I reached the registration table. The horde transformed into my co-runners. I think Indians are easily drawn to the idea of achieving the maximum benefit by making the minimum effort. I find that to be a persistent cultural trait. I was once invited to an Indian dinner party in honour of a visiting expert in mudra vigyan, or the science of fingers.

"You must be out of your mind to start running half marathons at the age of sixty-four," said the finger yogi. "You should stop immediately. Look at me. I was very sick for many years with liver complications. The doctors gave up. I started my own treatment using mudra vigyan. How old do you think I am?" he asked.

"You are not more than sixty."

"I'm sixty-five," he replied with pride. "All you have to do is to twist and turn your fingers in a certain way to solve all your problems. You will feel and stay healthy just by doing the finger exercises."

"At your age I climbed Kilimanjaro, and now you guess my age." I did not wait for his answer.

Many Indian friends, out of concern for me, tell me that according to doctors no other sport or exercise is better than walking. Indian doctors are absolutely right. And smart. They know that their patients have never indulged in exercise other than steering the car. For them even walking can be strenuous. Is there an exercise less than walking? When doctors hear about the rediscovery of mudra vigyan being more potent than any other yoga, they will prescribe it. This vigyan has a major advantage over walking - we can perform complex finger exercises while watching Bollywood movies. There is no need to move any other body part.

Judith is in her fifty-eighth year. She's wiry and fit and radiates pure health. She hails from Mangalore. Despite a touch of grey hair, she looks thirty-five. She has been running races since 1979 and has finished among the top ten many times. She is my inspiration. In Mandement, I was not surprised that she turned a time of one hour and twenty-one minutes, overall thirty-seventh out of eighty-nine women and fourth in her veteran category. I clocked one hour and thirty-nine minutes, three minutes more than the previous year. The lead guy in the group clocked one hour four minutes, which translates into an incredible speed of four minutes per kilometre.

My bionic watch indicated that my heart averaged one hundred and fifty-five beats and used twelve hundred calories. Surely my watch will not detect any energy loss when executing finger twisting as recommended by the Indian yogi.

A month later I saw Anne at the start of the Lausanne Half-Marathon. She ran brilliantly: sixty-fourth out of nine hundred and twenty-one women. I reduced my previous race-time by one minute, and I was two years older.

Since 1995, I have run over one hundred and fifty timed races, ranging between four and twenty-one kilometres, at an average speed of over ten kilometres per hour. Runners do not compare their times with others, but with their own previous record. The one who comes first is about one-third my age and runs at over twice that speed. My biggest expense in this sport is investing in a pair of good running shoes which minimise the shock to my old knees. The beauty is that you can run anywhere, at any time and in all weather conditions.

Recently I was thrilled to meet a young Indian couple, the Murlidhars, who have taken up running. "Congratulations," I said, greeting them with a broad smile at the second meeting. "It's nice to see you again. I see you have improved on last year's time."

"Just a little," said Murlidhar. "We cannot beat you yet."

"You will soon. You are young and have much greater scope for improving than I."

Lesson – never give up.

CHAPTER 36

WHEN THE WALL
CRUMBLED

~

I could not have asked for more in life. I have lived a happy life in a heavenly country with my children and grandchildren. On a hot mid-August Sunday we barbecued chicken and roasted potatoes for lunch in the back garden. The neighbours too were outside enjoying the summer day. The children chased each other on their bikes and the women exchanged the day's news. There was no other man with whom I could gossip.

At nine-thirty it was still sunny. To lighten my belly I decided to burn some calories and took off on my bike towards the lake without choosing a destination. I followed the cool lake breeze away from the city, cycling on the track along the lake road till I reached the next town twelve kilometres away. The sun slid down behind the Jura hills and the lake looked like an immense mirror with the skylight reflecting in it. I was thirsty and realized that I did not have my wallet. But I had a friend in Genthod, a small village sitting on top of the low hill a few minutes away. I rang his doorbell. It frightened the wife and their teenage son, who shouted from the upper window, "Who is it?"

"It's only me, Inder Uncle, not a thief."

"Why have you come?"

"I'm on my bike, I want a drink of water."

"On your bike? At this time?" the mother asked, opening the door.

"I'm sorry to scare you. I won't stay, just a glass of water."

I learned that my friend was on a business trip. After downing two glasses of water, I wished them good night feeling happy and relaxed. I thought of the probability of a Kenya-born Indian, educated in Europe, living in a beautiful country like Switzerland and biking on a track in the middle of the night. The probability, I estimated, was zero. A strange feeling crept into me. Malika wandered into my thoughts. But she almost does not exist for me, I reasoned. That was twelve years before I met her in Santa Fe.

The incessant flame of her memory continued to flicker inside me. I constantly found myself daydreaming about her. Does she think of me as well, I wondered? What would it have been like living with her? My memory had taken refuge behind a brick wall cemented with many distractions after our separation. I had a great job, I trekked in the Alps, ran an American Boy Scout troop, went to the gym regularly, performed in Indian cultural activities and learned new hobbies. I had little time to sit back and brood.

Suddenly I remembered the pain when the wall crumbled on me. Early in 1981, the weather was unusually mild. The snow melted early on the nearby ski runs. I decided we would not go to the ski resort, which was less than an hour's drive away, because crawling through the traffic takes away a big chunk of the fun. So we relaxed at home on Sunday.

I was enjoying a leisurely brunch in the kitchen when the telephone rang. In those days, it was rare to receive calls because phones were too expensive. Cordless phones and cellphones were unheard of. I rushed to the lounge. A man with an English accent spoke softly, "Good morning. I'm sorry for disturbing you. I'm calling from London. My name is Woodruff. Does Mr Inder live there?"

"Yes."

"Did he live in Eldore in Kenya before?"

"Yes, that's me."

"My friend here would like to talk to you."

"Is that Inder of Eldore?" My heart skipped a beat or two. It was a voice I knew from my past.

"It's Malika."

I was stunned. After so many years of silence, I hear her voice. But I was petrified at the same time, afraid that my wife's super-sensitive ears might overhear the conversation. For her, Malika did not exist any more.

"Can you call me in the office tomorrow morning?" I asked and gave my phone number and specified a time.

"Who was it?" my wife asked.

"Someone looking for a job wanted information," I lied. "I told him to call in the morning in the office."

I cannot hide a lie. There had been no reason for me to lie on any previous occasion and my wife looked at me quizzically. Suddenly the wall I had constructed twenty-five years before crumbled around me. My breath got stuck and the blood drained out of me. I felt like I was being carried away in a tornado.

"What's the matter?" my wife asked, concerned.

"Why did he call me here? How did he get our number?" I failed to suppress the fire of my emotions as a volcano erupted inside me. Molten lava engulfed my body. Lightning struck me from a cloudless sky. What happened to this confident self-made man, so used to confronting difficult situations in life? I realized, that was for self preservation and survival. Never before had I come face to face with such an emotional storm.

The following day, my office phone rang. I quickly closed the door and picked up the receiver. It was her. That unforgotten voice.

"How are you?" I stuttered.

"I hope you are not upset by my call." Malika used the plural form of the Punjabi 'you' as a mark of respect.

"I'm stunned," I replied. "I do not know what to say. How are you?"

We exchanged information about our parents, brothers and sisters. I admitted that I thought of her often. I heard her take a deep breath. And then she blew me away. She accused me of letting her down by not following her to India as I had promised.

"You got married soon after I left."

"Who told you that?"

"Babuji from Eldore, when he visited us."

"That is not true. A few months after you took the train I got a government scholarship and flew to a university in Dublin. I spent four years there. If I had known you were in England, surely I would have come to meet you whatever the consequences. No one told me. Dado wrote occasionally, but not a word about you. I got married a year after I returned from university and very reluctantly after Dado told me that you had got married in India. That is the truth."

For the next few days I phoned her from the Post Office cabin and listened to more of her sketchy story. She wanted to meet me. I started to behave strangely and became unusually quiet. I started to sweat. My nervousness turned into a fever. The mental torture began to wear me down until I could not bear it any more. The following Sunday morning, much to my wife's surprise, I took her to a new tea-room a few minutes from our house and told her about the phone calls. At first she was very upset. Then she surprised me completely by sympathising with me. My wife knew Malika, who had been her teacher in primary school. It was my wife who then phoned Malika to tell her we were coming to London. It had been in the pipeline because my father-in-law had recently passed away and we were to attend a memorial for him.

To my further astonishment, my wife fixed a meeting with Malika at Victoria Station. She even bought her a gift. And it was my wife who recognized her immediately at the station. Malika was wearing a light beige trouser suit and had short hair, and still looked very pretty. She walked with the same classy elegance. There was no sign of motherhood.

We shook hands and I felt uneasy. Outside I stopped a cab and we headed for Oxford Street. Malika and my wife were both very composed, while I was in a state of turmoil. I hoped it did not show. It was lunchtime. We entered an expensive restaurant and ordered steak and a bottle of red wine. We talked about family, work, common friends and schooldays.

We then walked across the street to have coffee in a bar. Malika showed us pictures of her three children. My wife needed to go to the washroom, but resisted, because she did not want to leave us alone, even for a moment. She gave Malika the gift before we bade goodbye. After that two-hour meeting with Malika, my wife was more relaxed and the issue of my past affair was never discussed again.

When I met Malika again in Santa Fe twenty-five years later, I did not carry the heavy baggage of an emotional hangover. Being with her for nearly two weeks completed my cycle. All that she asked of me was my shoulder to lean on, and I offered it to her.

CHAPTER 37

FAIRY POOL

∽

At the annual spring Geneva Book Show, the timetable was packed with book-signing, lectures and presentations by the authors. A pretty young women dressed in an orange-pink sari sat behind a stack of books in a stall. I had met her before at a dinner party but I did not know that she was a published writer. Ananda Devi is from Mauritius, the Pearl of Africa. My first contact with Mauritius goes back to my university days in Dublin, where I met students from that island and became good friends with them. Though they were of Indian origin, I was awed by them. They spoke French and English and played calypso music, giving me the impression that Mauritian Indians were culturally more advanced and westernized than their Kenyan counterparts. The French had ruled over them long enough to assimilate them into their culture, something that subsequent British rule could not undo.

I bought Ananda Devi's book *l'Arbre Fouet* (Whipping Tree) which she autographed 'Avec les amités de l'auteur' (with warm wishes from the author). It's a story of a girl tormented by a father who cannot tolerate modern Mauritius. I thought that such fathers existed only in caste-ridden orthodox India. After reading the book I telephoned her to express my appreciation of her literary talent. But I was critical of the heart-rending story based on the passé Hindu customs. A girl has violated her Brahmin caste by loving an untouchable. Her father's revenge is terrible. He ties her to a tree and whips her. The same tree was once used to whip slaves. He then takes her to the middle of a swampy pond with the intention of drowning her. But though crushed and mutilated, she finds courage and pushes him into the pond. She rows away without looking back or listening to his drowning gurgles.

I did not want Westerners to think that this perverse practice is still common among Mauritian Indians. It was dying fast among Kenyans.

Soon after that, destiny took me to Mauritius and I saw the reality. Mauritian Indians on the island live and think the way their ancestors did when they left their land of origin more than a century ago. Ananda Devi had depicted the picture faithfully. I made a mental note to apologize to her if we ever bumped into each other again.

I took the night flight from Paris to Mauritius in mid-June and woke in time to enjoy breakfast while gazing down over the deep blue sea. Landing at Ramgoolam International Airport in the southwest corner of the island, I joined a line of passengers from a British jumbo jet flight. We were jam-packed in the tiny immigration hall and I feared that our weight might sink the island. Before France ceded Mauritius to Britain in 1810, the slaves, mainly of African origin, and Tamil Indians from the former French colony of Pondicherry in India, worked on the sugar plantations. The British abolished the slave trade and replaced the slaves with Indian and Chinese workers shipped in from the east. In one of the ships was Vije Beeharry's grandfather from Bihar. Vije Beeharry is my nephew's father-in-law.

The story as told by Vije is that the English clerk asked his non-English-speaking grandfather, "What's your name?" The Indian, not quite understanding the Englishman's question but guessing that it would be related to his origin, answered "Bihari", implying he was from the province of Bihar. The English clerk, none-too-wise, scribbled Beeharry in the surname column and from then on the family acquired a new surname. This at least showed the origin of the man.

The new arrivals from India were lodged in a house close to the port until they were hired by the white planters. Originally called Coolie Ghat, it has been renamed Aapravasi (immigrants) Ghat. It's a long grey shed divided into small cubicles. Devoid of any distinctive features, it stands on the Port Louis harbour as a reminder of those days. Although the slave trade had been abolished, indentured labourers continued for a long time to be treated like slaves.

On the roadside by the Ghat is the statue of a Hindu woman martyr who had fought for their rights; it is unusual to hear of an Indian woman fighting for human rights in another land so long before the term 'human rights' came into fashion. The shipment of indentured labourers peaked between 1858 and 1859 when more than forty-four thousand men, woman and children arrived from Calcutta, Madras and Bombay. Under the British, the French continued to own most of the island, which measures sixty-eight by forty-five kilometres. Port Louis remains the business and industrial centre. The cool plateau around the picturesque volcanic crater, Trou aux Cerfs, twenty kilometres south of Port Louis, became the white community's residential area of Curepipe.

A fortnight before I landed in Mauritius, Vije Beeharry's daughter Ashi married my nephew Gulu in Delhi. They were now on their honeymoon in Mauritius near Grand Baie and I was there to attend their wedding reception. They came with Suresh, Ashi's friend, to pick me up from the airport. In a few minutes, we were in the town of Quatre Bornes. Vije is the chief inspector of schools and his wife, Mina, is a high-school chemistry teacher. They live in a two-storey house on the hill overlooking the town. Ashi, the eldest daughter, graduated with a Master's degree in English from Delhi University.

Gulu met Ashi in Delhi through his cousin who was her classmate. The encounter led to love, marriage, and the reason for my trip to Mauritius – to represent Gulu's parents.

After treating me to a delicious lunch of vegetable noodles, Vije took me to the local vegetable market. On the way we stopped at his younger brother's house, where I met his mother and his bedridden ninety-year-old father, a second-generation immigrant who had spent his life working on a sugar-cane plantation. Strolling through the shops and the market, I felt as if I was in Nairobi and India at the same time. The buildings and the roads were built in typical English colonial style. Driving on the left side is a British vestige of colonial Africa. The only difference was that all the stallkeepers in the market were Indians and not Africans. A whiff from a row of frying pans aroused my childhood yearning for Indian savouries. The streets were relatively clean with a range of shopping outlets - items sold on the footpath, narrow dukas, one-roomed shops and modern malls. I got a foretaste of the boundless Mauritian hospitality when I phoned friends I knew through my job. Each one insisted that I should spare at least one evening dining with them.

Vije's sister invited us for dinner. Her husband Ramdhaun, a jolly man, laughed at his own jokes based on his job working as a senior customs officer. His pre-knotted tie hung on the door hook over his white uniform.

"Everyone in Europe drinks" he concluded, handing me a glass of whisky. Laughing at his spicy stories, we munched savoury vegetarian titbits. His sister Rita, an equally jovial nursing teacher, joined us and added to her brother's exuberance. I spoke in a mixture of Hindi, French and English, which amused everyone. It was a little difficult to understand Vije and his family when they spoke in Creole–pidgin French mixed with local dialects. But in no time, I felt like one of the family.

I woke up at five the following morning, and had finished reading chapter eleven of The Autobiography of a Yogi when Vije called me for breakfast. "I love cooking," he stated while serving Indian fried vegetable rolls. "I also cook Chinese dishes."

After breakfast we went to the Arya Samaj temple. Arya Samaj is a Hindu reform society founded in India in 1875 by Dayananda, who believed in the infallible authority of the Vedas. Vije was its president. I watched the havan, which is the sacred fire ceremony. There were two parallel havans happening at the same time - one surrounded by women only and the other by men and one woman. After singing Om Shanti, the peace prayer, the secretary welcomed Vije's return from India and congratulated him on his daughter's marriage. A young accountant wearing a white kurta (pyjamas) was invited to give the Sunday morning talk, normally given by Vije. He pointed out the physical differences between the two havan platforms, for example one was smaller than the other. He did not mention the gender difference. He urged the devotees and the management to do things correctly, which meant learning Sanskrit and pronouncing consonants like 'p' correctly. I failed to distinguish the 'p' sounds he made. His message was, go back to the Vedic times.

When we returned home, the family was still asleep. I sneaked out to climb the small hill behind the house, five hundred metres above sea level. The road at the back, fouled with garbage, took me through a sugar-cane plantation to a stony track behind the police shooting range. Soon I was at the top. I was enjoying the panorama pierced by sharp volcanic outcrops amidst the green fields when out of the bushes a man emerged like a phantom, startling me. We exchanged greetings. Doomun was on his Sunday morning walk. He was the deputy director of a government office. Softly spoken, he pointed out the landmarks.

"Not long ago, all the cultivatable land in Mauritius was covered by sugar-cane plantations," he said. "But in the last thirty years, the towns have expanded, replacing a large chunk of the plantations. See the abandoned plantations on the right? We will have houses built there soon."

I accepted his offer to descend with him towards Phoenix. "This is truly a beautiful island," I remarked. "You live in heaven in the one and only speck on the globe governed by people of Indian origin other than India."

Doomun gave a snort. "What you see or have read is not real," he replied. "True, two-thirds of the population are of Indian origin and the Government is headed by one of them. But the real power is still in the hands of a few whites who own the sugar-cane plantations, big supermarkets and the flourishing tourist industry. The deputy prime minister, a white, has been promised that he will succeed the sick prime minister. He is playing the game of multiculturalism by supporting religious and caste groups and cleverly promoting division. The gap between Muslims and Hindus has widened. Cantankerous Hindu sects such as Arya Samaj and Sanatam Dharama are competing for government favours. The first is supposed to reform the society and the second to introduce a purist way of ethics based on natural and eternal law. But nothing happens because no one knows these ideologies. Both are limited to the ritual of worship.

"The caste differences have come to the forefront. Afraid of facing the future, they are seeking solutions to social problems in the long-forgotten Indian past. Severed from their roots generations ago, the Indian, Chinese and African people seem to feel uncomfortable with their new national Mauritian graft. The social insecurity limits the scope for economic expansion. We have failed to open out. You will encounter Asians churning in their own soup."

On the way down, absorbed in Doomun's talk, I lost my bearings.

"Everyone knows everyone here," Doomun comforted me. "I know where Vije lives. I'll take you there"

Walking towards Quatre Bornes, he continued to narrate the socio-political state of the island.

"You see, the Hindu social and religious institutions have only a rudimentary political sense. They are unfit to contribute to the overall management of society through a decision-making process and shaping government policy. Instead of coordinating their efforts nationally, each group hankers after small favours. An elected member of parliament receives little feedback from his electorate because institutions that would unite Hindu political and socio-economic opinion have yet to emerge. Struggle for personal promotion overrides all other considerations."

We reached Vije's house and Doomun bade me goodbye. Vije opened the door, visibly relieved to see me. "I was coming to look for you. I thought you had got lost somewhere" he said. He asked me to join him to attend another havan. A medical doctor had organized it to invoke the gods to bless his new house.

The havan ceremony was ending with the chanting of the peace prayer when we arrived. We sat down on the floor with the other devotees. When the prayer ceremony finished a short while later, we were led to the sacred lunch served under a marquee. There were many types of vegetables, some unknown to me, a variety of sauces, pickles and chutneys, and poories (small deep fried chapattis), served on green banana leaves. It turned out to be a real treat because I was starving. This was followed by a long siesta, after which I was refreshed for the wedding reception. The entire house was astir and buzzed with activity. Vije's younger brother, Puran, turned up in his new BMW 325D to pick up Ashi (who was wearing an exquisite bridal dress), Gulu and me. Puran was the permanent secretary to the deputy prime minister/minister of finance. A police car escorted us to the wedding hall. What an honour!

Ashi and Gulu received more than two hundred guests with handshakes and hugs, filling the decorated hall. They then sat with the family at the table. There was a gigantic bouquet of white lilies adorning it. On behalf of Gulu's parents I made a brief speech of thanks. A couple bearing broad smiles greeted me with a loud 'Sat Sri Akal'. Rajni and Colonel Bhima introduced themselves and were overjoyed to speak Punjabi, for Punjabis are not common on the island. Bhima originates from Ludhiana in India. After a career in the Indian army, he migrated to Mauritius and rose to head the Mauritian army and police.

Early on Monday morning Gulu and I boarded a bus that zigzagged through the villages before we got off at a deserted junction by the bridge over Grande Rivière Noire. We were visiting the National Park of Gorge de la Grande Rivière Noire. I've come to realize one thing – that places with big names are not grand or lofty like the Alps or the Himalayas. There were no signposts. It was beginning to get hot. Against Vije's advice, I had only taken a bottle of water and nothing to eat, expecting to find restaurants on the way. Two farm women confirmed in French that we were on the right track, but they were surprised to see us walking. People drive in to see the park. Gulu was bored, hot and not happy. To distract him, I narrated a story I had read the previous night of a young yogi named Mukunda.

"After a long stay in Benaras, young Yogi Mukunda and his friend Jitendra came to Agra where his elder brother rebuked him for wasting his life. Money first, God can come later, said his brother.

"God first, money is his slave, responded Mukunda. Next day Mukunda's brother sent the boys away to Brindaban, the birthplace of Krishna, with only a one-way rail ticket. He told them that they must not take any money with them, must not beg, must not reveal their predicament, must not go without a meal, must not be stranded there and must return to his house before midnight.

"Mukunda accepted the challenge, although his companion looked apprehensive. In the train Jitendra was famished and saw no sign that God was going to supply their next meal. At one station, two men joined them. They had come to collect two princes who had not turned up. So they invited the two boys to their hermitage.

After considerable reluctance the boys agreed and soon reached the stately hermitage to be welcomed by the motherly Gauri Ma to a royal thirty-course banquet. Jitendra burst into tears with happiness. After eating they stepped into the merciless heat outside, penniless, finding no way of reaching Brindaban. Jitendra had forgotten the good fortune they had just had. They were standing under a tree not knowing what to do when a young man approached them and asked if he could be their guide. Mukunda declined. The young man proclaimed, 'You are my guru, I have often seen you in my meditation and today I saw you standing forsaken under this very tree'. Mukunda gave in. The young man took them in a horse carriage to Lord Krishna's shrines and gave them an offering, which was a bundle of rupee notes. Well, the two boys returned home in Agra before midnight and placed the bundle of notes in the brother's hand."

Gulu gave me an annoyed look as I finished the tale and thumbed down the only car that passed. It was full. We had walked three kilometres and had two more to go when a police car offered to take us to the park's visitor centre. The policeman obtained maps for us and guided us to the hill track. Suddenly, I was hungry, but there was nothing to eat.

Walking along a dry stream, Gulu noticed a tree bearing ripe guavas, of which we ate our fill. I dug out a bar of Swiss chocolate from my backpack for dessert. Soon our track narrowed and branched off in three directions across the stream. I thought it unwise to go to the highest point of the island, which was over eight hundred meters above sea level. To get lost on this micro-part of a micro island would be shameful. Meekly we descended to the centre and looked for transport back to the bus stop. There was no car in sight. At the bridge on Rivière Noire, Gulu took off his shoes and dipped his feet in the cool water. Just then a white van braked noisily to a stop. Out poured a dozen youths with loud music blaring in the van. Two of them rushed to us and showered us with questions in broken Hindi: "Are you from India? Do you know Amitab Bachan? Sharukhan? The probability of getting a ride was almost zero, because the van was packed like a tin of sardines. Yet when I asked them if they would take us to the bus stop, they agreed and we squeezed in. After waving goodbye we entered a mini market run by a Chinese woman assisted by an Indian girl. Coke and potato crisps had never tasted so good, but Gulu was impatient. Waiting for the unpredictable bus was painful. He wished he was with Ashi.

"Can we get a taxi?" he asked the shop owner.

"I've not heard of anyone asking for a taxi here," she laughed, "There is no taxi here, wait for the bus. It will be cheaper."

As we waited for the bus, a young man driving a brand new car stopped when Gulu waved him down.

"How much to Quatre Bornes?" I asked the young driver.

"Three hundred rupees," he replied without batting an eyelid. He was taking advantage of our precarious situation. Deciding not to haggle with him, we got in and sat on the leather rear seat. Gulu's smile widened progressively as we got closer to home. Was Yogi Mukunda watching us? Did Lord Krishna's blessing-hand ensure that my urge for adventure did not spoil Gulu's happiness?

The days were filled with invitations from Beeharry's relatives and friends. Having tea with Puran, he informed me that Mauritius was trying hard to attract the rich of the world to use its offshore banking facility. Suresh and his wife Tara joined us. We all drove to King Dragon, a popular Chinese restaurant, and we resumed our talk. "Our biggest fear is from the rich Moslems supported by funds from abroad and the Hindu weaknesses" said Suresh.

"You are the majority and running the government. Why should you fear?"

"It's difficult to explain," replied Suresh. We closed the discussion until we had finished the meal. Outside, a Chinese girl working in the restaurant had stepped out for a break. I complimented her on the food. Suresh was surprised. "I'm amazed you talked so casually with a Chinese. We don't do that normally. I must get a white beard like you."

"It'll be a few years before you get one. I assure you that my white beard does not make me wiser."

Suresh's remark had revealed all. I did not need to ask any more questions about inter-ethnic issues.

The following day Ashi and Gulu were returning to their nest in Singapore. Vije saw me preparing my rucksack ready to leave the following morning also.

"Bhaiji," he addressed me with the respectful term for an older brother, "Why don't you extend your stay? We have planned to take you on the southwest circuit and we will all go to Ile aux Cerfs on Saturday. Tomorrow Puran will take you to the city."

I agreed. I figured I would not get a better opportunity than this to explore Mauritius. Besides, Vije had already arranged the trip and extending the stay was not a problem. Puran gave me a tour of Port Louis, stopping at St. Mary's Church on the hill to see the panoramic view of the city and port. After showing me the Parliament he returned to his office. I explored the city, enjoying an idyllic walk. The shops opened after nine-thirty. So I strolled along the beautiful waterfront, lined with restaurants and boutiques for tourists, also the meeting point for the old Indian men and women who come to the waterfront to see the crimson sunset over the ocean. Behind the main road, the narrow streets with their small shops reminded me of the shops in the rural towns in India and Nairobi's River Road. I walked through the vegetable market and Chinatown to board a bus to see Pamplemousse Botanical Garden. The noise of the Indian-made Tata buses and the competitive manner in which they are driven took me back to India. The only difference was that that the buses in Mauritius were cleaner and not crowded.

The following morning Vije took me in his Toyota to Curepipe crater, a wooded hole in the centre of a residential area. Looking down from the crater rim, Vije recalled, "I spent my childhood in this town. Often I used to walk to the bottom of the crater to collect firewood."

A dozen kilometres away Vije stopped on a hill overlooking a beautiful blue lake called Grand Bassin, hidden deep in a forest.

"In the early days, while the white men of Curepipe went to work in Port Louis, their women drove in the opposite direction to this lake to swim. The awestruck Indian plantation workers peeped from behind the trees, never having seen anything like this before. Wow! Look at those white fairies from heaven swimming like nymphs, they exclaimed. They had never seen scantily-dressed women swimming in crystal clear water or drying their wings in the sun like fairies. They named the lake 'Purry Talab', Fairy Pool."

I burst out laughing at the thought of those poor Indian men watching the white memsahibs frolicking half-naked in the lake.

"It so happened that Purry Talab took a spin and was renamed Ganga Talab a few years later," Vije continued. "It's now surrounded by temples dedicated to Lord Shiva and Lord Hanuman. The main temple was commissioned by an overtly pious Hindu named Dyal, who was then the head of the armed forces. He used the army's soldiers to build the main temple. As Indian lore demands, a miracle is associated with most sites where temples are built. With this temple, the miracle story is that while digging the foundation, people saw a bright flash of light, which was considered a holy sighting. Hence the temple was upgraded to become the Mauritiuseswarnath Shiv Jyothir Lingum Temple. There are thirteen of these lingum temples and all – except for this one – are in India. The temple is still run by the same family. The other Mauritian Hindus do not like it. This hilly part of the island was used for relaxing and to enjoy nature," Vije recalled sadly.

"The whites were not much better," I said. "They hunted the dodo to extinction."

"That's true. The ebony tree forest has also almost disappeared," replied Vije.

"You should dedicate the three temples that adorn Purry Talab to the dodo," I suggested.

This time it was Vije who laughed. Unlike the Kenya Indians who maintain close contact with the mother land, the Mauritian Hindus have lost contact with India.

"Our people came as labourers and they were illiterate," explains Vije. "The government connived with the plantation owners, who were white, to pay the labourers very little so that it would be extremely difficult for them to return to India. The Indian labourers longed to purify themselves with a dip in the holy Ganges River. They yearned for a jug of Gangajal, Ganges water, to consecrate their prayers in front of the idol of Lord Shiva especially on his birth night, the Shivaratree."

I could see Vije becoming nostalgic. The story of Purry Talab to Ganga Talab rests on a holy man, a Swami, who walked barefoot from the north of the Island to Grand Bassin and sanctified Purry Talab by pouring into it a bottle of water that someone had brought from the Ganges.

"People believe that the lake is now as holy as the Ganges" Vije told me.

"It's become customary for Hindus returning from India to carry water from the Ganges in bottles and ceremonially pour it into the lake, which keeps it pure eternally." During the week before Shivaratree, hundreds of thousands of Hindus come to Ganga Talab to get a jug of holy water.

Vije stopped in a parking area. "Can you believe that the government had to clear the forest to create this huge car park? For fifty-one weeks of the year it stays empty. Only a few learner drivers use it."

We descended to a paved walkway around the pool. A young Hindu couple were kneeling beside it. They tenderly floated a green leaf with a wax lamp lit on it and watched the leaf gently ride the ripples. They then stood up together, eyes closed and holding a small copper pitcher. They tilted it, pouring out the water slowly as if it would continue pouring forever. I photographed them, with their permission. When I came near they placed on my hand a piece of coconut and two bananas. It was the prasad, an offering usually given to the first person encountered after the prayer.

Sitting down on a concrete post I watched them finish the ceremony. Ramsurun and the girl were both twenty-three years old and had recently been betrothed to be married. He was a software expert working in a big company and the girl was looking for a long-term job. They had come to seek blessing from the gods, so that their marriage would be a happy one.

A short drive away was the picturesque Mare aux Vacaoas Reservoir, which at one time supplied water to the whole island. After a quick look at Alexandra Falls and Cascade Chamerel we stopped to see the Terre des Couleurs – the earth of many colours. The evening sun lit up an exposed volcanic hump displaying seven soothing pastel colours ranging from brick red to light purple.

On the shortest day of the year in that hemisphere, I took the bus to Port Louis and from there to Pereybere three kilometres north of the main tourist town of Grand Baie. Vije had booked a comfortable apartment in La Perdrix costing nine dollars. The owner, Nepaul, a wiry retired man, welcomed me and showed me food and drinks stocked as if I was going to spend all my life there.

Just before noon I started walking to Grand Baie. Everyone passing looked at me as if I was crazy to walk. A driver stopped and said, "No pay, I'll take you to Grand Baie". Evidently he wanted company, someone to talk with. He was very happy when he heard me speak Hindi. He pointed at the symbol painted prominently on his forehead proving his devotion to Lord Krishna. He started reciting religious verses and Hindi poetry. His name was Danny and he said he lived in the nearby rural town of Goodlands.

He parked in front of a supermarket and readily accepted an offer of coffee. For an hour he talked about himself and the people and then invited me for dinner at his house. I declined politely.

In Grand Baie, I rented a bicycle and pedalled through the sugar-cane plantations, visiting The Vale, Petit Raffray, and Roche Terre and making a tea stop in Grand Gaube Hotel, which was only one-tenth occupied. European tourists come in summer.

Cycling along the north coast road, which was lined with individual houses from colonial times, I passed through Cap Malheureux, cape of bad luck. The weather can change suddenly and the sea here can become very rough. Ships take shelter here.

The sun was about to set when I returned to my apartment. I ran to the public beach, spread the towel on the ground and sat down, leaning against a coconut tree trunk to watch it sink behind a glorious red horizon. In the morning, I cycled along the West Coast, which was dotted with many hotels. At Ganga Ghat I saw some devotees praying in front of colourful statues to a number of Hindu deities. From Pointe aux Piments I turned eastwards to Triolet, where a thunderstorm soaked me to the skin. Biking through plantations and small villages of Plaine des Papayes and Gowsal, I reached Chateau de Labourdonnais with its tall chimney stack, a remnant of an old sugar mill.

After a quick lunch of noodles at a roadside eating place I continued south-eastwards to Gokoola, Rivière du Rempart, Roches Noires and finally reached my destination, Pointe de Roches Noires on the East Coast. The rocks appear even blacker in the foam of the waves.

I was exhausted. I sat down and watched the wondrous play of the ocean. I listened to the roar of mighty waves breaking their heads against the coral reef a kilometre away. It was time to go. I began to doubt if I would be able to endure the return trip. I wished some bus or pickup would stop and offer to take me back across the island. It was three o'clock. The bike had to be returned before five.

Pedalling back was easier than I thought. The head wind which had confronted me earlier now pushed me northwards to Poudre d'Or and then to Goodlands.

Back in my apartment, Nepaul listened to my adventure. He took out a ripe papaya from the fridge. I relished it. "Now a swim in the warm sea should wash away my fatigue," I said.

"Careful, you are bound to get cramp after that exertion. Don't go into deep water, it is dangerous," he warned me.

The sea-water was cool and I suffered cramp in both legs. Remembering Nepaul, I quickly limped out and sat down against my palm tree. It was nearly five. People were thronging to the beach to watch a solar eclipse. Unfortunately, the clouds obscured this rare event.

A woman leaning against the palm next to me smiled. "I saw you in the bus from Grand Baie a little while ago," she said.

"Yes I returned the bike there."

"From your tee-shirt marked Lausanne Marathon I assumed you must be from Switzerland."

"You are correct. Are you from France?"

"I'm French, but I live in Trois Torrents in Valais."

"That's high up in the Alps. Isn't it just below the ski resort of Portes du Soleil?"

"That's right. Have you skied there?"

"No, I would like to one day. Right now I'm starving. Would you like to dine with me? We can then continue chatting."

"It would be nice, but only if we share the bill."

The following morning, I met Vije as planned at Aapravasi Ghat and drove to Quatre Bornes. Mina and Mridula, their younger daughter, had prepared picnic baskets and bottles of water. We reached Trou d'Eau Douce on the West Coast and boarded a tourist boat which zigzagged between the rocks to avoid the sand bars to reach Touessrok, a luxurious hotel sprawled over the entire green hillside sloping to the beach. The boat sailed past lle aux Cerfs and anchored near a popular public beach where we disembarked. The beach was not crowded and I enjoyed my last day on the island in bliss.

The Beeharrys were the epitome of Mauritian hospitality and I became a part of the family. At the airport bookshop I saw Ananda Devi's recently-published second book, *Pagli* (madwoman), a sequel to her earlier book in which the girl was nicknamed Gungi (dumb). Pagli lives in the village I visited. Like Gungi, she also traverses caste and racial and cultural barriers until her madness librates her. It was the best souvenir I could take from Mauritius. Reading it in the plane took me to the Ganga Talab, the villages I had biked through, waterfalls, lakes, Ile aux Cerfs, sacred havens and Nepaul's apartment. I could imagine Pagli standing in front of her shack in Triolet or Pointe aux Piments.

CHAPTER 38

THE SINS OF GRANTHOPHILES – A DIALOGUE

꩜

- It will be difficult for you to deny that religions have fermented more hatred between the world's peoples than any other human pursuit. Yet religions yell the loudest that they are champions of peace and love.

- That's a signal: the apocalypse is coming.

- Many have passed. Which one do you have in mind? Is it the one Christians are scared of?

- No, Christians have given up on that one.

- What do you mean?

- You have no idea what is happening in the world other than Afghanistan, Iraq and the fraudulent banks. Mahdi is coming.

- Who is Mahdi?

- Mahdi is believed to be the direct spiritual descendent of the Prophet, may God protect him. Under his command, armies will exterminate infidels, non-believers and bad followers and re-establish justice on Earth.

- Do you accept all this B.S.?

- Have you a choice? The worldwide campaign for the jihad has been proclaimed in printed and electronic media. That is going to be the latest face of the Apocalypse.

- I am an atheist, do not drag me into it.

- Sorry, that makes you a prime infidel. Sitting on the sidelines is not accepted: follow or lose your head.

- Are you out of your mind? Governments are not stupid. They know everything. The moment their fingers feel the world's pulse rate rise they inject some remote-controlled explosive medication. The old days are gone, my friend: information on the state of every part of the world is at hand all the time, press-button actions leave no scope for waiting.

- Thousands have taken the oath to join Mahdi's armies. They believe that Allah who has caused droughts, volcanic eruptions, earthquakes and tsunamis has also prepared the ground for the glorious day. Many American Christians also believe that the earthquake and cholera in Haiti are God's punishment.

- That is disinformation. It is not credible. Anyway, the Sikhs accept all religions and so we are not affected. In fact, ours is not even a religion. That's what Book-guru says. However, we have become a religion called Sikhism, equal to or better than Buddhism, Judaism, Islam and Christianity.

- We need a name. Sikhism is a good one.

- Sikhism and the Sikh way are not synonymous. The Sikh way is all-inclusive, looking over all other isms. The universal Sikh way is open to any person of any faith or of no faith to follow it. There are no pre-conditions imposed, no conversion, no baptism, no absurd rituals, symbols, ceremonies and restrictions. Sikhism as religion has become a pain in the neck, as someone has said.

- Now now!

- I do not have to repeat that the Book-guru is clear.

- We do not need a religion.

- Are you sure?

- Why do you think Nanak had proclaimed: There is neither Hindu nor Muslim, only brotherhood of human beings? Surely he did not want to set up another religion, convinced that the world already had too many? They fight each other and divide humankind. All we need is to walk on the righteous path and live in peace. Sorry for being verbose, listen to Nanak himself:

If you look for meaning in life, do not look for it in religions, do not go from one cult to another or from one guru to the next. You can expend all your life or look for eternity and will find nothing but disappointment and disillusionment. Look instead in service to humanity. You will find meaning in your love for other human beings. You can experience God when you help someone who needs your help. The only truth that exists is the love that we have for each other. This is absolute and real. The rest is mirage, fancies of human imagination and fallacies of our own making.

- That's exquisitely explicit.

- Actually, that's the theme of the entire Book-guru. You will not find absurdities in it that one finds in other religious books. We have a treasure in our hands and we cannot see it. Could we be more stupid? Sikhs brand me an atheist for talking like this.

- You mean we have many standards.

- Of course. I may recite the five daily prayers upholding equality of men and women, equality of all people regardless of race, religion, caste, creed and status. Yet as a father, I would kill my daughter if she married outside the clan.

- Has Book-guru failed in its mission?

- We are a stuck-up people. Those who question the way priests manipulate Book-guru stay away from religious institutions. They know that there are no shortcomings in its teachings.

- The problem is with the followers.

- To show that they are modern, the misled followers want to be equal with Christianity and Islam, thus transforming the Sikh way into Sikhism, an inflexible religion.

- Are you not muddying the entire people, throwing the baby out with the bath water?

- I do not have to resort to research to see that the Sikh farmers settled in British Columbia and around Sacramento, the taxi drivers of Los Angles, the bricklayers, shopkeepers, and mechanics of Birmingham, in fact, even the rural people of the Punjab know that they have a great dharma, a remarkable practical way of life. But they do not know that Book-guru talks about a round earth, the Big Bang, many universes, evolution, and even possible life on other planets, all integrated in the form of an eternal flow or flux maintaining a perfect equilibrium. In it, human beings are insignificant.

- I did not know that Book-guru refers to such matters. I can find absurdities by the thousand in what Sikhs practice.

- Have you heard of Bertrand Russell?

- Wasn't he the skinny British philosopher? Young people adored him.

- That's him. Very few know how he glorified the Sikh way: it is capable of guiding humankind before the onslaught of the third world war. If some lucky men survive it, then the Sikh way will be the only means of guiding them. The Sikhs have not brought out into broad daylight the splendid doctrines of this religion. This is their greatest sin and the Sikhs cannot be freed of it.

- What a compliment. How nice of him.

- Other thinkers like Arnold Toynbee, Pearl S. Buck and George Bernard Shaw were of the view that Book-guru's universal message of human brotherhood should be conveyed to the entire world. However, the backward-thinking Sikh institutions are unable to take the message fully, even to the Sikhs.

- Is that why we make so much fuss of Book-guru?

- Yes and no. We are extraordinary Book-guru lovers, Granthophiles.

- That sounds like paedophiles. Careful, the Sikhs might get you for tagging them with such names. Don't you think it is a question of our absolute faith in it?

- We suffer from a dysfunction, not acting upon the teachings of Book-guru which we love so deeply. Having got rid of the idols and images that are pertinent in other religions, we found ourselves at a loose end with nothing tangible to hold on to. We needed a physical image. Book-guru served the purpose. Earlier, the Muslims had replaced images with a colossal cube of black granite, and aspire to go round it once in their life.

- Many Christians are bibliomancers with total faith in the Bible, and believe that just reading it or any part of it randomly, without even understanding it, can solve all problems and enlighten them.

- I call our love of Book-guru, Adi Granth, Granthophilia. We love it more than we love a living guru. No one can beat us. Unlike the Bible and the Koran, Book-guru is a living embodiment of the gurus. It's a person, not an ordinary person but our Perfect Emperor, a Maharaja, holding court like a Mogul emperor. At the same time, it's our prisoner.

- A prisoner?

- Yes. Once I entered a well-known London gurdwara to pay my respects to Book-guru. I confronted eight cells, actually cubicles each with a living Book-guru enthroned on a well-cushioned mini-bed exquisitely adorned with precious silks studded with stars twinkling in brilliant lights. I was confused. I bowed down and rubbed my nose in front of each cell. Naturally, no prisoner would give up such comfort. A turbanned and bearded man guards each prisoner. He has a white muslin cloth wrapped round the lower half of his face, I believe to hide his identity. He talks continuously to Book-guru. No one outside can hear what he is saying. Once I used to be a guardian as well, but not shut in a cell.

- You don't have to twist things, they were performing eight uninterrupted readings.

- When I straightened up in front of the eighth cubicle, I noticed that it was empty.

- You mean, one Baba had escaped [another commonly-used name for Book-guru honouring its wisdom].

- I guess so. Later I heard a rumour that appeared in the local press. The guard-reader had to go to pee, and he forgot to close the door. A group called the Guardians of the Book-guru tracked him down and located his exact whereabouts through the internet and the GPS. Book-guru was riding on a man's head in the nearby suburb. They attacked and respectfully guided Book-guru back to the cell.

- You are mistaken. Devotees often take Baba (Book-guru) to their houses for some ceremony or a wedding. In the villages, it is still a common practice.

- In the UK, there is a new religious edict: Book-guru must not be taken to private houses because people may be drinking alcohol there. It is especially forbidden at the marriage palaces, hotels and community halls that are often used for partying and dancing. The wedding ceremony must be performed in a gurdwara.

- That does not make sense. The tradition in Punjab has been that a marriage ceremony must take place in the girl's house. Otherwise, the village takes it as a disgrace and dishonour. Only very poor parents, with the consent of the village elders, allow a wedding ceremony to take place in a gurdwara.

- I believe the guardians have a hidden motive. They have imprisoned Book-guru's ideas that reject absurd rituals and blind worship because it harms their source of income.

- I believe you are correct. Book-guru is serving a life sentence with hard labour. It must do public service at all hours. The waiting list of demands for uninterrupted reading is long. Have you heard the latest rumour from the UK? All privately owned Book-gurus will be confiscated and enslaved.

- I have told you how I lost my three-quarter Book-guru. There won't be a shortage for funds for building new cells. The Sikhs believe that donating to Book-guru is a true service and genuine charity. In Eldore, I remember, Babuji used to make us sing hymns on weekends. After prolonged bowing in front of Book-guru, he would invariably perform the ritual of a clockwise circumambulation and pause behind Book-guru. Then he would bend down to hold the right leg of the palanquin with both hands and squeeze it up and down as if massaging a living guru, and then proceed to the left leg. He would then pick up the flywhisk and swing it a few times reverently over Book-guru, driving away imaginary flies and dust. He would then bow down again with utmost respect to complete the ritual. In those days, it looked quite normal to me.

- Don't you realise how tired Book-guru gets? His workload has increased exponentially — a good case for labour unions to protest.

- Do you recall that in October 2008 we celebrated the 300th anniversary of bestowing the guruship on the Adi Granth? I was in Jatpur then. The village pledged five hundred uninterrupted readings.

- Poor Book-guru, no holiday even on his birthday. How did you fulfil the pledge?

- In my village, it's difficult to find so many readers. Therefore, they did line reading and performed akhri darshan, script vision.

- Wait a minute, I'm lost. What are line reading and akhri darshan?

- The reader passes his eyes over each line without reading it. I heard that in the neighbouring village of Bheni, the reader viewed or scanned each page with his eyes and kept on turning the pages. We have infallible faith in the miraculous power of Book-guru: merely seeing it is enough. Boundless is our Granthophilia, astounding our devotion. The leader of a group of villagers going on yatra, pilgrimage, to Hazur Sahib invited me to join them.

- Why Hazur Sahib? Isn't it far in the south?

- Yes, a few days by train to the Deccan. That's where Gobind

Singh enthroned the Adi Granth as the final guru. Sikhs from all over the world gather there. Indian Railways has arranged special trains to take Punjab Sikhs to Nader. The Government renamed the railway station Nader Hazur Sahib. Helicopters rained flowers on Nader Gurdwara on October 28 and 30. Besides the fireworks in the evening, the Sikhs laid on three hundred varieties of food and sixty varieties of sweets as well as burgers and noodles. A machine produced fifteen tons of ice cream per hour. The communal kitchen served five thousand worshipers at a go. What a superb Khalsa Diners' Club. It serves well-fed pilgrims, and ignores the country's millions of hungry and the poor, a slap on Nanak's sacha sauda, true trade.

- These ostentatious celebrations feed the Sikh megalomania. They get bigger and better organized than the Hindu Kumbh Mela.

- That's what I've been saying: by imitating Hindus we have become more Hindu than the Hindus - but we never admit it.

- Gurdwaras are burgeoning everywhere, perpetuating Granthophilia.

- People need adulation and belief in something. That is the basis of a successful religion. Book-guru is not a terrifying book like the Bible with its legends, fables and miracles. Unlike the Koran, it does not admonish its followers and non-followers. It shows the practical way for a happy life, discarding mythological chaff except frequent poetic allegorical references to Hindu mythology. Unfortunately, the Sikh preachers have built on similar myths cleverly linking, or rather interfacing, miracles performed by the authors of Book-guru and other gurus with verses from the Book-guru. However, they are unable to beat the exhilarating Hindu mythology. People love listening to miraculous stories and our preachers continue to exploit this frailty, recounting miraculous incidents from Ramayana, Mahabharata and other similar literature with tales of gods, yamas and dharmaraj who keeps an account of each person's karma and waits, like Saint Peter, for the arrival of souls at the gate and assigns them to paradise or hell or keeps them in limbo.

- That is true. My family has modified meal times in order to watch the television series of Hindu epics. Every Punjabi villager has been drawn to the Hindu fold.

- When the television breaks down, it's a disaster.

- The Sikhs, like the Muslims, do not permit filming of legends and myths associated with Sikh gurus and saints. Naturally, they watch those of others. They have overcome this shortcoming partly by idolatrous and credulous worship of Book-guru. Frankly, pilgrimages do not attract me. Worshipping Book-guru like an idol is not my cup of tea. I know Nader is our fourth throne, as holy as Amritsar. Was it here where two agents sent by the Muslim Governor of Sirhand stabbed Gobind Singh, our tenth guru? We attribute miraculous powers to Gobind Singh. Couldn't he see his assassins coming? I wish he could have lived longer, to put the Khalsa on a solid footing and save the world. Before he died, he bestowed the guruship on the Pothi [book] which became the Adi Granth, the First Book. Some fifty years later, it became the Guru Granth, Book-guru. Subsequently it received honorific titles of Sri, Sahib and 'Ji', I believe in recognition of its hard work.

- How did we fall into this trap?

- Hindu traditions and rituals in a modified form which are intrinsically more insidious have penetrated the Sikh psyche. Book-guru and its authors were elevated above God with Book-guru becoming the focus of adoration and worship. Some blame the Brahmin priests for manipulating the illiterate people. It's our fault.

- Nevertheless, you also adore Book-guru.

- Yes, I perform the ritual in order not to be different from the others. However, I find much peace by being in a like-minded assembly of devotees, lovers of Book-guru. It reminds me of an elderly Sikh reverently carrying his old Book-guru, not yet dead, on his head. He walked many kilometres from his village to Amritsar. With utmost respect, he handed it to a well-known publisher near the Golden Temple and bought a new one. He recited his abridged prayer and respectfully placed it on his head. Behold, the shopkeeper flung his beloved old Book-guru over his shoulder on to a heap of paper and other books. Shocked and dumbfounded, he could not believe his eyes. Such an ignominious end to Book-guru happening a few yards away from the place where the Book-guru was first compiled.

- We bribe Book-guru with money. To ensure that he is never hungry, we place food and water under his bed. Some fastidious disciples even place a vessel as a toilet. In summer, it has its own air-conditioning unit because fanning with a flywhisk is not enough. Baba gets fine cotton underclothes to wear in summer and woollens in winter. Recently I was in Toronto, Canada where there are over one hundred and forty gurdwaras.

- So many?

- Book-guru helps the owners to obtain tax relief.

- You are joking?

- No, having a Book-guru in a room makes it a public place of worship; hence the owner is entitled to tax relief, according to some law.

- Occasionally I think of my three-quarter Book-guru. When I installed it on the top shelf of my wardrobe with its clothes, the flywhisk and a small sword, I thought of the Egyptian pharaohs buried under the Pyramids with precious objects placed next to them. I often worry about its state, residing in Langenthal gurdwara. I believe it should be all right, secure and comfortable in heavenly Switzerland. When I got used to the Gurbani CD, happy memories have replaced my guilt feeling. Now Book-guru is ever-present and easily accessible. I can search for any song, copy, cut and paste without worrying about the spit escaping from the mouth and wetting the pages. It lodges comfortably in a USB memory key in my breast pocket next to my heart. Yesterday my cousin wanted the text of a hymn to sing in the morning. I got it from here and printed it. Do you think Baba is angry with me?

- You are blessed.

- There is no need for messy garlands, burning essence, perfumes and offerings of money and food. There will be no problem of cremating it or recycling it.

- But then, why has the Granthophilia strengthened?

- Book-guru's message is clear and easy to understand. However, it is much easier to accept and follow the belief that the all-powerful Book-guru will resolve our problems and fulfil our desires. All I need to do is to place my wishes in front of Book-guru, sing its songs, or let someone read it for me.

- Do you mean to say that if I do not obey Book-guru I do not have a guru and I'm not its disciple, a Sikh?

- We often melodiously sing Book-guru's couplet: If you seek anything other than Him, you will accumulate pain and grief.

- Punjab is one of the most literate and prosperous states of India. Do its people have any excuse for not following the Sikh path?

- Many Sikh preachers are like the Brahmin priest who could earn his living only by perpetuating rituals and false beliefs. They have overpowered even the educated who have stopped protesting. Like the Brahmin priest, they have the Sikh society in their grip. Any person can read, preach and sing verses from Book-guru and perform ceremonies, but the Brahmin way has entered the Sikh psyche more subtly. Firstly, the Book-guru has been elevated above God. It is Maharajah, Patshah and the All-knower. With the permission of Book-guru, we start every ceremony: social, religious, commercial and family. Book-guru receives all donations and offerings. Poor God has lost its throne, even though Book-guru says repeatedly that whoever would equate the gurus to God would go to hell.

- In that case, many Sikhs purchase their ticket to hell daily. Is it binding for me to go to a gurdwara?

- Book-guru says that God is everywhere and one can pray anywhere at any time - in fact a Sikh should be at prayer all the time, even his work is prayer. Book-guru also says that associating with good people is beneficial spiritually and builds the willpower.

- For many, unquestioned faith blindly followed keeps them going.

- It's a good crutch. My understanding of sadh sangat, company of good people, corresponds less to preaching and more to conferences, exchange of experiences and debates. I do know how God comes into it.

- God has shaken off his responsibility by according human beings the freedom to do good or evil. They carry the weight of errors.

- Therefore, God is not all-powerful.

- He offers love, His force. Otherwise, He is weak and suffering with human beings.

- In that case, we must save God. But what is wrong with singing the sacred songs?

- Singing is very therapeutic and calming. The problem is that what they sing is not always a prayer or meditation. It is usually instructions, descriptions and recommendations for action. For example Nanak describes the Jain practice:

They have their head-hair plucked, drink dirty water
And eat by begging other's leavings.
They spread out their shit and inhale by mouth its stinking odour...

Do you see what I mean? Am I disparaging the Book-guru?

- I just sing as if it were a prayer and never question. The melody transports me to the realm of bliss. For me each word of Book-guru is potent.

- Then why do you need to read one thousand four hundred and thirty pages? Book-guru was written in relatively short poems so that even the illiterate could learn and understand them. In the present times, the young go to universities and acquire academic and professional knowledge, caring little about what semi-educated priests preach. They tend to follow the Sikh way without acquiring knowledge from Book-guru.

- I see your point. If we don't change, we will not grow. If we do not grow, we are not really living. Growing requires giving up many traditions and rituals that provide only temporary hope but do not conform to the Sikh path.

- It is extremely difficult, if not too late, for the Sikh religious institutions to change now. They will follow the way of other religions. Not long ago in Birmingham a group staged a play, *Dishonour*. One scene with sexual connotations was set in a gurdwara. It angered many Sikhs, both young and old. There were violent demonstrations that were an affront to the broadmindedness of the Sikh credo.

- Why do we blame others and conceal our shortcomings by taking refuge in Book-guru's universality? We beat our chests for the success of save-the-turban campaigns in England and Canada as if the turban safeguards Book-guru's teachings. We did not dare liberate our Book-guru from the holy prison in case it became alive and condemned us to the painful fate of the masands, regional representatives of the gurus who kept stealing tax money and misused their position. Gobind Singh had them arrested and burnt alive. Our modern slippery masands know this cannot happen to them and continue to flourish.

- Book-guru is not our prisoner. We love him. Or should I say 'her' or 'it'?

- If a man has a beautiful wife whom he loves dearly, he wants to keep her for himself and protect her from other men. He cannot allow her to leave the house except with him. Her beauty cannot be shared.

- The prison authorities earn handsome reading fees, doubling it if the demand is urgent. A request for slower interrupted reading costs less. That's how the law of demand-supply works.

- Where does the money go?

- Don't be naïve. The guardian-readers deserve a good salary for conversing with Book-guru. According to the Sikh mindset, this is the best form of charity money - the safest investment.

- Where do they find so many guardian-readers?

- It is no longer a problem. The stock of jobless super-fast readers, especially from lower castes, is inexhaustible.

- This morning I was waving the flywhisk over Book-guru. The priest miraculously found a randomly chosen hymn that exactly matched the ceremony for naming a child. He had marked the page with a hair from his beard. He raised his voice to stress key words. Wonderstruck, the devotees nodded and acknowledged All-knowing Book-guru's power by uttering soulfully: Waheguru, Waheguru, the wonderful Guru-God.

- New religious anniversaries never celebrated before have come on the annual agenda. The fourth centenary in 2004 of compiling Book-guru was celebrated with an incredible ceremony and pageantry. Did we celebrate previous centenaries?

- Without realizing, we copy the Hindus. But Hindus have a numerous religious festivals spread though out the year. There are fasts, sacrifices to Kali, Holi, Diwali, Dusehra, the new moon and the full moon and numerous others. They celebrate in a variety of ways: prayers, dance, music, singing, theatre, processions, pilgrimages, bathing, burning effigies, splashing people with coloured powder and water. Bollywood and television have magnified these festivals dramatically. One benefit of these celebrations is that people can safely vent their frustrations and maintain some level of psychological balance and mental health, control their passions and live in relative peace. These festivities enhance the feeling of belonging to a social group. Sikh religious festivals are devoid of such variety. This is not a criticism.

- Do you mean Sikhs have invented rituals to replace Hindu and Muslim ones?

- They don't have to; they never abandoned the Hindu rituals. They have simply modified them and found some folklore or historical incident associated with some guru to justify celebration of a purely Hindu festival. Nothing wrong, the more we celebrate the better the social health.

CHAPTER 39

GOD IS NOT A WOMAN

❧

"Sikh dharma is without equal. It is unique. Our gurus have given us a flawless Book-guru," the leader of a trio of ballad singers vociferously sermonized, standing on the back of a small truck. His companion played a rapid sequence of doleful beats on a small two-faced drum held in his left hand with a strap round the drum cords. Squeezing the strap throttled the drum sound into a wail.

Simultaneously the third man slid the bow on the sarangi cords, producing woeful music as if someone was in pain. With Jas I followed the Jatpur village Nagar Keertan (holy procession), led by a truck carrying Book-guru enthroned in the modified front cab. A dozen tractor-drawn trolleys and singing groups trailed behind. This was the finale of the vigil when people play religious music and sing all night. The procession came to a halt in the village square. Women sat on mats spread out on the dusty ground in front of their houses. We joined the men sitting on the concrete pedestal under a banyan tree. Scanning the big gathering, the ballad singer-storyteller raised his voice and repeated, "Our Book-guru is extraordinary. It is the word of God. Everyone repeat after me a roaring Waheguru."

The response was half-hearted.

"The Muslim Koran gives very low status to women. In the Christian Bible women are almost like slaves." He exposed some other shortcomings of the two holy books. Surely he had not read them.

"The supreme, honoured and all-knowing Book-guru of the Sikhs is different. It categorically declares that men and women are equal. The trio sing Nanak's song:

Of a woman we are conceived,

Of a woman we are born,

To a woman we are betrothed and wedded,

She is the friend and partner of life,

She keeps the race going.

Why curse and condemn them,

When from women are born leaders and rulers.

Without her there can be no human birth.

"He then made a passionate outburst against female foeticide. His plea for protecting girls culminated in singing a heart-rending ode: "girls are precious, they are wealth, and we must not commit this sin". The man's well-argued and convincing appeal touched my heart. However, I did not notice any impact on the faces of the folks. I asked Jas "Why isn't there even one woman in the procession? Why do you keep on claiming around the world that men and women among Sikhs are equal just because Nanak has said so? It's the practice that counts."

"In cities some educated women participate actively. Overall, Sikh women are much better off than other women in India."

"I agree. What would Nanak say if he saw that women are not allowed to sing his hymns in the Golden Temple?"

"You know, men think that women are enchantresses. Their enticing voices and natural musical talent would not only beat male singers but perturb the gathering in deep meditation," Jas laughed.

Just then the bard snapped, "We should be ashamed of what we are doing! We produce a lot and feed the rest of India, but we commit female foeticide more than any other state. There aren't enough girls left for young men to marry."

Jas continued, "Newspapers and television point out daily the danger and immorality of foeticide. People have stopped listening to it."

"Why do women allow this to happen if they are equal to men? They are better educated than men. They occupy high posts, lecture in universities and the law defends them. Your aunt in Chandigarh became the first woman vice-chancellor of a university in India. Women must suffer emotionally. Don't their wishes count?"

"All that is true, but the man still heads the family and community. What you do not know is that wives collaborate fully in female foeticide. They do not want to bear the burden of marrying off a daughter because of the dowry system. The majority of girl-killers go scot free. Then they are scared of the girl getting pregnant before marriage. No one will marry her. But a boy can do anything. His errant ways are tolerated and misdeeds easily forgotten."

"Why don't the gurdwaras enforce Nanak's instruction?"

"Our temples, preachers and institutions are useless. They like to quote verses from Book-guru to show our superiority over other faiths. They do nothing to stop the wicked practice."

"That is not the Sikh way?"

"Shamming has become our tradition. No one wants to know the right way."

"Muslims stick staunchly to their religious codes, good or bad. Our Book-guru clearly interdicts female foeticide and mistreating women. But we do not refrain from committing these sins. Who are guiltier, more sinful and more disobedient: Muslims or Sikhs?"

"We are."

"Sikhs are proud of being the bravest people in the country. How do they feel being at the top in female foeticide? How many millions of girls have they killed?"

"I read that the Jains are the worst, although their religion requires them not to kill even germs."

"Are you telling me that the most religious people of India are incorrigible killers?"

"Don't get angry, Baiji. See the situation in a proper context. You know the story of Adam and Eve. Eve enticed Adam to have sex with her against God's instruction. They have become parents of all Jews, Christians and Muslims. The entire blame for human misbehaviour is attributed to a woman's original sin, not men. The Bible and the Koran ordained man to rule over women. It is an eternal decree which we have no right and no power to alter. Don't forget that Manu, a well-known ancient Hindu sage, set laws giving men similar authority over women."

"Yes, we often hear about him. For many years I have wondered why for five thousand years the world has had only male prophets. Of our ten gurus not even one was a woman. Imagine if we had one woman guru."

Reluctant to react, Jas asked, "Are women in Europe totally free? Can they do what they like?"

"They are, especially in countries where education and social reforms brought about by thinkers and philosophers overrode the Christian orthodoxy. Many Roman Catholics and Christian fundamentalist communities still stick to the old values, especially in America. The Muslim countries have not advanced much. In fact many try to return to the past and enforce Sharia laws."

"I have read about stoning of women, splashing acid on the face of young girls, it's horrible. Thank God we don't do that. Do you think the world will have at least one woman prophet in the next five thousand years?" Jas laughed.

"I doubt if human beings will survive that long. But by then, women will have no desire or aspiration to become prophets. "

"Why?"

"Because they have always been profoundly spiritual. In fact they do not need any prophet. Spirituality is in short supply in men. By nature a woman has to be very human in order to raise and protect her children. This trait is not so strong in man. To preserve the human race she tolerates man being the master, keeps him happy and even slaves for him."

"Doesn't Book-guru say that the laws of nature are true and whoever tries to change them will cause trouble?"

"Human beings consider themselves to be above nature. Even if all the past prophets got together today they would not know what to do with human beings, particularly men, not even Book-guru."

"Not even Book-guru?" Jas frowned.

"Haven't you ever noticed that Book-guru portrays a human being as a woman and a wife and God as a man, a lover and a husband? It has retained the Hindu real-life image of the man–woman relationship: master and servant, just like Lord Krishna with his gopis [milkmaids]. Book-guru uses this unfortunate metaphor in hundreds of poems epitomizing man's spiritual union with God similar to sexual fulfilment of a woman by a husband. That has fixed our mindset, not easy to change. It does not help the women's cause. In order to erase this engraved image should we first edit Book-guru?"

"I never thought of it that way. What you say is true."

"We actually reinforce the male dominance over females by singing this poetic analogy in the marriage ceremony. At Atima's marriage, when I handed her the end of the groom's red palla [scarf] signifying that she was now leaving my care to join her husband, the singer-priest sang the chorus:

All flattery and slander I have given up and renounced.
I found all other relationships false,
Therefore I have clung to the end of your scarf."

"But it refers to God's scarf," Jas protested.

"No, the congregation singing with him turned the boy into

God. At the end of the ceremony the priest proudly sang another refrain:

I have found the Eternal Immortal Being as Spouse
Who never dies nor is born.
O my Father, I have married
And through the guru I have obtained God."

Then I teased Jas, "Soon you will marry and then you will be a god."

"But it is meant to apply to both, the girl and the boy," Jas defended himself.

"Yes, I know, but the words of the song are clear: The girl has found God."

"You're right. Just because the word marriage occurs in a verse we use it blindly."

"The funniest part was when Atima entered the hall and walked towards the Book-guru. The singer switched to a charming hymn.

Graceful is your walk and sweet is Your speech,
like the singing of a nightingale.
Lively is your youth...
With the graceful walk of an elephant
You walk unperturbed absorbed in your own self.

Atima did not know that she was being called an elephant."

"She is more like a giraffe," Jas laughed.

Atima, led by Yaniss, walked around Book-guru's palanquin four times. The priest, a professor of physics in England, defined the duties of the couple. He carefully avoided the commonly used term 'pati parmeshar', husband-God. Instead he said that a man and a woman are like the two wheels of a cart, equal in every way. Then he explained why the boy leads the girl: When walking in a circle there is no leader, it's like electrons circling round a nucleus, none is the leader. The entire congregation had a good laugh.

"Here in the villages it is very difficult to bring about change,"

Jas said. "You have seen my mother. She gets up well before dawn. Fortunately, these days she doesn't have to grind flour. She feeds the cattle and then milks the buffalos and the cows. She lights the fire in the hearth and boils milk. The smoke has ruined her eyes. After sweeping the yard she churns curdled milk to make butter. She cooks breakfast for everyone. Somehow she fits washing and sewing clothes, embroidery and weaving into her morning. She rushes to cook lunch and sends it to the workshop. The process is repeated in the afternoon. She finds time to visit the temple briefly. With a smile she cleans the pots and pans, makes the beds and is the last to bed. And all this is just to keep Papa happy."

CHAPTER 40

WHO ARE YOU, SIR?

❧

Two curious Sikh teenagers, Kabir and Navi, sat down with me and wrote a dialogue using Taylor Morris's idea from his *Message from the Sparrows*, a book of esoteric wisdom. They refined it with the help of Kabir's mother Sunita, who is articulate in English and has good communication skills. They were ready to present it on Sunday morning for Guru Nanak Dev's birthday anniversary celebration. At the end of the hymn singing and recitations from Book-guru, the trio got their turn.

Navi: Kabir, was Nanak a guru and a leader of the Sikhs?

Kabir: Navi, he was a guru, not a leader and there were no Sikhs then.

Navi: What's the difference?

Kabir: Leaders want us to follow, and in following they want us to believe. This is the main thing: they want us to believe.

Navi: And a guru?

Kabir: A guru is a teacher. A teacher wants to help us see the truth and think for ourselves. He wants us to understand. He is not looking for followers as leaders are.

Sunita: Nanak in his poem called Japu, meditation, has written:
If you listen to the Guru's teachings, even once,
Your mind will shine like gems, jewels and rubies.

Navi: We are celebrating Nanak's birthday. We sang his songs. Are we not his followers?

Kabir: Those who sing or read but do not understand what the guru wants to teach us are followers. In his song Nanak said:

One may read a cartload of books
And spend every month of the year in reading only,
And thus read all one's life,
Right up to the last breath.
A thoughtful life is really what matters.

Sunita: Nanak also wrote: *A person will be known as good or bad judged by his actions and deeds.*

Navi: You said there were no Sikhs during Nanak's time. Where were they?

Kabir: The word 'sikh' comes from the Sanskrit word 'shishya' which means a student, learner or disciple. So anybody who is ready to learn from the guru is a sikh. Nanak has explained:

Understanding and accepting the Name,
A student of the guru saves himself and others.

Sunita: *Manai terai tare gur sikh.*

Navi: In the Gita, Krishna is the teacher and answers questions put by his student, Arjun.

Kabir: Yes, Arjun was not a follower of Krishna. He listened to Krishna's advice carefully, understood it and then acted upon it. He was a true sikh or learner.

Navi: So Sikhs must be the most learned people in the world?

Kabir: Why do you say that?

Navi: Because they are Sikhs. They are expected to learn all the time. I also know that they read the entire Granth non-stop more than people of other religions read their holy books.

Kabir: I wish you were right. Sikhs have become followers and believe that by simply reading the book every problem will be solved. That is not what the Granth and other similar books say.

Navi: Aren't they like salesmen? When they tell us to drink Coke they want us to believe that it's a magic potion, that if we drink Coke we'll be young and popular, and we'll have plenty of fun as well. They don't want us to understand that it's really only sugary water with a little flavour.

Kabir: Exactly, we're almost back to Nanak's times when people and even their teachers didn't properly understand the advice given in holy books.

Sunita: Nanak wrote: "*They read the Simritees, the Shastras and the Puranas, they argue and debate, but do not know the true meaning of reality.*" Well, people continue to recite and sing from these writings in prayers, ceremonies, and marriages. These songs continue to provide a useful way of worship and socialising and give us mental comfort and peace.

Navi: Why did Nanak start writing and preaching when all knowledge and ideas were already there?

Kabir: Don't you know that all previous sacred writings were in Sanskrit and Arabic? Only a few could speak or read these languages. Those who could read could not understand the ideas contained in them. Well, they serve no useful purpose. So Nanak and others started writing in the language of their people and informed the ordinary people of the ideas contained in old books. Most Pundits and Mullahs did not like this.

Navi: Don't tell me that Nanak and other holy people went to school to learn Sanskrit. I'm told that they learnt many languages without going to school. They knew them when they were born. Is that possible?

Kabir: These stories have convinced many followers. But that is not true. Nanak put in a lot of effort to learn not only different languages but also many other things about people, their customs, beliefs, traditions, rituals, and about nature, animals, and forests.

Navi: He must be very gifted and interested. That's why he learnt very fast.

Kabir: Yes, in addition, Nanak travelled to many countries to see for himself and expand his experience and be able to teach better. He believed in the old saying "doing is knowing". For him acquiring knowledge, gyan, was the basis for leading a good active life.

Navi: Did he not care for heaven and hell or salvation and nirvana?

Kabir: You know what Nanak said: "*He who has the company of God, what has he to do with salvation or heaven?*"

Navi: Didn't Nanak start the Sikh religion?

Kabir: Nanak did not accept that religions are different. There is only one religion. That's why he proclaimed "There is neither Hindu nor Muslim".

Navi: If Nanak were with us now, would he have said that there are no Sikhs either?

Kabir: Because most Sikhs have also become blind followers, using songs from the Book-guru mainly to perform ceremonies without getting the meaning and acting on them, he would, if he were with us, certainly include them in the list, as well as Christians, Buddhists and others.

Sunita: Nanak wanted peace among religions and nations. He sang:

I have made a pact with the Supreme Lord
All other pacts are for worldly power.
For worldly gains fools dispute and struggle.
In this Dark Age, five dominant passions cause factions:
Lust, anger, greed, attachment, and self-will.
I am in the Lord's faction,
Which has destroyed all other factions!
False is all love besides that of God
Which divides men into warring groups.

Navi: Kabir, What exactly did Nanak want to teach?

Kabir: There's an old story about a Greek philosopher who went about with a lighted lamp in the daytime. People asked, what are you looking for? He said, I'm looking for human beings. Well, Nanak was also looking for loving human beings. But he saw only Hindus, Buddhists, Jains and Muslims.

Navi: But what good are stories about Nanak performing miracles if we don't take them to heart and if we don't live them?

Kabir: Many stories about Nanak are teaching tales. They might not be true. We do not have to believe them. We should use our imagination so that from the unreal in the story we take something that we can apply to our life.

Sunita: Nanak has written a lot about haunmain ego. He says, *haunmain dheerag rog hai daru bhi is mahe*, which means, I-ness is a grave disease and the medicine is also in it. What are "I" and our bodies? According to him we are not our bodies. We are our consciousness, the thing that sparks us, which uses our muscles, our eyes, our ears, and our brains through which we function. And, without that consciousness we die. In fact that is life itself.

Now if the life in us is the same as the life in everything else, then we must truly identify not with our skins and our physical shells but with the real, the thing that moves all of us, the life in all of us. That spark, that fire, that life thing, that consciousness, is the same in you and me and everyone else. That is the reason why Nanak proclaimed:

Navi & Kabir: There is neither Hindu nor Muslim.

Sunita: And he added,

Navi & Kabir: but only the brotherhood of human beings.

Kabir: Did Nanak write only about life and people and nothing else?

Sunita: Nanak was an outstanding poet. No other poet can write like him. In his songs he embraces nature in all its aspects: sky and stars, birds and animals, seasons and seasonal activities of people around him. He has written in many local dialects and in Persian. He acquired first-hand knowledge by travelling all over India,

Afghanistan, Arabia, Iraq, Iran, Tibet and Sri Lanka. He went to the Himalayas specifically to meet and talk with highly learned and respected Charpat yogis. He has recorded his dialogue with them in Book-guru. His knowledge was vast because he was one with nature, his true guru. He was one with the power that we call God. Nanak repeats: I am that. That is I.

Listen to some of his poetry, first the spring:

Kabir:

It is the month of Chet
It is spring.
All is seemly,
The beautiful honeybee can be seen
In the flower-adorned woodland,
The home of my childhood days.
But there is sorrow of separation in my soul,
Longing I wait for the Lord'.

Navi: Summer

In Asad the sun scorches,
Skies are hot,
The earth burns like an oven,
Waters give up their vapours,
The sun burns and scorches the earth relentlessly.

Sunita: Monsoon,

The season of rain has come,
My heart is full of joy,
Rivers and land are one expanse of water
For it is the monsoon, the season of merry-making.
It rains.
Peacocks cry with joy,
The papiha calls … peeoo, peeoo,
The fangs of serpents that crawl,

The stings of mosquitoes that fly
Are venomous
The seas have burst their bounds in the ecstasy of fulfilment
I alone am deprived of joy.
Kabir: A beautiful evening worship
The sky is the plate,
In it, the sun and the moon are the lamps
And the celestial stars are like pearls.
The sandalwood-scented wind from the Malai hills
Is the incense,
It sways like a whisk,
The entire plant life supplies sacred flowers for You, O Light.
What a wonderful evening worship!

Sunita: Most songs in the Book-guru are easy to understand, but the desire to make that little effort to understand seems to be lacking. So, let's pray.

Kabir, Navi and Sunita: O Waheguru, help us to learn to translate and reinterpret old writings and traditions and make them applicable to the daily lives of human beings in the present times and where they live. There is neither Hindu nor Muslim nor Christian nor Buddhist nor Sikh nor any other similar bodies but only the brotherhood of human beings.

Sunita concluded by reciting Ibn Arabi's poem that conveys Nanak's message beautifully.

Simran was first to react after the ceremony. "What you are saying is that Sikhs are not sikhs. Do you want to be lynched?" she asked.

"I do not doubt that, fundamentalists can do it, but the chances are much less than if I had said the same thing about Muslims," I retorted. "The truth when articulated can become a bitter pill. The educated take what the trio said with gratitude, the majority will not notice it, and a few will certainly protest."

And that is exactly what happened.

The gathering included two ambassadors of India who were Sikhs and many other cultured persons of various faiths. They came to congratulate the three speakers. One of them said, "This is what we need in modern India. Why can't our religious leaders take this approach to teaching?" The other commented, "I agree. Sikhs need to look at things differently if they want to carry out Nanak's mission. You are safe here. But in Punjab you can expect to be grilled."

They took our copies of the dialogue. While I was soaking in glory, a bearded and turbanned young Sikh approached me and asked, "Who are you, sir? I am sorry if I'm being rude but you're simply misreading vital information about Sikhism. It is different from what you preach - Sikhism evolved from Guru Nanak Dev Ji's teaching into the Khalsa-hood religion. Guru Gobind Singh Ji upheld Guru Nanak Dev Ji's teachings and also lessons. Sikhism does teach about brotherhood but it also teaches God praising. Please peruse the Jaap by Guru Gobind Singh Ji and see if you can find any flaw in it. It's written with finesse and pure love towards God. Why are you publicising such messages?"

"Apparently you did not hear the praise from the ambassadors and others" I said, trying to keep calm. "All I can tell you is that young Kabir and Navi immensely enjoyed preparing the dialogue and even more presenting it. It sharpened their curiosity and desire to learn more about the message of Book-guru. They acquired quality knowledge by articulating what they had produced. It has become part of them. They did not understand anything of what was earlier sung or recited."

I've stopped trying to persuade people, it doesn't work. The young man did not look satisfied. I adopted a sterner tone, "I assume you have acquired much love by reading the Jaap. God is love. You must be God or about to become one. Now please save the world, or at least stop female foeticide and save the girls in the Punjab, the land of your gurus. Soon there won't be any left."

He turned away, crestfallen.

CHAPTER 41

TO BE MALIKA

⌒

The Sikh people of India, America, Europe and Africa have a profound faith in Book-guru, gurdwaras and deras (monasteries). Yet no community of Sikh people exists. There is a nebulous religious consensus. The gurus have not left any sermons, dogmas or commandments which are frozen in time or cast in stone forbidding change. Not to change is to deny reality, scientific knowledge, rational thinking and progress. Sikh intellectuals occupy key positions in the political, economic, social and educational sectors. There is no dearth of research and media support. But so far, they have failed to modernize a society atrophied by orthodoxy.

A short time before going to Santa Fe I was sitting in Bhola's workshop in Raikot and read in the Punjabi daily *Ajit* a report by a conformist Sikh on his experience of attending a Radha Soami lecture in Delhi. This is a splinter sect excommunicated by the central Sikh authority.

The traffic was heavy – unusual for a Sunday morning - but flowing smoothly, even though there was not a single policeman in sight. Radha Soami volunteers dressed in white and equipped with walkie-talkies were guiding the cars to prearranged parking areas, all very efficient, not common in that country.

The gigantic tent was full. There were ministers, tycoons, scholars

366

and writers seated on clean mats. Electric fans fanned some three hundred thousand people. He walked quietly into the hall so as not to disturb the deathly silence – unusual for India. In front, he saw a high dais covered in a white sheet. At nine-thirty sharp, the head of the Radha Soami sect, Gurinder Singh, walked up the steps and sat down in the middle of the dais with two companions on his right. There was continued absolute silence during the ninety-minute discourse on the concept of Nam, Name, from Book-guru . His excellent presentation captured the audience. The reporter was quite surprised to see only a handful of Sikhs recognizable from their turbans and beards in such a big audience. He realized that Gurinder was taking Book-guru's message to millions who remain outside the Sikh fold.

I recounted this to Malika. She suddenly became quite excited.

"You won't believe this, I am married to Gurinder's distant cousin."

"Tell me more" I said, equally excited.

"There are many Radha Soami centres in the world," began Malika. "The headquarters is located on River Beas not far from Amritsar. My husband's aunt was married to the previous guru, Charan Singh, a rich jat. She tried for years to persuade me to convert into a Radha Soami. The Book-guru is not enough, she would tell me. It does not speak. No one has the time to search for guidance from it. It is no more than an idol. Sikhs are only good at singing sacred songs and expect that everything they wish for will happen. We need a living guru. There is no salvation without him. Come to our dera and see for yourself."

"Oh..." I raised an eyebrow. Malika gave me a sceptical look and continued.

"Like any staunch Sikh I responded that my guru was the Book-guru and I did not accept anybody else to replace it - living or dead. When Charan Singh died, his nephew, Gurinder, was enthroned as guru. My in-laws insisted that I must pay my respects to him. Many of his followers wear Sikh symbols but do not accept the baptism and martial codes of the Khalsa. A majority of members are clean-shaven.

"I told you that I returned to India to be with my husband after a few years in England," continued Malika. "I did not go to the dera because I wanted to protect my teenage sons from such cults. But I could not get used to village life in India and returned to England with the children. Before I left, I did visit the Radha Soami centre."

She stopped, taking a moment to remember something.

"We rented a Maruti. It was a long drive – almost two hours on a very hot day. At the Radha Soami centre, we were stopped at the gate by armed men.

'You cannot enter with your car', the guard said. 'Who do you want to see?'

'My aunt', I replied.

'What's her name?'

'I can't remember her name, but she lives in that house on the right.'

'What's the guru's name?' I could not remember his name either. 'I was told to contact SP Sharma', I blurted out.

'What car have you got?' asked the guard. He must have thought that I was mad.

'Maruti.'

'What colour?'

'Have you seen a Maruti in India other than white?' I retorted, a little upset now.

'What is its number?'

'It's a hire car. Ask the driver.'

'This security man will escort you', said the man.

"I realized at that point that Gurinder was under constant threat from Sikh fundamentalists. The security in the dera was very heavy" continued Malika.

"My aunt received us. She is not very educated but plays the role of a guru-mother well. After some refreshments, she addressed me with authority, 'Malika, you're not a Radha Soami member. Strictly the dera does not admit non-members. Walk with me in a dignified manner, but say nothing. We went to the dining hall for a meal before the lecture. There were devotees holding five-rupee notes to pay for lunch. Some looked very poor and miserable. We bypassed them and entered a door that led us to a well-laid table. We were served a huge lunch. Before we got up, the guru-mother reminded me, 'As I said earlier, you walk behind me heads up, like a queen. The monitors have not seen you before. Just follow me quietly.'

"The hall was packed. I followed my aunt to the front, led by a monitor. My aunt sat down on a comfortable cushion. The second monitor stuck out his arm in front of me and guided me to the row behind. A little later, as if she had returned to earth, my aunt saw me. 'Why are you sitting there?' she said. 'You come here and sit on the cushion.' I obeyed. 'The monitors have seen you with me, you won't have any problem in the future. You'll be treated with respect.'

"The guru and four attendants walked in at the prescribed time and sat down on the raised platform facing the audience. They sang hymns - it was impressive. Within the compound they have built a huge modern hospital offering free treatment. Gurinder is very knowledgeable. Assisted by well-educated people, he has put in a lot of effort to modernize his institutions as a model for others."

"Your name means queen, but you did not know how to act like one. Your aunt gave you the first lesson on becoming a true Malika, the queen of my heart," I laughed.

Roshan came to the lounge looking fresh after her siesta. "Go and sit in the garden," she said. "It's nice and warm there. I'll clean up and bring the coffee." It was my last day with Malika and Roshan before I was to fly home to Geneva. Malika strolled around the garden for a few minutes before sitting down. I sat down on the bench opposite her.

"You are Malika, the queen, I can be a raja if I marry you," I said playfully.

"You are dreaming," she replied blushing.

We were laughing when Roshan walked out carrying the tray of coffee.

"I'm so happy to see you together," she said. "I wish this could have happened years ago."

It was three o'clock. I had to be at the airport at six.

"Malika, where shall we meet next?" I asked her. "Let's go to Spain, Italy or Bali. And Roshan, you're invited."

"Of course, I'll be there. I can't leave you two together alone," Roshan joked.

"Bali will be great," I said. "It's a beautiful island. Malika, I'll wait for you there."

Malika did not say anything, but smiled.

"Roshan, you are an angel. Without you I would never have met my Malika. I hope she does not regret meeting me."

"No," said Malika.

My heart skipped a beat.

"The last few days have been a dream come true," Malika continued. I felt my heart beating fast now.

"There are moments when I began to doubt myself. I had to pinch myself to make sure that the days were real and not a figment of my imagination."

She smiled at me – the old Malika I had fallen in love with. Her eyes shone and her face glowed. We were both grandparents, but love is strange. Does it ever fade? Not for me.

"I'm so glad that we finally met and had time to talk," she continued. "I'm deeply touched that you and Roshan went out of your way to look after me so lovingly. Thanks is a miserly word, but for the lack of a better one please accept it."

Roshan gave Malika a hug. I just sat immobile, waiting for her to say more.

"I will return home with a renewed zest for life, thanks to you and Inder," she said, this time looking at me. "I can handle the biopsy and whatever the results are. I'm going to work out, eat healthy and you have been bugging me Inder, I will get fit."

Roshan and I gave her a round of applause.

"That's my girl," I said, getting up to give her a hug too.

"Stay busy, Malika. It will keep you active," said Roshan.

"I agree," Malika replied. "It might not be fulfilling, or provide the happiness an individual seeks. But it will keep me off the anti-depressants and out of loony-bins. I hope you don't have too many regrets meeting me like this."

Malika was looking at me when she said that.

"No, not at all. I'm so lucky to have finally met you. It will be easier from now on. So when do we go to Bali?"

Malika laughed. "Inder, you are really incorrigible. You'll have to wait for that."

"Why?" I asked. "We are not teenagers, we have a lot of time."

"Sometimes," replied Malika, "it's better to let a dream be than to chase it."

It was so ambiguous a statement and I had no time to pursue it. We had to leave for the airport.

At the airport I hugged Roshan, and then Malika. I held her tighter and longer in silence. There was nothing either of us could have said. Then I disappeared through the departure gate, not allowing my brain to wonder if we would ever meet again.

CHAPTER 42

HOPPING TO PARADISE

～

For fifteen years, no matter what the weather, I showed up at the Stade du Bout du Monde – World's End Sports Stadium. World's End is real. It was a constant in my life, every Thursday afternoon at two thirty, to exercise in the open-air gym and jog. The stadium is located in the perfect loop of the River Arve before it joins the Rhône. Save for one or two afternoons, it never rained or snowed until we finished our training. The weather man and the climatologist might not accept this phenomenon, but we veterans have complete faith that climate change has no influence on those safe hours on Thursdays. So the weather was never an excuse for not turning up.

The number of participants varied. In autumn until the annual Geneva race in December there would be at least one hundred and fifty people training, which would drop to less than sixty after the race.

Three years ago on Thursday, the regular training day, there was a heavy storm which stopped at exactly 2 pm. Our group of forty took the riverside track through the wood. I was running behind a blonde who looked much younger than the rest of us. For that reason she should not have been with us. No one questioned her. I had not spoken to her before, although she was there when I joined the group a few years ago. She was struggling a little. In order to encourage her I ran beside her.

"I hate jogging," Carine confessed.

"Why?" I asked.

"It's boring and I get tired very quickly. I feel my heart rate goes up and I feel uncomfortable."

"You will get used to it soon," I said. "You need to build up your stamina."

"I've tried, but I get breathless quickly and give up. I can cycle hundreds of kilometres but not jog. I prefer yoga. I have noticed that you are never tired. I'm sure you do yoga."

"My yoga is jogging."

"Then you cannot be an Indian."

"Why?"

"I haven't seen Indians running," Carine said.

"I haven't seen many Indians doing yoga either, here or in India," I countered.

"That's unbelievable. I thought all Indians practised yoga."

Carine spoke fluent English and French. I switched to English.

"No, most Indians do not practise yoga, jogging even less. Yoga is very good. But it has become a business. Other than asanas, its gurus reject other types of physical exercise and make people believe that their type of yoga will keep one perpetually healthy. The gurus do not encourage people, especially the old, to do strenuous exercise which makes the body function naturally as a whole, resulting in a fast heartbeat, maximum breathing and sweat."

Carine gave me a sideways glance.

"Are you Swiss?" I asked out of curiosity.

"No, I'm from Sweden."

"You speak French very well," I complimented her.

"I came here when I was seventeen as a family help and stayed for good."

"You need to run with someone who can help you to gradually increase the running time and build your stamina," I said. "After that you will be the master of your destiny. You know, my son-in-law hated jogging. Now he runs fifteen kilometres twice a week and cannot live without it. If you want, I can run with you when we train. I'm afraid that after a few weeks you will run much faster than me and leave me behind struggling."

We became running mates and a month later she gave up yoga. Every time she feels stressed she goes out for a run on her own.

I have run hundreds of races. Each race becomes a new objective for me. Without these objectives, I could not exercise. Instead I would become lazy and good for nothing. I like to stay fit. Staying fit is great fun. It's not about how long I live, but how well I live.

One day, I phoned my doctor for my annual check-up.

"What's the problem?" Dr Françoise asked.

"I want to see if you are well and if you have changed your mind about dining with me this evening?"

Dr Françoise gave the rendezvous. Her stand has been that a doctor-patient relationship is different and should be left at that. We have run many half marathons together, so when I go for a regular medical check up, we chat about the marathons.

"How have you been since I last saw you more than a year ago?" she asked.

"Young as when I was forty. That makes me younger than you," I kidded.

She pointed to the weighing scale.

"Oh dear, I've put on two kilos!" I exclaimed.

Without commenting she strapped my arm to check the blood pressure. "It is within the norm, but it continues to stay on the high side."

"It's always high when I'm with you" I joked.

"You should measure it once a week and keep a record."

Her assistant entered and handed her the result of the blood and urine tests. "Everything looks all right except your cholesterol - the bad one, it has not come down."

"It's genetic with Indians," I defended myself. "I do not eat fatty food, not even Swiss cheese. Do you see my end approaching?"

"Nothing like that. On the other hand you have a very high level of the good cholesterol."

"People with high cholesterol tend to die suddenly, like my father. People in my village say that he died a saint's death. I also want a swift ending, like the click of a finger." I made a loud flick with my fingers. "I do not want to linger on and be a headache to the family. Nevertheless, I would love to stay afloat for a while and watch you trying to drag my life back and see people crying over my corpse and soften their strings of attachment with their tears."

"There's nothing wrong with you," announced Dr Françoise. "Stay active. But I have been lazy. I do not take time to jog."

"We can jog together," I said. "I usually pass by your apartment building on the way to Bois des Frères. Fix a time and I'll wait for you."

I am convinced that life continues after death in some form as part of the overall Flow. It loses it individuality and identity. It does not reincarnate directly into some animal being. The talk of life with a soul after death is a human invention. It is to cushion the fear of death with the hope of being received by a welcoming Dharamraj or Yama or God's Angel of Death or Saint Peter at the famous gates in front of his hut, holding a ledger containing a balance sheet for each individual. Strangely, he has no time to receive other forms of life. I wonder how Dharamraj is able to condemn a human being to be born in some lower form of life if he does not account in the ledgers for millions of other beings which die every second. Surely he limits his search to the eight million four hundred thousand transmigrations of life fixed by the Hindu census carried out thousands of years ago and mentioned in the Book-guru quite a few times. Even so, Dharamraj has difficulty in managing these transactions. In his ledger, the credit balance of human beings has continued to increase dramatically in the last few decades, because the human population has increased many times while that of other beings has decreased. By simple logic and judged according to religious ratings, all human beings are good, and all other forms of beings are not good enough to satisfy God's Angel of Death.

Carine is now my companion. She is a nurse in an old people's residence. For seventeen years, she has been singing in the city's oldest popular choral group. In return for my helping her in jogging she persuaded me to join the singing group. She also recruited me to join the bike-trekking club. She has cycled around Lake Geneva and most other lakes in central Europe, descended along the Rhône River valley to the Mediterranean, crossed from the Atlantic coast to the Mediterranean and criss-crossed the hills of Sri Lanka. With her, I have island-hopped, cycling over the hilly islands of Croatia and Greece, the remnant summits of the legendary submerged continent of Atlantis. Each time, we have shared a boat with two dozen other cyclists from countries as far apart as New Zealand and USA.

Cycling uphill under the blistering sun was torturous. Once at the top, the view of the deep blue sea below was like a hop to paradise with all suffering forgotten. This is the type of holiday I like, not lazing on sunbeds. Biking is less taxing than running half-marathons.

A few months later I stacked our bikes inside my little Honda and drove to Passau in Germany. Carine loves doing things the difficult way to torture me. En route, as a warm up, we biked around the Alpensee in southern Bavaria because she wanted to photograph the two famous castles. From the half-way point we had a spectacular view of the castles mirrored in the lake in the light of the setting sun. The internet describes the castles and the eccentric builder, King

Ludwig II, exquisitely. The cycle track ended there. We had to push or carry our bikes for nearly three kilometres over tree roots and rocks. It was a good preparation for the days to come.

It was Carine's idea to bike instead of taking a bus or a horse-drawn carriage to the fairy-tale Neuschwanstein castle two hundred metres higher immortalized in a Walt Disney film and in the Disneyland amusement parks. It tested my aging legs and lungs.

The next day we set off from Passau along the left bank of the Danube to Vienna, four hundred kilometres away. It would not have been so difficult to pedal for six days on the level towpath once used by teams of horses towing barges upstream. But Carine kept testing my willpower with side trips into the hills.

She took the first diversion to seek blessings at Maria Taferl, an Austrian equivalent of Lourdes - a pilgrimage to absolve my sins. The three-and-a-half-kilometre climb to the Cathedral was so steep that my bike refused to go up, obstinate as mule. I had to push it two-thirds of the way. But then, blessing is earned only through suffering! The eight-minute ride down was delightful. I quickly realized that on a flat track I would have to pedal continuously with no time to rest.

The riverbank trees shaded us from temperatures of over 34°C for most of the time. The beautiful scenery and long barges struggling against the river flow kept my mind off fatigue, though my thighs felt like lead. The view of the famous Schlogen bend from the viewpoint on the hill was simply stunning. Exhausted, we arrived at the Gasthof for the night stop and the cold beer served by pretty waitresses dressed in traditional Austrian costumes was great. That evening, I could not email my travel log to friends around the world because the WiFi communication broke down, thanks to a violent squall preceding a thunderstorm which cut our TV reception. We almost missed the football championship final, but luckily the storm cleared just before the match began.

A day later, we biked to Melk to visit the famous monastery, once stupendously rich. Then followed an enjoyable ride through Austria's famous vineyards as far as Krems before the longest stretch of ninety kilometres through picturesque villages until we reached the Vienna city limit.

Every time I meet Carine, which is frequently, she has a story to tell me about the old people she looks after, alive or dead. "The most difficult ones to handle are those with reduced mental functions," she has told me many times. "Your time will come earlier if you stop jogging," she teases me.

"I'm not worried about dying," I have replied many a time. "But I want to die quickly while I am fit."

Preachers tell terrifying tales of hellfire waiting for sinners to frighten the gullible. I think it was Tagore, the Indian Nobel laureate, who said that these preachers and priests and their disciples croak together like frogs in the rainy season. When my time comes, I just want to hop across the line while jogging and continue on the other side.

Did I speak too soon? One Sunday morning, a thunderstorm left many puddles in the narrow track that snakes through the wood along the Rhône near my house. It was still drizzling when our group of oldies began to jog the ten-kilometre La Course des Ponts, the Race of Bridges. I enjoy running in the rain. It keeps me cool and the sound of my shoes splashing in the puddles provides a hypnotic rhythm.

After two kilometres Carine said, "You go on, I cannot keep pace with you." Just then I approached a puddle and jumped over it. I saw a flash. I did not land. The earth's gravity did not pull me back, I was aloft. Carine disappeared. I swung my arms and kicked with my legs, trying to avoid a nasty fall. Once I had sprained my ankle just like that.

I found myself walking, a little breathless and enveloped in a translucent cloud. I looked for my bearings. In the haze I saw some gates in front of me. Was it the Passerelle du Lignon, the high footbridge over the Rhône? The path I was on fused into a white cloud in front of the gates. I could not judge the distance.

I bent down and tied the loose lace of my left shoe and resumed my jog. I saw many shadowy figures loitering around and wondered what they were up to. I raised my hand a few times at people, but no one took any notice. I pressed the button of my Polar watch to check my heartbeat and see if the sensor belt on my chest was in place. After a short spurt I settled into my cruising speed. Many young people overtook me. My heartbeat dropped to normal at one hundred and forty-five. I lost track of time. There was no sweat or knee aches.

Not far from the gated wall I saw a hut. Standing in front of it was a phantom-like man scratching his long-bearded chin. Surely he was Saint Peter? But how come he was wearing a turban? Had he become a Sikh? Suddenly his turban disappeared. Instead, he had long, neatly-combed hair over his shoulders.

I approached him and asked, "Hello, a moment ago you were wearing a turban. Why did you take it off?"

"People call me Long Beard Singh, LBS for short," said the phantom-man. "Why do you wear a turban and why is your beard so tightly bound that your cheeks bulge out?"

I was offended. "It's the symbol of bravery, it makes me look distinguished" I replied. "In the good old days, my appearance frightened the enemy."

"Do you mean to say that clean-shaven people are not as courageous as you? What about the Gurkhas?"

I felt stupid at that. "Actually, I have put on my turban to please you," I replied.

"Who told you about me?" he asked.

"Aren't you Dharamraj Singh?" I asked. "All the sacred books, including my Book-guru, talk about you."

Dharamraj Singh was holding a long computer printout. I felt rebellious. "I presume your computer list is of my deeds. That's very smart. I hope your memory is not failing with age. Will you judge me for my actions on earth only, or will you cover my entire travel through evolution, what you call karmic cycle?"

"All your books are wrong, but their intention is right," replied Dharamraj.

"What do you mean, wrong and right?" I frowned.

"Because they want to frighten you into playing your role correctly in nature's cycle," he replied.

"And you, what are you doing here?" I asked. "Has Waheguru, I mean God, appointed you to this post?"

"There is no God. You have twisted Waheguru to look like a superhuman being holding the world with strings. The universe with its multitude of manifestations is the wonderful giver of light, your Waheguru. The light, the reality, what you call truth, envelops everything. On Earth only animals and plants benefit from it automatically. But most human beings don't, because you do not consider nature to be your God."

"My Book-guru taught me that there is a God," I replied.

"Are you sure?" asked Dharamraj. "Nowhere does it define God. In its preamble, which you repeat all the time, it describes a power and force. There is no mention of God or Ram or Bhagwan or Allah or Waheguru or any other name. These names make the force look like a human being. Everything has originated from random forces and chance mutations. Nothing can escape the laws of nature."

"How can the Big Bang, matter, energy, and the universe be laws of nature?" I questioned.

"There is no reason," said Dharamraj. "The universe may not exist. It's all chance, no cause. Even God, if it exits, is a chance."

"I'm beginning to understand," I replied. "I was a nobody, motherless and fatherless, and now I'm somebody. Pure chance."

"That's not correct," said Dharamraj. "You are a product of circumstances, many unforeseeable, which you handled positively. You just do not know that."

"Who are you, then?" I questioned. My Sikh blood was beginning to rage.

"I'm nothing, it's your imagination, I don't exist."

"Who am I talking to?" I asked confused.

"To yourself. Delusion is a common human problem," replied Dharamraj. I retorted quickly. "Our tenth Guru has extracted our people from delusion by creating the Khalsa, fearless, brave...." LBS interrupted, "And reckless. I watched your Khalistanis blow up the Air India plane over the Irish Sea."

"These people were misled, mad, they were ignorant," I tried to defend Khalistan.

LBS smiled and replied: "Beards, turbans or any other symbols do not distinguish courage from madness. You know it. The world admires the Sikh virtues and spiritual values. Your code of conduct requires that you wear a turban and maintain an uncut and undyed beard to be virtuous. Many believe that goodness is directly proportional to the size of a Sikh's turban."

"So what we need is knowledge and to be aware of the good and bad at all times. I admit, these qualities stand head and shoulders above beards and turbans," I submitted.

"You're learning fast," said Dharamraj. "A final word before I examine your listing. Your Book-guru is clear. If you have acquired and used wealth, high and honourable office and other facilities justly and righteously, you are entitled to be called a virtuous person and a saint. The size of your turban, length of beard and level of wealth are not measures of your moral worth or virtue."

LBS turned to the printout in his hand.

"How are you going to assess me?" I asked.

"I'm looking at your genome - what your Book-guru calls

karmic chart," replied Dharamraj. "The results of your past actions are recorded here. All I'm looking for is if there is a recent change in your gene chain."

"You are cheating, you have stolen a human-patented invention. Anyway it cannot reveal my goodness or badness," I protested.

"Your pride is making you forget what you have been telling your close and dear friends Roshan and Malika about the Big Bang, information, interdependence, light, vital energy, spirituality" retorted Dharamraj.

"Of course, I remember all that now," I replied. "Yes, humans have invented nothing, all these things exist in the eternal integrated Flow, and we carry traces of it with us."

"Exactly. Your Nanak has told you that it's all written in you."

"You mean it's in our genes?" I questioned.

"He also said that you can change your genes any time," replied Dharamraj.

There was a few minutes' silence as I absorbed this.

"Does my genome show any changes in me?" I asked curiously, raising my hand to adjust my turban as it was biting into my ears. But there was no turban. It had disappeared.

"Do you know why you jogged to see me?" LBS asked, his eyes looking piercingly over his reading glasses. They were my old glasses. I'm glad I had not thrown them away, but I wondered how he had got them.

"Well, I jog twice a week and whenever I feel stressed. Today is nothing unusual, I did not know I would cross your path, but I'm glad I met you."

"I'll tell you something you do not know," said Dharamraj. "You inhaled your first breath on the high plateau of Eldore, the birthplace of many great long-distance runners. You did not know that your genes were modified a little. Nobody had heard of such things then. It took almost sixty years before your modified genes asserted themselves and prompted you to jog, and you have done well, although you could have done better. I'm happy with you. Then I wonder why it took you so long."

"Can it be my childhood trauma when my mother died? Maybe I was preoccupied with other essential matters," I suggested.

"You are nearly right," said Dharamraj. "Scientists have found out that childhood trauma inflicted by wars, cruel parents, loss of a mother or other reasons can modify a small chain in a child's genes. This defect can be treated if detected early. Otherwise the defective genes persist for three generations."

"You scare me!" I exclaimed. "Are my children and grandchildren now genetically malformed? Why didn't you tell me before?"

"Even if I had told you there were no psychologists who could have treated you. But don't worry. You have handled your trauma well and circumstances helped you, like returning to your birthplace, and all the things you learnt and did – manual and intellectual."

"So my children's genes are OK?" I asked, relieved.

"You need not worry, they are doing well."

"What a relief!" I sighed. I was beginning to feel cold.

"I had better continue jogging before I get cramp," I said to LBS.

"Wait a minute. What do you think you are and where do you think you are going?" LBS asked.

"I have told you, haven't I? Why do you ask me again?"

"You are not what you think," replied LBS.

"I'm me, Inder, with a body and soul," I stated.

"No, you are not," LBS laughed. "You are one of the particles of your ash. Just a particle, nothing more."

"Can you stop joking at my expense?" I complained.

"I'm not joking. You were cremated, or rather gassed, in Saint George Cemetery just across the bridge from your house at the Confluence of the River Arve and the Rhône."

I move my hands frantically to feel my body. There's no turban, no head, and no arm! It's there, it's not there. I'm everywhere at the same time, able to move to any place near and far. Distance does not exist, I fill the space, the universe.

I did not want to lose my hold on the situation. I pressed the button to start my Pulsar stop-watch again to resume my jogging. Nothing.

"Do you mean I'm my soul?" I asked.

"To be a soul, a God has to exist," replied LBS. "I have told you before that there is no God. Both God and soul are an invention of human imagination, simply to keep people under some fear so that they do not fight each other to extinction. Now you are free and yet connected to everything. Your scientists call you electron, or photon or some other on. When you hopped over the puddle you landed in the Flow. Your conscience is awakening and has begun to interact freely with all elements that are interdependent. You are downloading all the information or knowledge that surrounds you. You are in the state of Nam. You have abandoned the human flow and rejoined the Real Flow. You have access to the vital energy and light."

I lifted my foot to resume jogging, but the ground disappeared. I swung my arms up and down like a bird to save myself from falling into a bottomless abyss. Was it hell? I did not see any scorching flames. I was afloat.

LBS assured me, "I can see that you have found your feet. You are not floating randomly. You are navigating admirably within the Flow in the right direction. Soon you will reach your destination."

It felt good just floating in the Universe.

"Tell me LBS, why can't we be like this on the Earth?" I asked.

"You can. Your guru Nanak and many others were like that. Telling human beings to live simply, they guided them towards the Flow. But few see the path. Now his task has fallen on the shoulders of ecologists, environmentalists and lovers of nature."

"Where can I find Malika?" I asked.

"I have seen her waiting-listed on my computer," replied LBS. "You are free to visit her in California or Roshan in Santa Fe. Her family will not know. It's so easy. But..." LBS paused. "But she will not know that you are there even if you criss-cross her body. You have the capability of travelling in space. Wait a minute." He thrust his finger into his beard to reflect. "Actually, for her to see you, she has to work very hard to learn how to teleport. Some yogis are said to possess such powers. Probably it's too late now. Why don't you meet your other friends?"

I thought of Jote and Amra. I saw them having tea in the garden not too far away. They did not notice me. My brother, Mohi, was walking with a smart woman in white. She must be my mother. I closed up on them. Surely it was her. I recognized the mole near her right temple - I have one in exactly the same spot but a little smaller.

I returned to LBS to find out why my mother ignored me. But before I could open my mouth, he had disappeared through a hazy door. The door vanished as well.

I swirled around and felt that I was everything and everything was me — a perfect balance. The future did not bother me. Chance might merge me with other particles to form something more tangible: a rock, a seed, a volcanic eruption, water, an animal, a plant, a gas, or float away to explore the universe. There is a remote chance of returning in the human form. But I did not care. I was curious: how can a particle think and recall the past? I am not Inder any more. There is no eternal human soul. It is only a selfish human idea, an artifice, to console ourselves. Do donkeys, oaks, ants, streptococci and sharks think of souls? Am I being an egotist?

Yes and no. On my own, I'm nothing, but with my fellow particles we together make up the entire universe, including the Earth.

With my hop, I have landed myself in bliss - a state of equipoise, nectar, amrit - union with the Flow.

So will you.

ND - #0062 - 270225 - C0 - 229/152/22 - PB - 9781861510242 - Matt Lamination